DATE DUE

OC 24 '97		
DE 12 '97		
DE 17 '97		
MY 28 '98		
JY 21 '98		
AP 8 '00		
AG 3 '00		
DE 2 '00		
NO 5 '01		
FE 4 '03		
FE 13 '03		
MY 14 '03		
JE 11 '03		

DEMCO 38-296

ELDER SUICIDE: RESEARCH, THEORY AND TREATMENT

ELDER SUICIDE: RESEARCH, THEORY, AND TREATMENT

JOHN L. McINTOSH,

JOHN F. SANTOS,

RICHARD W. HUBBARD, AND

JAMES C. OVERHOLSER

AMERICAN PSYCHOLOGICAL ASSOCIATION
WASHINGTON, DC

Copies may be ordered from
APA Order Department
P.O. Box 2710
Hyattsville, MD 20784

In the UK and Europe, copies may be ordered from
American Psychological Association
3 Henrietta Street
Covent Garden, London
WC2E 8LU England

This book was typeset in Palatino by Beacon Graphics, Ashland, OH

Printer: United Book Press, Baltimore, MD
Cover designer: Minker Design, Bethesda, MD
Cover illustrator: Stephanie Shieldhouse
Technical/production editor: Olin J. Nettles

Library of Congress Cataloging-in-Publication Data
Elder suicide : research, theory, and treatment / John L. McIntosh ... [et al.].
    p. cm.
    Includes bibliographical references and index.
    ISBN 1-55798-240-6 (hard). — ISBN 1-55798-242-2 (soft) (acid-free paper)
    1. Aged—Suicidal behavior. 2. Aged—Suicidal behavior—Prevention.
    I. McIntosh, John L.
    HV6545.2.E58 1994
    362.2′8084′—dc20   94-4604
                                        CIP

British Library Cataloguing-in-Publication Data
A CIP record is available from the British Library.

Printed in the United States of America
First Edition

To the trustees and staff of the Retirement Research Foundation, for their help and support of the research and training that made this book possible.

Contents

Foreword

The endgame years of the human life course are a mixed bag. They are both an Indian summer of life—a time of relative repose and reward (the children are grown, the life's work is essentially done, realistic responsibilities are lightened)—and a time of special anxieties related to deteriorating health (that ol' devil catabolism), unwelcome loneliness, incapacities—rheumatism, sciatica, arthritis, lumbago—and the growing specter of imminent death.

Suicide among the elderly is a double paradox. Why advertently end life toward the very end of it? Why the hurry? What are the special conditions of psychache associated with those twilight years? Are there tangible desiderata related to elderly suicide? Is being old a special state of mind that is coterminous with self-destruction?

If these are questions that are of personal or professional interest or importance to you, *Elder Suicide* is the book you will want to read. It is scholarly, lucid, unobtrusively organized, and well illustrated with vignette examples—a pleasure to use as a source of information and insights. I sighed with intellectual contentment as I read it and learned from it. It is one of the most mature textbooks in suicidology, a happy sign of that discipline's coming of age. I have it on my shelf along with my other basic suicidological texts relating to the life course. I recommend *Elder Suicide* with that quiet enthusiasm that one reserves for solid, indispensable books that make up one's own private library of the best in the field.

Edwin S. Shneidman, PhD
Professor of Thanatology Emeritus,
University of California, Los Angeles;
Founder, American Association of Suicidology

Preface

A t no life period is there a more complex causative picture of suicide than in older adulthood. The self-destructive acts of the elderly are most often produced by multiple factors (biological/medical, social, and psychological) that are present simultaneously and that interact to produce the ultimate feelings of hopelessness and unbearable psychological pain that make suicide an acceptable solution to the individual. Suicidal tendencies in older adults create many perplexing dilemmas for the mental health professional. This book was written to address the complexity of this behavior, to convey present knowledge about the topic, and to identify important gaps in that knowledge that remain to be filled. More important, it was intended to help clinicians, researchers, educators, and others to better understand the general and personal aspects involved in the suicidal acts of older adults.

To address this complex problem, several individuals were involved whose talents and backgrounds complemented one another. Training and experience in gerontology were combined with expertise in suicidology, psychology, and mental health. Clinical experience in working with suicidal clients was added to backgrounds in epidemiology and research. Each author brought several areas of expertise that were required to communicate the complicated picture of elderly suicide and show how it might better be identified, prevented, and treated.

The first three authors (McIntosh, Santos, and Hubbard) have collaborated on many projects, including several that dealt with suicide in late life. Their careers have largely been devoted to gerontological research, training, and services. Dr. Overholser was invited to join the group because of his clinical expertise with suicidal clients. This collaboration has resulted in a book that uniquely brings together epidemiological, theoretical, and treatment perspectives along with empirical research findings and assessment approaches, as well as ethical and philosophical aspects of elderly suicide. To our knowledge, no other book on this topic has dealt with these varied components.

An important goal of the book is to provide clinicians with both data-based information and experience derived from clinical contacts with suicidal clients. An important part of that information is conveyed in the clinical and public cases that are included in the book. Case studies have a long history in clinical psychology of providing valuable insights that may not be gained from demographic and other research sources alone. On the other hand, additional knowledge can be gained from cases that are derived from nonclinical sources. Minimal assessment- and therapy-related information are generally provided in newspaper and book accounts of real-life events that occur outside the therapeutic setting. However, such portrayals can provide their own set of insights, making abstract concepts and ideas more concrete. If sufficient and varied public information appear, it may be possible to begin to understand the factors that led the individual to suicide. For this reason, public as well as more traditional clinical cases have been included to provide a richer variety of suicidal behaviors in older adults.

Another part of this book deals with the debate surrounding the currently volatile ethical issues involving the terminally ill, the elderly, and suicide. Events of recent years have made the topics of rational, assisted, and physician-assisted suicide hotly debated issues in such diverse fields as psychology, theology, psychiatry, social work, philosophy, and medical ethics, as well as in judicial and legislative arenas. This is also one of the most important issues in contemporary suicidology. Certainly it will not disappear, and it is hoped that the coverage here will help to illuminate and add relevant information to the topic. To ignore or omit this sensitive and emerging debate would not help in the understanding of this ethical, religious, and medical quandary. The timing of the book permits the inclusion of these ethical discussions and the events that have fueled them, and, we feel, adds to its value.

Acknowledgments

The authors wish to thank the many individuals and institutions that have supported us during this project, including Indiana University South Bend and Case Western Reserve University. In more personal ways, this book would not have been possible without the understanding of our significant others, including Charleen, Kimberly, and Shawn McIntosh; Mary Alice Santos; Floyd and Arlene Hubbard; and Patti, Katie, and Nicky Overholser. They exhibited tremendous patience and indulgence over an extended time in the writing of this book. They also provided encouragement, love, and emotional support throughout the endeavor. We were also helped greatly by the editorial suggestions of two outside reviewers and Theodore J. Baroody, our APA development editor. Ted's suggestions and guidance were extremely helpful as we completed the book. We also wish to express our gratitude to the APA for the opportunity to write this book and particularly for their patience, indulgence, and continued confidence in us through a longer-than-expected time period.

Introduction

Suicide occurs in all periods across the life span. Official records indicate that individuals as young as 5 and as old as 100 years of age kill themselves. Suicide is a tragic and unnecessary cause of death among all age groups in that it is most often recognizable, treatable, and preventable. What is not widely recognized is that the highest risk for suicide occurs among the elders in our society.

Until recently, suicidologists have focused their attention largely on young people and, in comparison, have virtually ignored this problem among older adults. To illustrate this predominant focus, it should be noted that, to date, there have been only 8 professionally oriented books devoted exclusively to elderly suicide (Leenaars, Maris, McIntosh, & Richman, 1992; Miller, 1979; Osgood, 1985, 1992; Osgood, Brant, & Lipman, 1991; Osgood & McIntosh, 1986; Prado, 1990; Richman, 1993), whereas at least 15 since 1990 have dealt with youth suicide (e.g., Bergman, 1990; Berman & Jobes, 1991; Cimbolic & Jobes, 1990; Davidson & Linniola, 1990; Davis & Sandoval, 1991; Hicks, 1990; Kirk, 1993; Leenaars & Wenkstern, 1990; MacLean, 1990; Muse, 1990; Northrup & Garfinkel, 1990; Rotheram-Borus, Bradley, & Obolensky, 1990; Shamoo & Patros, 1990; Trad, 1990; Whitaker & Slimak, 1990). Although this list is not exhaustive, it is meant to illustrate the discrepancy in the available literature on youthful and geriatric suicide. Bibliographies of the literature on suicide among the young (McIntosh, 1984, 1988, 1994; McIntosh & Santos, 1981) include no less than 51 books prior to 1990, but this number does not adequately represent the huge and rapidly expanding research literature on suicide in the earlier life periods. By comparison, there is a modest but growing research literature on elderly suicides. The literature on elder suicide will be reviewed in the present text along with its implications for intervention and prevention. The intent here is not to deemphasize the importance of self-destructive behavior among young populations, but rather to focus more attention

1

on the greater problem among older persons who demonstrate the highest risks of suicidal behavior.

Recent events have brought elderly suicide to the fore of national and even international awareness. Much of this attention was initiated by the case of Janet Adkins, a 53-year-old Alzheimer's patient who in 1990 was "assisted" by a Michigan physician and his "suicide machine" in bringing about her death (see Public Case Numbers 3.2 and 6.2). The physician, Jack Kevorkian, has given the name "medicide" to the issue of physician-assisted suicide (Kevorkian, 1991). In October 1991, Dr. Kevorkian also aided two other persons (neither of whom was elderly or terminally ill) to commit suicide, along with another nonelderly individual in May 1992. At the time of this writing, the number of cases has reached a total of 20 and Michigan has passed legislation banning assisted suicide. The law has been contested and is under appeal, but for the present it remains in force (see Chapter 6).

A short time after Adkins's death, another physician wrote a public letter in the *New England Journal of Medicine* (Quill, 1991) in which he openly admitted his assistance in the death of one of his longtime patients (in some of these cases legal action was initiated and pursued, and in others it was investigated, but charges in all cases were ultimately either dropped or never formally made). Finally, the *New York Times* identified on its front page a book that specifically detailed a number of ways of committing suicide as the number one best-seller for hardcover "how-to" books for the week of August 18, 1991 (Humphry, 1991). That book was intended to aid the terminally ill in carrying out more effective suicides, but, unfortunately, it may have an appeal for the many older adults who are also likely candidates for physician-assisted suicide. The issues raised by these recent and ongoing events have grown into much more than a theological or philosophical question. The problems associated with physician-assisted suicides have generated much heated debate and will be addressed in more detail in the final chapter of this book.

Chapter 1 of this book begins with a presentation of official and other data illustrating the past, present, and future levels of suicide among older adults and provides an overview of the empirical literature dealing with the various forms of suicidal behavior. Chapter 2 reviews general theoretical explanations of suicide and those specifically related to older adults. Chapter 3 discusses some special issues with respect to elderly suicide and high risk. An overview of clinical aspects of geriatric suicide provides the focus of chapter 4, and chapter 5 deals with assessment and treatment modalities and procedures that may be used by mental health professionals in working with suicidal elders. These two chapters provide the clinical direction for the text and emphasize the cognitive–behavioral orientation of the clinical authors. We give more detailed coverage of the cognitive–behavioral approach because it is in keeping with most recent outcome studies and because this approach is well established in the assessment and treatment of depression and hopelessness, two factors that play a prominent role in suicidal tendencies. However, brief coverage of other intervention orientations is also provided, including psychopharmacology. Throughout the book, cases of elderly suicides that illustrate the psychological state of suicidal elders are discussed along with the recommended therapeutic/interventive actions. Cases from both clinical and public sources are used to better illustrate epidemiological, case management, and theoretical issues. The book concludes with some critical observations regarding elderly suicide and identifies questions and problems that urgently require further elaboration and understanding. Also included in the final chapter is a brief discussion of the timely and important ethical issues that have been raised by elderly suicide in general and rational as well as physician-assisted suicide in particular.

References

Bergman, D. B. (1990). *Kids on the brink: Understanding the teen suicide epidemic.* Summit, NJ: PIA Press.

Berman, A. L., & Jobes, D. A. (1991). *Adolescent suicide: Assessment and intervention*. Washington, DC: American Psychological Association.

Cimbolic, P., & Jobes, D. A. (Eds.). (1990). *Youth suicide: Issues, assessment, and intervention*. Springfield, IL: Charles C Thomas.

Davidson, L., & Linniola, M. (1990). *Risk factors for youth suicide*. Bristol, PA: Hemisphere.

Davis, J. M., & Sandoval, J. (1991). *Suicidal youth: School-based intervention and prevention*. San Francisco: Jossey-Bass.

Hicks, B. B. (1990). *Youth suicide: A comprehensive manual for prevention and intervention*. Bloomington, IN: Research for Better Schools/National Educational Service.

Humphry, D. (1991). *Final exit: The practicalities of self-deliverance and assisted suicide for the dying*. Secaucus, NJ: Carol.

Kevorkian, J. (1991). *Prescription: Medicide—The goodness of planned death*. Buffalo, NY: Prometheus.

Kirk, W. G. (1993). *Adolescent suicide: Guidelines for educators, practitioners, parents*. Champaign, IL: Research Press.

Leenaars, A. A., Maris, R. W., McIntosh, J. L., & Richman, J. (Eds.). (1992). *Suicide and the older adult*. New York: Guilford Press.

Leenaars, A., & Wenkstern, S. (Eds.). (1990). *Suicide prevention in schools*. New York: Hemisphere.

MacLean, G. (Ed.). (1990). *Suicide in children and adolescents*. Lewiston, NY: Hogrefe & Huber.

McIntosh, J. L. (1984). *Suicide among children, adolescents, and students, 1980–1984: A comprehensive bibliography*. Monticello, IL: Vance Bibliographies, Public Administration Series Bibliography P-1586.

McIntosh, J. L. (1988). *Suicide among children, adolescents, and students, 1984–1988: A comprehensive bibliography*. Monticello, IL: Vance Bibliographies, Public Administration Series Bibliography P-2540.

McIntosh, J. L. (1994). *Suicide among children, adolescents, and students: A comprehensive bibliography, 1988–1994*. Unpublished manuscript.

McIntosh, J. L., & Santos, J. F. (1981). *Suicide among children, adolescents, and students: A comprehensive bibliography*. Monticello, IL: Vance Bibliographies, Public Administration Series Bibliography P-685.

Miller, M. (1979). *Suicide after sixty: The final alternative*. New York: Springer.

Muse, N. J. (1990). *Depression and suicide in children and adolescents*. Austin, TX: PRO-ED.

Northrup, G., & Garfinkel, B. (Eds.). (1990). *Adolescent suicide: Recognition, treatment, and prevention*. Redding, CA: Haworth Press.

Osgood, N. J. (1985). *Suicide in the elderly: A practitioner's guide to diagnosis and mental health intervention*. Rockville, MD: Aspen.

Osgood, N. J. (1992). *Suicide in later life: Recognizing the warning signs*. New York: Lexington Books.

Osgood, N. J., Brant, B. A., & Lipman, A. (1991). *Suicide among the elderly in long-term care facilities*. Westport, CT: Greenwood Press.

Osgood, N. J., & McIntosh, J. L. (1986). *Suicide and the elderly: An annotated bibliography and review.* Westport, CT: Greenwood Press.

Prado, C. G. (1990). *The last choice: Preemptive suicide in advanced age.* Westport, CT: Greenwood Press.

Quill, T. E. (1991). Death and dignity: A case of individualized decision making. *New England Journal of Medicine, 324,* 691–694.

Richman, J. (1993). *Preventing elderly suicide: Overcoming personal despair, professional neglect, and social bias.* New York: Springer.

Rotheram-Borus, M. J., Bradley, J., & Obolensky, N. (Eds.). (1990). *Planning to live: Evaluating and treating suicidal teens in community settings.* Tulsa: National Resource Center for Youth Services/University of Oklahoma Press.

Shamoo, T. K., & Patros, P. G. (1990). *I want to kill myself: Helping your child cope with depression and suicidal thoughts.* Lexington, MA: Lexington Books.

Trad, P. V. (1990). *Treating suicide-like behavior in a preschooler.* New York: International Universities Press.

Whitaker, L. C., & Slimak, R. E. (Eds.). (1990). *College student suicide.* Binghamton, NY: Haworth Press.

Chapter 1

Epidemiology: The Variety and Extent of Suicidal Behavior in Older Adulthood

An 86-year-old widowed resident of a nursing home takes some pills, places a plastic bag over his head, and dies from suffocation. This sad course of events may come as a shock and surprise when it is revealed that the person involved was the famous psychologist Bruno Bettelheim. For those familiar with the career of this unusual and reknowned professional, the question is inevitably raised as to why someone who had helped so many, who had survived the Nazi concentration camps, would end up taking his own life. (As we will show later, Bettelheim's suicide, along with those of many other elderly persons, was likely the result of intense psychological pain and feelings of hopelessness.)

Although college students have been found to believe that suicide is more common among the young than the old (e.g., McIntosh, Hubbard, & Santos, 1985), the elderly actually represent a clearly and consistently higher risk. Several sources of information are available to help us determine the prevalence of death by suicide and other, related suicidal behaviors among older adults. Mortality data based on death certificates provide one measure of suicidal deaths along with studies of

Some portions of this chapter are substantially revised and expanded from McIntosh (1987d, 1992a, 1992c, 1992d); McIntosh and Hubbard (1988); and McIntosh, Hubbard, and Santos (1981).

attempted suicides and individuals displaying life-threatening behavior and suicidal thoughts that broaden and further complicate the extent of the problem. The number of individuals affected by the suicidal death of a loved one is not known, but some rough estimates have been proposed. A separate consideration of each of these aspects in the spectrum of suicidal behavior is presented here.

Completed Suicide

Estimates of deaths by suicide are usually derived from official statistics. Available and published official mortality data are collected and compiled by local and national governmental agencies (in the United States, this agency is the Mortality Branch of the National Center for Health Statistics [NCHS]). Official suicide statistics have been questioned with respect to bias and underreporting (e.g., Douglas, 1967, chapter 23; Lester, 1972, chapter 12), but not without dispute (e.g., Sainsbury & Jenkins, 1982; Walsh, Cullen, Cullivan, & O'Donnell, 1990; see Jarvis, Boldt, & Butt, 1991, and Schmidtke & Weinacker, 1991, with respect to older adults and underreporting). Undoubtedly, official figures are not a completely accurate representation of the number of suicides that occur, but they may be regarded as conservative estimates (e.g., Allen, 1984), and, clearly, they are the only systematically collected and available data. The mortality statistics presented here will focus on the United States and then will briefly deal with some international figures. It should be noted, however, that the relative risk of suicide among the elderly compared to other age groups is generally similar across nations. This similarity with respect to relatively high risk is true despite tremendous cultural variability for overall suicide rates (e.g., Ruzicka, 1976; Shulman, 1978).

It should be kept in mind that official statistics, which are nearly always presented in the form of aggregate data, have the limitation of representing groups rather than the individuals therein. That is, although these statistics may reflect which aggregate groupings demonstrate high risk of suicide, they may also lead us to incorrectly assign high (or low) risk to individual cases (this has been referred to as the "ecological fallacy"). Obviously, clinical experience and skills must be used along with demographic data information in any individual assessment of suicide risk. The latter may provide some gross indications of risk but should not be substituted for clinical judgment on an individual level. For example, although older women are at much lower suicide risk than elderly men, they do commit suicide in late life, and in fact, the risk may be high for some individual elderly women.

Official Statistics on Suicide: United States of America

Current levels. Currently in the United States, approximately 30,000 annual deaths are officially recorded as suicide. Among these, more than 6,000 are carried out by older adults. In other words, one of every five Americans who kill themselves is over the age of 65. The most recent year for which final and complete official figures are available is 1989 (NCHS, 1992), and these data reported 30,232 U.S. suicides. Of these, 6,228 were committed by Americans age 65 and above. Therefore, in 1989 a suicide occurred, on the average, every 17.4 minutes in the United States, with an elderly person dying in this manner every 84 minutes. Calculated another way, of the 83 suicides recorded per day, 17 were committed by someone age 65 or above.

It is often indicated in the literature that suicides are overrepresented among older adults. That is, whereas older persons made up 12.5% of the U.S. population in 1989 (U.S. Bureau of the Census, 1990b), they accounted for 20.6% of the suicides in that year (see Figure 1). If the elderly were represented equally in these data, they would have contributed a proportion of the suicides only equivalent to their relative size in the population (i.e., 12.5%, or 3,779, of the 30,232 suicides in 1989). By way of comparison, the young (15–24 years of age) represented 14.7% of the population and a fairly close 16.1% of the suicides (4,870 in 1989).

The largest *number* of suicides actually occur among the adult population, defined as those either 25 to 44 or 25 to 64 years of age. However, these two age groupings also constitute the largest segment of the U.S. population. For 1989, the comparable proportions of population and suicides for those 25 to 44 years of age were 32.4% of the population and 39.3%

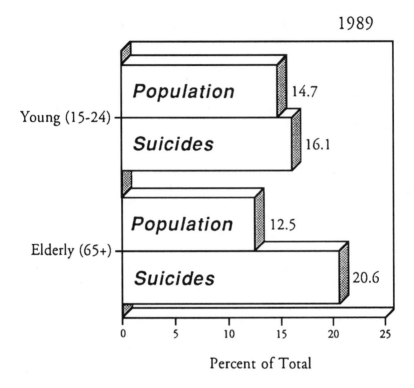

Figure 1.   The contribution of the elderly to population and suicide in the United States, 1989.

of the suicides (for ages 25–64 the figures were 51.1% and 62.5%, respectively).

A more revealing and accurate way to compare suicide risk is to look at rates rather than raw numbers by age or for any particular group. A suicide rate is determined by dividing the number of suicides within a population or subpopulation by the number of individuals in that same population or subpopulation and multiplying by a constant. The constant most often used is 100,000, so that a given rate indicates the risk of suicide for each 100,000 persons in the population. It reflects a measure of risk that takes into account the number of individuals contributing to the number of suicides. This computation also makes the rates comparable across subpopulations where raw numbers may not (the misleading nature of numbers as compared with rates can be seen clearly in the example of marital status below).

The rate of suicide in the United States as a whole was 12.2 per 100,000 population in 1989, as compared with 20.1 for elderly Americans (the rate for those 15–24 years of age was 13.3). Older adults are therefore at higher risk than that for the nation (and the young) by more than 50%. As can be seen in Figure 2, the rate for older adults has always exceeded the national levels by at least 50% and, in fact, by much more in earlier decades. If data on the elderly are eliminated from the national figures, the rate of suicide for the population under age 65 would drop to 11.0 for 1989. Furthermore, if the population under age 5 were eliminated (because no death under 5 can

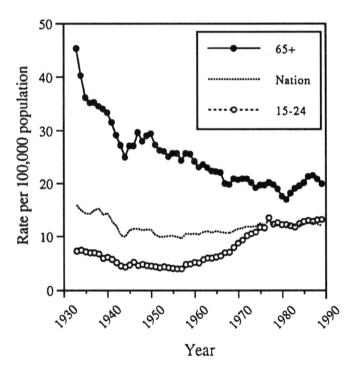

Figure 2.   Elderly, youth, and national suicide rates, United States, 1933–1989.

be classified as a suicide), the national rate without the aged would be 12.1. The rate for the nation that included the aged but excluded those under age 5 was 13.2 for 1989. Thus, the geriatric suicide risk is not only higher than that for the nation, but also contributes significantly to the overall rate for the United States.

Suicide rates for the nation reveal a pattern that may best be described as increasing with age (although a nearly flat pattern may be seen for young adults prior to a higher peak in older ages), with the highest rates emerging after the age of 65. Indeed, Figure 3 shows that the rate is higher for each elderly group than for any of those younger than 65.

The results of Figure 3 reveal that suicides are highest among the old-old (those 75 years of age and above) and slightly lower among the young-old (those age 65–74 years). It should also

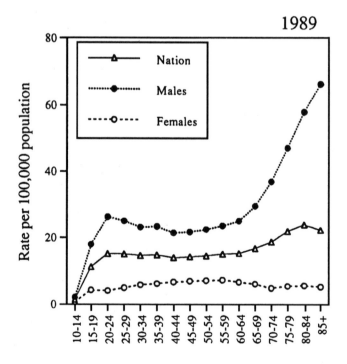

Figure 3.   Suicide rates by 5-year age groups and sex: United States, 1989.

be noted, however, that the rates among even the young-old exceed all other younger groups. Gerontologists have recently differentiated among the old-old, with the oldest old being further delineated (e.g., Rosenwaike, 1985). For the nation as a whole, these oldest of the older adults (85 years and above in these data) represent a high-risk group. Although the risk for them is slightly lower than for the 75-to-84 age group, it remains higher than that for any other lower age grouping, including the young-old in the 65-to-74 category (the comparison of 75–84 to 85+, as noted later, is greatly influenced by sex differences). These higher rates among the old-old are particularly important for a variety of future education, prevention, and intervention programs, because this is the fastest growing subpopulation of older adults.

The extreme aged form a special subgroup of old-old adults. These oldest citizens over age 90 and 100 account for very few suicides (see Figure 4) annually. Of course, it must be kept in mind that accurate and consistently available population data from which these and other suicide rates are calculated are not often available. However, low rates as well as few suicide deaths have been reported for these oldest old. For instance, Masaryk (1881/1970) and Bromley (1974) have suggested that the very old are a highly select group from their cohort. They are the hardiest of their original cohort and may be low in self-destructive tendencies, whereas those with stronger tendencies may have already succumbed to suicide (or death by other means) in response to life's stressors. As theorized by others (e.g., Maris, 1981; Shneidman, 1985; also see chapter 2 of the present volume), life-long patterns of behavior, including coping mechanisms and personality characteristics, may contribute to the predispositions of those who will commit suicide and those who will not. In any event, it seems likely that, for whatever reasons, the very old may be at somewhat lower risk as a subgroup of older adults.

The national age pattern of Figure 3 masks differential risk factors across groups that combine to produce the total population picture. Most notable and consistent among these demographic factors are sex, race, marital status, and methods of suicide. For suicide in general, the single demographic variable

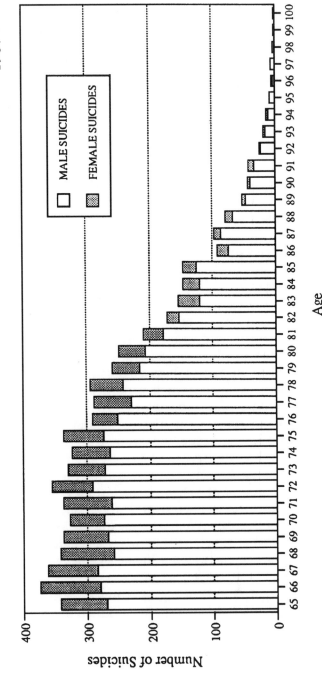

Figure 4.   Number of elderly suicides by single years of age: United States, 1987.

with the greatest predictive power is sex. As can be seen in Figure 3, males and females display differential levels of suicidal risk throughout the life span, and the characteristic pattern by age is also distinct for each sex. Male rates exceed those for females at all ages, consistently increasing with age and reaching their highest levels in the oldest age grouping. On the other hand, female rates increase only slightly with age (but always at noticeably lower levels than for men), peak in middle adulthood (the 40s to 50s, most often 45–54), and decline slightly with advancing age. Because male rates continue to rise throughout older adulthood while those for women decrease, the difference in rates for the sexes is greatest during old age and smallest in middle age, where female rates peak. The 1989 rate for men age 65 and above was 40.7, compared with 5.9 for elderly women (this compares with 19.9 and 4.8 for men and women, respectively, in the population as a whole). Therefore, although the number of women exceeds that of men in the population of older adults, the suicide rates (and the numbers as well in this case, with 5,137 suicides by men and 1,091 by women age 65 and above in 1989) are markedly higher among elderly men.

Racial differences, like those for sex, tend to be at their greatest in older adulthood. Rates for the White population increase with age, peaking in older adulthood, as noted earlier, for the nation as a whole (see Figure 5). Non-White suicide rates, on the other hand, peak in the younger years (generally by age 35) and decline to lower levels in older adulthood. The White suicide rate for the elderly (65+) in 1989 was 21.5, whereas that for non-Whites was 8.1 (compared with 13.1 and 7.1 for these groups, respectively, in the nation as a whole).

Combining suicide data for race with sex shows that men of both races are at higher risk than women of either race and that Whites exhibit higher suicide rates than their same-sex non-White counterparts in each case. White men older than 65 have the highest rates of suicide (43.5 in 1989), followed by non-White men (15.7), White women (6.3), and, finally, non-White women (2.8). Although the relative rankings of these rates across the four groups are similar to those for the nation as a whole for each race–sex group (21.4, 12.0, 5.2, and 2.7, respectively),

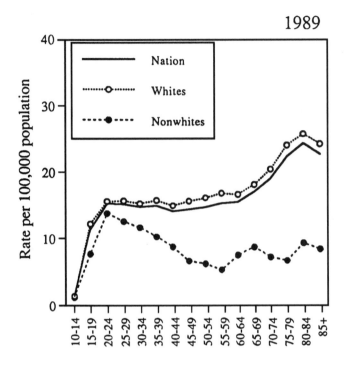

Figure 5.   Suicide rates by 5-year age groups and race: United States, 1989.

the differences among these groups are largest in old age (see Figure 6).

Although as a whole, Whites display higher rates than non-Whites, there are distinct ethnic differences among and between the groups that constitute the non-White category (McIntosh & Santos, 1981). The population data needed to calculate rates for ethnic minorities are consistently available only for census years. McIntosh (1985, 1986) compiled data from official sources by age for the 3-year period 1979 to 1981 for each racial/ethnic minority for which national data were available. Even among those groups whose patterns of suicide by age were similar (i.e., group rates increase with age or decrease with age), tremendous variability was still observed in overall rates. For example, for all ages combined, the highest rates were ob-

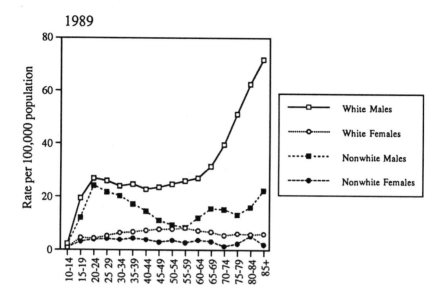

Figure 6. Suicide rates by 5-year age groups, race, and sex: United States, 1989.

tained for Native Americans (13.6), followed in decreasing order by Whites (12.9), Japanese Americans (9.1), Chinese Americans (8.3), African Americans (5.7), and Filipino Americans (3.6). Suicides peaked in young adulthood among both Native Americans and African Americans and declined to low rates for them in the later years. As was the case for Whites and the nation as a whole, peaks in suicide among the elderly were observed for Chinese, Japanese, and Filipino Americans. The rates for those 65 and older were 28.7 for Chinese Americans, 19.2 for Whites, 18.3 for Japanese Americans, and 9.3, 6.2, and 3.6 for Filipino Americans, African Americans, and Native Americans, respectively. In a study of 10 states from which suicide data for Hispanics were available, McIntosh (1987a) found rates that were similar to those for African Americans and lower than those for Whites when all ages were combined (Hispanics are generally included in the White aggregate data). Also similar to African Americans, Hispanic suicides peaked in young adulthood and were low in old age (the rate was 10.4 for 1979–1981 among Hispanics age 65 and above, with an overall rate of 7.5). Therefore, although suicide data often combine all non-Whites/minorities into a single category, it should be recognized that heterogeneity exists within that grouping.

Another demographic variable that has shown a reliable pattern is the marital status of the deceased. The *number* of suicides is much greater among married persons in the population as a whole, as well as those in older adulthood. However, the overwhelming proportion of both groups are married individuals. Therefore, when suicide *rates* are calculated, married persons demonstrate the lowest risk among the marital status categories. The divorced and widowed exhibit the highest rates, with the single (never married) population generally falling between the married and marital-disruption groups.

In the case of marital status, the high risk of suicide in the elderly is quite apparent when they are compared to the nation as a whole (with an exception being the widowed). As can be seen in Table 1 for 1989, the rate of suicide in each marital category except the widowed is higher for the corresponding older adult group than for the nation (calculated for the population age 15 and above, using figures from the U.S. Bureau of the Census, 1990a). The rate differential is particularly large for men. (The issue of widowhood will be further discussed in chapter 3.)

Finally, the methods that are used to commit suicide also exhibit age-related patterns. Although the use of firearms has become the most common suicide technique for nearly all groups in the United States (e.g., McIntosh & Santos, 1982; great cultural differences exist in this regard, as cited by McIntosh, 1992b), the proportion of suicides attributable to firearms is greater among the elderly than for any other age group (McIntosh & Santos, 1985–1986). For instance, in the United States as a whole in 1989, firearms were top-ranked and associated with 60.1% of all suicides (18,178 of 30,232 suicides), compared with 68.2% of such deaths in the elderly in the same year (4,247 of 6,228). Hanging, another highly lethal method, ranked second for the elderly and for the nation (12.2% and 14.8%, respectively). Gas and solid or liquid poisons represented the next largest means after firearms and hanging, with older persons using both methods less frequently than was observed for the nation as a whole.

Table 1

United States Suicide Rates by Marital Status and Sex: Elderly[a] and National Rates, 1989

Marital status	Both sexes combined		Men		Women	
	Nation	Elderly	Nation	Elderly	Nation	Elderly
Married	11.3	19.7	18.2	30.8	4.5	5.1
Single (never married)	17.5	25.2	27.3	52.3	5.8	7.1
Widowed	20.2	19.9	81.8	83.5	8.0	6.9
Divorced	35.1	48.0	65.0	99.8	14.0	12.7
Total[b]	15.8	21.5	26.3	42.5	6.1	6.4

Note. Population source: U.S. Bureau of the Census (1990a). Because the population data differ for this table and the other figures in the text (U.S. Bureau of the Census, 1990b), rates for the elderly will differ in the two places. Similarly, the use of different population estimates, as well as defining "total" as age 15 and above, will produce differing rates for national data as well. Other than comparisons among these tabled data, the other figures in the text are comparable to traditionally available official data.
[a]"Elderly" refers to age 65 years and above.
[b]"Total" refers to age 15 and above.

For suicidal methods, however, differences by sex have been found to be large (e.g., McIntosh & Santos, 1981, 1985–1986). Women in the population as a whole have come to use firearms most often (40.8%), thus exceeding the historical preference that they have exhibited for solid or liquid poisons (27.6%). However, it should be pointed out that McIntosh and Santos (1985–1986) studied official data through 1978 but did not find this reversal of the traditional preferences among elderly women. Between 1978 and 1989, a pattern of suicides similar to that for women in the nation as a whole occurred (25.1% by solid/liquid poisons compared with 32.9% by firearms in 1989). For men, firearm usage is the most common means of suicide at all ages, and the proportions for elderly men exceed those for all other age groups (75.7% for elderly men, compared with 65.1% for men of all ages combined). Although both older men and women used firearms most often, the use of solid and liquid poisons was markedly higher among women than men (25.1% vs. 3.1%).

A summary of the data above provides a picture of a modal- or highest-suicidal-risk older person (keeping in mind the ecological fallacy noted earlier). It is likely that the most common picture would be an old-old White man who is divorced or widowed and who used a gun to kill himself. Although such a person does not represent the only older adult at high risk, demographic data strongly suggest that these variables are associated with a high probability of death by suicide.

Trends

Past and recent trends.   Returning to Figure 2, it can be clearly seen that over the long term, rates of suicide among the old have declined dramatically. In fact, this decreasing tendency has been of longer duration (beginning in the 1930s) than the more recent increases observed among the young (beginning in the 1950s). The increase of over 200% for young people occurred concomitantly with a dramatic decrease of more than 50% among the old. From the extremely high levels of approximately 35 to 40 per 100,000 population among older adults during the economically depressed 1930s, the rates have declined to around 20 for the 1980s. In comparison, the rate of approximately 4 per 100,000 for young people in the 1950s rose to 13 per 100,000 in the late 1970s and 1980s. The national rates have remained between 10 and 13 since 1941 after being between 14 and 15 per 100,000 during the 1930s.

Although the best characterization of long-term trends in elderly suicides is that of decline, the more recent short-term trends are upward. Following 1981, in which the lowest rates were recorded for older adults (17.1) since the United States began keeping mortality records in 1900, suicides among those 65 and above have increased every year through 1987 and decreased minimally for 1988 and 1989. By comparison, during the period from 1977 to 1989, the comparable rates for those 15 to 24 years old have remained stable or dropped slightly. In the 7-year time period from 1981 to 1989, the rate of elderly suicide increased approximately 20% while the number increased by nearly 40%. The implications of these short-term trends for the future are unclear (see the discussion below). However, during the 1980s, older adults have become slightly more likely to commit suicide, and a downward trend covering several decades has apparently been reversed or at least halted or slowed.

The long-term decline in elderly suicides demonstrated in Figure 2 has received minimal attention in the literature so far as explanations or recognition of its occurrence is concerned. However, McIntosh (1984) has shown that the declines were due almost exclusively to decreased risk among elderly men, whereas older women showed stable to slight declines over the same period. He also found that the lower rates were largely the result of trends for older Whites, because non-White elderly rates changed relatively little. McIntosh also noted that the observed rate declines were greater for the young-old than for the old-old.

Of those few explanations that have surfaced to explain the long-term reductions in elderly suicide, some have speculated about the possible positive influence of developments such as access to hospitals associated with Medicare, elderly political and social activism (e.g., the Gray Panthers and the American Association of Retired Persons), improved social services for the elderly (Ford, Rushforth, Rushforth, Hirsch, & Adelson, 1979), the use of antidepressants (Busse, 1974), changing attitudes toward retirement (Kruijt, 1977), and increased economic security. Economic factors have been identified in at least two correlational studies of elderly White males (Marshall, 1978; McCall, 1991). Hamermesh and Soss (1974) also noted that there was a decline in elderly suicide rates in the late 1930s associated with the initiation of the Social Security Act.

Along somewhat different lines, a few studies have investigated the role of population size and change on elderly suicides. Holinger and Offer (1982) found no relationship between the increasing number of elderly adults and their suicide rates, whereas McIntosh, Hubbard, and Santos (1980) obtained a significant correlation between sex ratio and suicide rates for older persons. Thus, the increase in the number of older adults alone does not appear to account for the decreased rates, but the increasing proportion of women to men in the older groups was a relevant factor. No studies of the recent rise in rates have been published at this time, but McIntosh (1992c) has speculated that growing concern about economic security among older adults might be involved.

It should be noted that the long-term decline in suicides among older adults represents only one aspect of the larger picture of this century's changing rates by age over time. That is, the rates for the overall adult groups over age 45 have generally decreased, whereas those for younger groups have increased. The trends noted above for the 65+ and 15-to-24-year olds are the most extreme of these general age tendencies, and the net result has been a lessening of differences by age over time (see Figure 7). Despite these trends, however, old persons remain at highest risk across the successive age groupings.

Future trends.   As indicated elsewhere (McIntosh, 1992c), there have been predictions that elderly suicides will be extremely high in the future because of the large number of "baby boomers" and the higher rates that they have exhibited in comparison with earlier cohorts at similar age levels (Manton, Blazer, & Woodbury, 1987; Pollinger-Haas & Hendin, 1983). The sole issue involved in these predictions has been the size of the cohort and the resultant effects on its social and psychological well-being. On the other hand, McIntosh (1992c) has argued that the size of the baby boomer group across their adult life span may actually work to their benefit and result in more attention and resources dedicated to their needs as older adults. Logically, this would seem to produce lower rather than higher rates of suicide. It would also follow that the higher rates for baby boomers at younger ages would serve to reduce the number of survivors that are more suicide prone when they

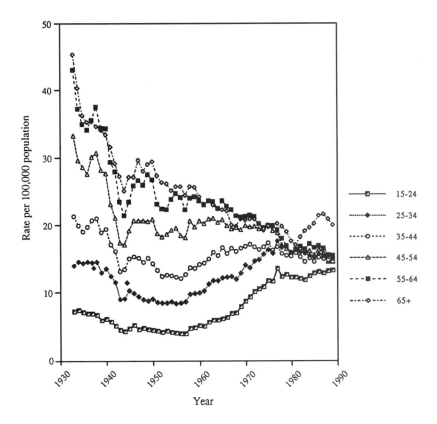

Figure 7. Suicide rates by 10-year age groups: United States, 1933–1989.

reach older adulthood, thus lowering rather than raising the suicide rates.

It is McIntosh's (1992c) contention that there is great uncertainty regarding future levels of elderly suicide for both the near and distant future. Forces and factors that cannot be predicted may well arise, such as future attitudes toward aging, old age, and suicide; health and disease control; pain management and increased availability of services for the terminally ill and dying; economic conditions; and more effective treatment of mental health problems such as depression and Alzheimer's Disease. The development of programs targeted specifically to older suicidal adults or those with other mental health problems, along with advances in biological, medical, and technological knowledge, is another change that could easily influence the likelihood of suicide among the elderly. The quality and nature of living within a particular period such as late life can certainly be a crucial factor for suicide risk. Thus, the outcomes are not predetermined simply by the size of the cohort. Of course, the ready availability of a suicide "how-to manual," such as Derek Humphry's (1991) *Final Exit,* along with more accepting future attitudes toward self-destruction, may also influence future levels. These and other related issues will be further considered in chapter 6 in connection with the prevention of elderly suicide.

Although we cannot predict levels of suicide among older adults with great certainty, that does not mean that predictions are impossible. McIntosh (1992c), for instance, has advanced some estimates based on quite conservative data. For instance, what would suicide levels among older adults of the future be if there were no changes from present levels? That is, if we cannot predict with great certainty that future rates will change significantly, what levels would result solely as a result of rate stability from the late 1980s through 2030?

By using conservative figures for population size and stability of suicide rates alone in making future projections, McIntosh has estimated that the number of suicides by older Americans would increase dramatically by the year 2030. The average number of older adults committing suicide would rise from 15.4 per day for 1981 to 1988, to 35.8 per day in the year 2030; or from one elderly suicide every 93.3 minutes to one every 40.3 minutes. If these data are considered from still another perspective, from 1981 to 1988 older adults were one of every eight Americans and they were responsible for one of every five suicides. By 2030, one of every five Americans will be 65 or older but they will account for one of every three individuals who kill themselves. It seems, then, that even with no increase in risk (and, therefore, stable rates per 100,000 population), an "epidemic" of sorts may be likely for the future aged. As the size of the elderly population increases at a faster pace than that for the nation as a whole or other age groups, there will be large numbers of elderly who kill themselves. Thus, the old will influence the overall suicide picture even more significantly than they do today.

A final and important prognostic issue is that post-baby boomers of the future may display unique suicidal character-istics not only related to the size of their cohort, but also in terms of their experiences along the way to older adulthood and their experience of old age as it is at that time. For ex-ample, will the "baby busters" (those immediately following the baby boomers) have less economic resources available to them in old age both individually and collectively because of lessened lifetime income, more lifelong competition with baby boomers for jobs and opportunities, and the depletion of soci-etal resources and revenues that will be needed to care for the aged baby boomers? Similarly, what might be the future life-long and old-age risk of suicide among the offspring of the baby boomers (sometimes called the "echo" or the "baby boomlet"; e.g., Edmondson, 1991)? The important point is that the relative risk of suicide among cohorts cannot be easily predicted, be-cause it will be influenced by the complex interactions of social, psychological, and historical factors that are unique to each co-hort. Thus, suicide prevention for each cohort and time, for ex-ample, may well present unique and different problems and thus require different solutions than those currently used.

Official Statistics on Suicide: International Data

Many nations compile and make available a variety of mortality statistics. The World Health Organization (WHO), for example, collects these figures from contributing nations and publishes them in regular reports. The most recent figures (WHO, 1991) that are available cover the years 1988 and 1989 (however, in some cases only pre-1988 figures are available). Before proceed-ing to a brief consideration of international figures on the extent of elderly suicide (for more detailed reviews of suicide in vari-ous cultures, see, e.g., Diekstra, 1990; Farberow, 1975; Kruijt, 1977; Tousignant & Mishara, 1981), a few points should be made to clarify some of the problems inherent in cross-cultural sta-tistical comparisons and comparability. Chief among these are the questions of bias and underreporting already mentioned and the difficulties inherent in dealing with various procedural, political, and cultural factors that can influence death certification among different nations. Therefore, some caution must be exercised in coming to definite conclusions on the basis of direct comparisons of rates from nation to nation or from culture to culture.

Current levels. As can be seen in Table 2 and Figure 8, international suicide rates show wide variations, with the United States falling within the moderate range. With only one exception (Scotland), among the countries for which data are available, elderly rates are higher than those for the nation as a whole (see also de Leo & Diekstra, 1990; Diekstra, 1993, chapter 12;

Table 2

International Suicide Data: National and Elderly Rates

Country	All ages combined (national data)			Older adults (65+ years of age)			
	Total	Men	Women	Total	Men	Women	Year
Hungary	41.6	61.4	23.1	83.8	127.2	56.8	1989
East Germany	25.8	36.1	16.3	70.6	119.7	47.6	1989
Sri Lanka	35.8	48.8	22.3	57.6	92.6	18.5	1985
China	17.1	14.7	19.6	57.1	63.2	52.0	1989
Bulgaria	16.2	23.5	9.2	50.0	76.8	29.0	1989
Austria	24.9	36.1	14.7	48.5	82.2	30.6	1989
Yugoslavia	16.2	22.4	10.2	47.2	74.9	28.6	1988
Denmark	26.0	33.3	19.0	43.8	55.8	34.5	1988
France	20.8	30.2	11.7	43.8	74.2	24.2	1988
Japan	17.3	21.5	13.1	43.1	49.7	38.7	1989
Czechoslovakia	17.7	27.1	8.8	39.5	67.8	21.9	1989
Switzerland	22.8	32.8	13.2	38.9	64.9	21.7	1989
U.S.S.R.	19.5	30.9	9.4	36.6	64.5	25.7	1988
West Germany	16.5	23.5	10.0	32.2	55.0	20.5	1989

(table continues)

Table 2   *(continued)*

Country	All ages combined (national data)			Older adults (65+ years of age)			Year
	Total	Men	Women	Total	Men	Women	
Finland	28.3	46.2	11.6	32.1	62.4	15.8	1988
Uruguay	8.5	12.9	4.2	25.5	45.4	10.6	1987
Argentina	7.5	10.8	4.2	24	43.9	9.0	1986
Israel	6.2	8.9	3.6	23.4	33.3	14.8	1987
United States	12.4	20.1	5.0	21.0	41.9	6.6	1988
Italy	7.6	11.1	4.4	20.5	35.7	10.4	1988
Puerto Rico	7.7	13.5	2.1	20.3	39.4	3.8	1987
Portugal	7.2	11.0	3.7	20.1	35.7	9.3	1989
New Zealand	14.0	22.2	6.0	18.9	34.2	7.8	1987
Netherlands	10.3	13.2	7.5	18.6	28.6	12.0	1988
Spain	7.1	10.7	3.7	18.6	30.8	10.2	1986
Australia	13.3	21.0	5.6	18.4	31.8	8.5	1988
Norway	16.8	24.5	9.3	18.1	28.5	10.6	1988
Canada	13.5	21.4	5.9	15.2	27.7	6.2	1988
Poland	11.3	19.3	3.7	14.3	27.2	6.5	1989
Venezuela	4.1	6.6	1.5	11.3	22.2	2.1	1987
England & Wales	7.4	11.2	3.7	10.2	16.0	6.3	1989
Scotland	10.4	15.4	5.6	9.7	15.4	6.2	1989
Ireland	7.5	11.0	4.0	9.4	16.4	4.1	1988
Greece	4.0	5.9	2.3	8.8	11.7	6.5	1988
Ecuador	4.6	6.3	2.8	8.2	14.9	2.5	1988
Colombia	3.8	6.0	1.6	5.7	11.9	0.7	1984

Source.   WHO (1991); rates for 65 years of age and above as well as both sexes combined ("Total") were calculated from figures included in tabular material in WHO (1991). The countries included here are all those for which at least 20 suicides total occurred among those age 65 years of age and above.

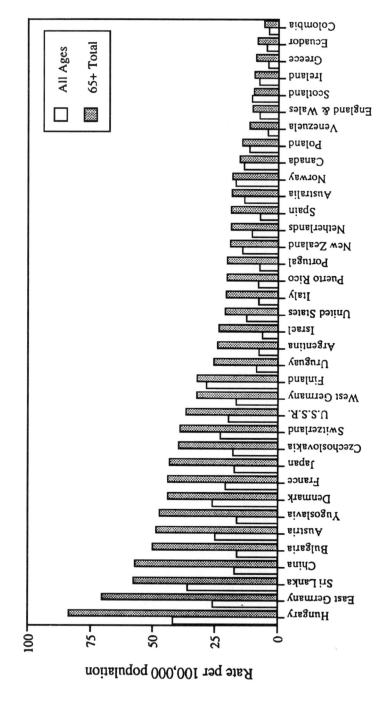

Figure 8.   International suicide data: National and elderly (65+ years of age) suicide rates.

Retterstøl, 1993, pp. 77–78). Although the patterns of rates by age have long been observed to be somewhat variable across countries (e.g., Ruzicka, 1976), these patterns most often display a peak in late adulthood among the nations reporting to the WHO (1991). Many countries show an escalation in rates among increasingly older male and female age groups that results in a highest peak in old age (see Figure 9, Pattern A; Figure 9 displays patterns for representative countries). However, other patterns by age have been observed. For example, one rate pattern peaks in young adulthood followed by slightly lower rates among the middle-aged, with subsequent increases to a high peak in older adulthood (see Figure 9, Pattern B) for men (e.g., the United States, Greece, the Netherlands, Switzerland, China, Australia) and women (e.g., Bulgaria, Israel, China). A third pattern (found for men in Denmark, Poland, the former U.S.S.R., England and Wales, and, to a lesser degree, Finland) demonstrates increases with age that show a peak in middle age. This initial peak is followed by lower rates among the young-old and a second, larger peak in the old-old age groups (see Figure 9, Pattern C). Rates that peak in middle age then decline throughout older adulthood for American women appear for women in several other countries (e.g., Scotland, Canada, Finland, the Netherlands, Ireland, Norway). However, this pattern is not observed among men in any country except Scotland (Pattern D). For a small number of nations (e.g., Australia, Denmark), women exhibit suicide rates that increase into middle age then remain at nearly stable levels across the remainder of the life span (Pattern E). For New Zealanders of both sexes, as well as Irish and Norwegian men, suicide rates increase and decrease repeatedly over the life cycle, but also show higher peaks in older adulthood than at earlier life periods.

In accordance with the information presented above, male suicide rates in old age (defined as age 65 and above), virtually without exception internationally, are markedly higher than those observed among elderly women. Interestingly, in both China and Japan, although rates are high for both sexes and although male rates do exceed those for women, the differences

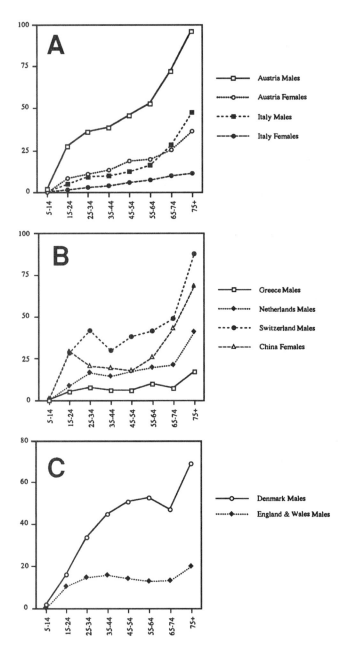

Figure 9. International suicide data: Patterns of suicide rates by age (various countries). Scales differ for graph ordinates. Therefore, graphs are not directly comparable. All rates per 100,000 population.

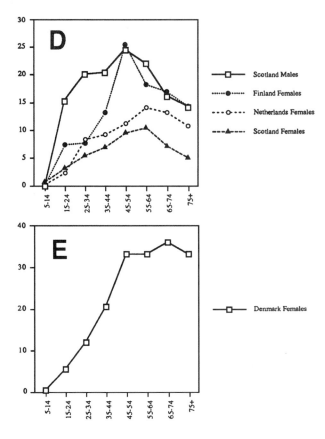

Figure 9.   (*continued*)

are much less than those generally seen for other cultures or nations (see Table 2).

Trends. A complete coverage and demonstration of international trends would require annual data for the elderly population of each of the nations represented. Such coverage is beyond the scope of this book, although a rough estimation of trends may be obtained by comparing the currently available national levels of suicide among elderly men and women with those compiled previously by Ruzicka (1976). In his report, Ruzicka (p. 410) presented rates compiled from WHO statistics for men and women age 65 to 74 years for approximately the year 1970 (in some cases, 1970 was not available and the closest year was used). Ruzicka categorized rates for men and women differently because of the much lower levels generally observed among women across the world. He categorized the rates by increments of 10 per 100,000 population for men (i.e., 0–9.9, 10.0–19.9, . . . 70.0 and over) and 5 per 100,000 for women (i.e., 0–4.9, 5.0–9.9, . . . 30.0 and over). The data for nations that are available in the WHO (1991) report for around the year 1988 can be similarly categorized as one measure of changes in rates over time. In this way, a comparison of the current rates with Ruzicka's categorized rates shows that many countries evidenced no substantial categorical changes in their rates for either elderly men or women age 65 to 74 years for the period 1970 to 1988. This was true for Scotland, Canada, Italy, Poland, the Netherlands, the United States, and Hungary, whereas several other countries each showed declines for both sexes (e.g., England and Wales, Portugal, Australia, New Zealand, West Germany [the former German Federal Republic], Japan, Czechoslovakia) or increases for both sexes (e.g., Ireland, Norway, Bulgaria, Yugoslavia, Sri Lanka).

The data from other countries that were available in both 1970 and 1988 displayed either mixed rate changes (one sex increased while the other decreased; e.g., Greece, France) or a change for one sex of older adults but not for the other (e.g., Northern Ireland, Israel, Switzerland, Denmark, Finland, Austria). The general conclusion from these comparisons is that little change in the overall levels of elderly suicide has appeared internationally and no single trend in elderly suicide has occurred in all or most nations of the world from which data were available over the past two decades. However, it is also obvious that the elderly as a group are at high risk for suicide in all of the countries compared in relation to their own national levels.

Public Case Number 1.1: Bruno Bettelheim

> Bruno Bettelheim was an eminent psychologist, psychoanalyst, and author ("Bruno Bettelheim," 1990; Ekstein, 1991). He was well-known for his lifelong contributions to the treatment of emotionally disturbed, psychotic, and autistic children, as well as many general contributions to the field of

psychoanalysis and parenting. Soon after receiving his doctoral degree from the University of Vienna, he was arrested in 1938 and sent to Nazi concentration camps in Buchenwald and Dachau. His release in 1939 after a year and his move to the United States were the result of Eleanor Roosevelt's intervention on his behalf. Bettelheim wrote a landmark article in 1943 that detailed the methods by which the Nazis dehumanized their prisoners, destroyed their identity, and created extreme personal distress and problems for those who were submitted to their methods.

Following a lifetime career as a college professor and head of an innovative school for disturbed children at the University of Chicago, he retired in 1973. His wife of 43 years died in 1984, a loss that friends said devastated him (Plummer, Wilheim, & Matsumoto, 1990). His distance and apparent lack of frequent contact may also have contributed to his social isolation and feelings of loss (Goleman, 1990). Bettelheim continued to write following his retirement, but after his wife's death this became more difficult when he also suffered a stroke in 1987 along with other illnesses. Plummer et al. (1990) quoted one of Bettelheim's coauthors as noting that the stroke affected his thinking, and "for a man so used to vigorous thought, that was the greatest threat of all" (p. 52).

In early 1990, he decided to move east from his apartment in California to a retirement/nursing home in Maryland. Bettelheim "apparently found [the retirement home] unsatisfactory" (Friedrich, 1990, p. 65), and the loss of independence made the situation particularly difficult for him (Goleman, 1990; Plummer et al., 1990). In the context of his concentration camp experiences and some of his later writings on institutionalization, it is likely that a nursing home environment would have been more problematic for him than for other older adults. He had written in *The Empty Fortress* (Bettelheim, 1967), "I had experienced being at the mercy of forces that seemed beyond one's ability to influence, and with no knowledge of whether or when the experience would end. It was an experience of living isolated from family and friends, of being severely restricted in the sending and receiving of information" (p. 8). Certainly nursing home life cannot be equated to the extreme concentration camp experiences that Bettelheim described, but the loss of control and the feelings of isolation and dehumanization that may occur in institutional settings might understandably represent special stressors to which he was particularly vulnerable. For whatever reason or combination of reasons (i.e., loss of spouse, loss of work, health problems, institutionalization), after only six weeks in the home Bettelheim took pills, placed a plastic bag over his head, and died of asphyxiation. A note that he left was found, but its contents have not been made public (Goleman, 1990).

Bettelheim represents the demographic/modal suicide case in some ways but not in others. Like the majority of suicides in late life, he was male. As will be noted later, the loss and health problems that were present in his case are also common in many geriatric suicides. However, the method of suicide that Bettelheim chose was not typical. Only 121 of 6,464 (1.9%) elderly suicides in 1987 occurred by asphyxiation with plastic bags. In terms of accessibility and availability, this method may simply represent an easy means of committing suicide in nursing home settings rather than one of "choice" (see the discussion, in the section "Indirect Self-Destructive Behavior" below, of indirect self-destruction in nursing homes). Related to this, it should be pointed out that Osgood, Brant, and Lipman (1991) found that 13% of suicidal acts reported to them by nursing home administrators in a national survey were accomplished by means of asphyxiation. Concerning the suicide note, it should be realized that leaving such a note does not occur in the majority of suicides, but higher levels of suicidal risk are associated with the writing of final notes (see Leenaars, 1988).

Public Case Number 1.2: Wanda Bauer

Wanda Bauer, a resident of a Colorado community of 750, was a 69-year-old widow. She had been diagnosed with fatal liver and pancreatic cancer following symptoms of excruciating and unrelenting abdominal pain. Mrs. Bauer had undergone an expensive CAT scan but refused to have a biopsy of her liver performed and checked herself out of the hospital because of the expenses already incurred and her desire not to financially burden her family. Convinced that she was dying anyway, her wish was to die quickly. On her return to her home after leaving the hospital, her 49-year-old son, and only child, helped make her as comfortable as he could, in a setting where she could see the mountains outside their home. Wanda, described as an independent mountain woman, then asked her son to bring her the .22-caliber gun that she owned. He brought the gun to her, as she had asked, and moments later, from another room, he heard a gunshot. She had fatally shot herself in the head. An autopsy revealed what she and her son had never imagined: that her illness was serious but was not cancer as they had been told. Instead, she had a liver infection. Her son was charged with aiding and abetting a suicide, an illegal act in Colorado (Bartimus, 1991; Miller, 1991), but was acquitted by a jury at his trial.

This case is an excellent illustration of the potential dangers that can arise with overreliance on demographic high-risk categories as predictive indices of individual suicide. Wanda was an elderly woman in a low-risk group, and although widowed, she had the strong emotional support of her son. Her illness, and particularly her unrelenting pain and terminal diagnosis, created a high-risk situation (see chapter 3) for suicide on the basis of the helplessness and hopelessness that it generated. If the significant gender variable alone were considered, Wanda might well be viewed as a relatively low risk for suicide despite her illness, pain, and independent life style patterns. Thus, experienced clinical assessment of each individual case is essential in determining suicidal potential. Demographic factors provide only one aspect or component to be considered in such an assessment. This case also underscores the tremendous need for health professionals to recognize the warning signs and high risk factors for suicide so that appropriate consultation and intervention can occur (see chapter 6).

As will be further discussed in chapter 6, the example of Wanda Bauer illustrates the inconsistency with which assisted suicides are prosecuted. This case has some similarity to that of Roswell Gilbert of Florida, who was prosecuted for and convicted of killing his ill wife at her request (and in August 1990 granted clemency). However, other cases in which family members openly admitted their part in assisting in the suicide of a loved one have gone unprosecuted. Such was true with Betty Rollin, who aided her mother's suicide (as described in her book *Last Wish*, 1985; see the description of this case in chapter 3, Public Case 3.1), and Derek Humphry, the founder of the Hemlock Society, who helped his wife die (as chronicled in his *Jean's Way*, 1978).

Attempted Suicide/Parasuicide

Another aspect of elderly life-threatening behavior relates to suicide attempts (i.e., nonfatal actions). Although official national figures are available for deaths by suicide, there are no such data for nonfatal suicidal actions. These intentional actions are similar to suicide completions but do not result in death and are referred to as *attempted suicides*. It should be noted that the term *parasuicide* is increasingly used to describe this behavior (e.g., Kreitman, 1977). The lack of consistently maintained figures on parasuicide necessitates the use of data from epidemiological studies in specific locations (i.e., cities, hospitals, etc.) in order to investigate this phenomenon. Although the variety of information relating to various demographic variables and trends discussed above in connection with completed suicides is not available from this research, the findings are relatively consistent with respect to age and sex differences.

Unlike completed suicides, rates for attempted suicide have consistently been shown to peak at high levels among the young and to decline with increasing age to much lower levels among the elderly for both sexes (for reviews, see Bille-Brahe, 1993; Kreitman, 1977; Platt, 1992; Platt et al., 1991; Weissman, 1974; Wexler, Weissman, & Kasl, 1978). Thus, across the life span, older adults have the lowest rates of attempted suicide. It appears that, when older adults attempt suicide, in comparison with younger persons, they are more often "successful" in that their act ends fatally. Estimates of the ratio of attempted to completed suicides further support this point. For the population as a whole, there are between 8 and 20 attempts for every completion (i.e., a ratio of 8–20:1; Shneidman, 1969; Wolff, 1970). Ratios for the young have been placed as high as 200:1 (McIntire &

Angle, 1981) or 300:1 (Curran, 1987), whereas for the old they are generally estimated to be around 4:1 or lower (Stenback, 1980). These extreme differences in the ratios again suggest that, relatively speaking, when an older adult attempts suicide the likelihood of a fatality is high (particularly when compared with the young). An interesting possibility involved in this very high risk of death among elderly attempters is that older adults who attempt suicide and live may be more similar to older adults who attempt and succeed than is true in other age groups. Also, elderly suicide attempters may be quite different from younger attempters in a number of ways (see, e.g., Frierson, 1991).

Several explanations may account for the increased risk of death among older adults who attempt suicide (see McIntosh, 1987c; McIntosh, Hubbard, & Santos, 1981; McIntosh & Santos, 1985–1986). For example, it has been suggested that older adults may have a greater intent to die when they try than do younger individuals and, thus, their motivation differs. Also, the elderly more often use lethal methods in their suicides than do younger persons. Physical changes associated with age likewise increase the likelihood of succumbing to the bodily damage that may result from a suicide attempt in an older adult as compared with a younger individual. Social isolation is also greater among older adults and is generally associated with high suicide risk partly because the isolation will increase the probability of fatality following injuries. In addition, it reduces the chances that someone will rescue or intervene in a suicidal situation. Individually or in combination, these factors probably increase the likelihood of death among those older adults who attempt suicide.

As with completed suicide, sex differences in attempted cases are so clear-cut that a dramatic and revealing picture emerges when this variable is examined. Both for the population as a whole and for all age groups (including older adults), attempted suicide is most prevalent among women. Also, in contrast with completed suicides, attempt rates are markedly higher among women of all ages, and the differences between men and women tend to be greatest among the young and less so among the elderly (but nonetheless higher for women). The findings of an older study by Schmid and Van Arsdol (1955) demonstrate these differences. The authors calculated the proportion of those who *completed* suicide among those who *attempted* suicide in Seattle in the period 1948 to 1952 and found that only 30.7% of the entire sample of attempters actually died. Interestingly enough, the proportion of women who died was much lower than that of men (15.1% vs. 46.5%). For young people age 20 to 29, only 14.7% died among those who attempted suicide, and, of those, women and men accounted for 7.5% and 26.4%, respectively. By contrast, the proportion of deaths among older attempters (age 60 and above) was 62.9% for both sexes combined, with 38.2% for elderly women and 67.8% for elderly men. Thus, the number and rates of suicide attempts are much higher among the young and much lower among the old of both sexes, and the probability of a fatal attempt increases with age. One interesting but ignored fact in these findings, given that there are many more attempts than completions, is that women actually exhibit a greater number of total suicidal behaviors (nonfatal attempts combined with completions) than do men at all ages.

A final aspect regarding the elderly and attempted suicide emerges when past attempts and age are considered. Other than a single study where no differences were observed by age (Chynoweth, 1981), available research results have shown that older persons of both sexes are less likely to have made a previous attempt compared with younger individuals. This was true in comparisons of elderly attempters (i.e., nonfatal acts) and young attempters (Lester & Beck, 1974; Lönnqvist & Achté, 1985) and with elderly completers and younger completers (Chia, 1979). Among older completers, then, their fatal act was more likely to have been their one and only "try" at suicide. This, of course, has some definite implications with respect to clues and warning signs (see chapter 5), because the elderly are less likely to have made a previous attempt that might help to identify those at currently higher risk for suicidal behaviors.

Clinical Case Number 1.1: Mrs. W.

Mrs. W. had a history of chronic depression that had led to suicide attempts in middle age. At the age of 64, she made two additional attempts, one shortly after the death of her husband and another four months later. After the last attempt, she was institutionalized and referred to a parapro-fessional mental health outreach program for the elderly. Mrs. W.'s history included chronic depression and alco-holism, which seemed to interact in precipitating her suicidal attempts. Her later years of life included increased trauma and loss, which brought about more suicidal behavior. Out-reach workers participated in discharge planning for Mrs. W. and continued weekly visits to her at home. Six weeks af-ter her discharge, Mrs. W.'s son was given a job transfer that moved him far away from his mother. When alerted to this new development, the outreach workers contacted Mrs. W.'s psychiatrist and began visiting her three times a week. A suicidal threat made by Mrs. W. during this time resulted in short-term institutionalization.

Although suicidal behavior is not generally thought of in terms of chronicity (see, however, Maris, 1981, and Shneidman, 1985, chapter Q, as well as chapter 2 of the present volume), it is clear that many individuals who are predisposed to suici-dal behavior may well suffer losses and trauma in old age that may tend to further increase the likelihood of suicidal attempts. In Mrs. W.'s case, three significant factors were involved that would suggest a high suicidal risk: prior attempts, chronic de-pression and alcohol use, and recent trauma and loss.

By recognizing Mrs. W.'s suicidal pattern, the caseworker came to an early identification of intent and was able to initiate appropriate preventive measures. While continuing to work with the problems of depression and alcoholism, the caseworker also began to develop informal supports for Mrs. W. and alerted them to the importance of early identification of clues so that the caseworker and psychiatrist could be contacted as quickly as possible.

As this case demonstrates, with advanced age many people may become more isolated, less visible in the community, and less willing or able to use available mental health services. Al-though psychiatric intervention was used in Mrs. W.'s case dur-ing her suicidal crises, she steadfastly refused regular treatment. This is a good example of vigorous community-based efforts, properly used, reducing the likelihood of successful suicidal at-tempts in older and at-risk individuals.

Indirect Self-Destructive Behavior

Much of the data cited above reflect official mortality statistics, that is, cases for which death certificates have indicated suicide as the cause. It is generally accepted that such data underestimate the incidence of suicide for any given population (for a review of these problems, see, e.g., Lester, 1972, chapter 12), and these underestimates may be particularly misleading in the case of the aged (see, e.g., Jarvis et al., 1991). There are at least two reasons for this assumption. First, coroners and medical examiners may be less likely to pursue a cause of death such as suicide when the person is old. For instance, it has been noted that there is a decline with increasing age in the percentage of deaths in which an autopsy is performed. From a high of 55.5% in 1980 for those age 25 to 34, the percentages fell with each older age group to 11.1% among those 65 to 74, 6.6% for 75 to 84, and only 3.3% among those 85 and above (NCHS, 1985, Table 1-26, p. 1-302).

One explanation of these findings may be that the old are perceived as close to death anyway, so "Why stir things up? They were going to die soon anyway." As Kastenbaum and Mishara (1971) have put it, "Less seems to hinge upon the final diagnosis" (p. 74) when the certification deals with an elderly person's death. Sympathy for or belief in such an attitude may tend to reduce the likelihood that a death will be classified as a suicide, and a conclusion other than suicide is more likely to avoid the stigma and taboo of society toward the surviving family members of the deceased.

A second reason for the underreporting of suicide as a cause of death for the aged relates to the methods that they are likely to use. Many potential methods are available to older persons that can result in premature, avoidable death but these may not be obvious as an attempt to kill oneself. The mental images that come to mind in connection with "suicide" usually involve acts such as putting a gun to the head, slitting wrists, putting a noose around the neck, or taking an overdose of pills. There are, however, much more subtle means of self-destruction, and although these covert, indirect, and perhaps unconscious methods may be used at all age levels, they appear to be more prevalent in old age.

Among the behaviors that result in death more slowly and indirectly than might be expected in a "suicide" are overeating and obesity; smoking, alcoholism, and other drug addiction; risk-taking behaviors; and accident-proneness (see Farberow, 1980b, for a more complete coverage of these behaviors). Another relevant category involves the omission of behaviors that are helpful or essential in sustaining life and health. Examples would include neglect in taking prescribed medication for illnesses; neglect of routine medical examinations; ignoring or delaying medical aid when needed; refusal of medications or nourishment; smoking or drinking against medical advice; and placing oneself in a hazardous situation or environment (see, e.g., Kastenbaum & Mishara, 1971; Patterson, Abrahams, & Baker, 1974). Although deaths related to these behaviors would rarely be classified as suicide, they could clearly play a significant role in hastening or causing deaths.

The concept of indirect suicide has been discussed in the literature for some time. For instance, Durkheim wrote in 1897 of "exaggerated form[s] of common practices" (1897/1951, p. 45), which differ from direct suicide only by degree and "form a sort of embryonic suicide" (p. 46). Such actions have been given many names and have been discussed by Menninger (1938) when he referred to "partial," "focal," and "chronic" suicides; by Meerloo (1968) as "hidden" suicide; by Kastenbaum and Mishara (1971) as "premature death"; by Shneidman (1973) in suggesting "subintentioned death"; and most recently and extensively by Farberow and Nelson (Farberow, 1980a, 1980b; Nelson & Farberow, 1980, 1982) as "indirect self-destructive behavior" (ISDB). In the field of health psychology, behaviors that persist in spite of dangers to health and well-being are referred to as "behavioral pathogens" (Matarazzo, 1980) and have been the focus of a great deal of recent research (see e.g., Gatchel, Baum, & Singer, 1982).

Despite the rather long history of the concept of ISDB, the extent and incidence of such behavior is largely unknown. However, although the incidence of ISDB may be unclear, the opinion of many writers on the topic is that direct self-destructive behavior (i.e., what we refer to when we use the term *suicide*) is not nearly as common as ISDB, particularly for the aged. Kastenbaum and Mishara (1971) summarized their position on the subject when they stated that "the number of self-aided deaths in old age that cannot be classified as suicide equals or exceeds those which properly would be classified as suicidal were all facts known" (p. 74).

In a study of institutionalized elderly, Kastenbaum and Mishara (1971) noted that 44% of the men and 22% of the women who were observed exhibited self-injurious behavior during a one-week period. Patterson et al. (1974) found lower percentages but various forms of self-injurious behavior among a representative sample of community-dwelling elderly. Subsequent research has followed the initial attempts by Nelson and Farberow (1977, 1980, 1982) to develop a scale to measure ISDB. In one such investigation, a sample of chronically ill elderly male patients in an intermediate care unit of a Veterans Administration medical center were studied by Nelson and Farberow (1982), and their findings indicated that 88% had engaged in some form of ISDB during the week-long observation period. Using a different approach, Osgood and colleagues (Osgood et al., 1991) conducted a national survey of nursing home administrators in which they asked for information about overt as well as covert forms of suicide among nursing home residents. The results indicated that some form of suicidal behavior was reported by 84 of the 463 facilities, and this represented 1% of the residents as engaging in either direct or indirect self-destructive behavior. Over 80% of all of the suicidal behaviors reported by these administrators were classifiable as ISDB and involved rates several times higher than that for overt suicidal behaviors. This was true for both those who lived and those who died among the persons regarded as attempting direct and indirect self-destructive behaviors. Thus, from these scant research results, it would seem that ISDB among older persons is a significant problem and warrants more attention and study by gerontologists as well as suicidologists.

Public Case Number 1.3: Gramp (Frank Tugend)

A well-known book (and film produced by the Children's Television Workshop) presents an excellent example of ISDB. The sensitive and emotional pictorial essay titled *Gramp* by Mark and Dan Jury (1976a) portrays the life and final months of the authors' 81-year-old grandfather, Frank Tugend. Affectionately known as "Gramp," Mr. Tugend was a retired Pennsylvania coal miner who still resided with his wife of more than 50 years and one of their daughters in the house he had personally built over 40 years earlier on a tract of land in the country. Their grandson, Mark Jury, and his family lived on a farm two miles away, and Mark's brother Dan lived in the same town.

Following his retirement, Gramp spent "his days working on his 'estate,' and his evenings devouring the daily newspaper and listening to the ball games" (Jury & Jury, 1976a, p. 8). The family, an extended and close-knit group, began to notice subtle and more obvious cognitive, social, and behavioral changes in Gramp that were later diagnosed as symptoms of Alzheimer's Disease. The Jurys' book poignantly describes approximately four years of the day-to-day changes and the progressively downward course associated with the disease, including the loss of independence and increasing cognitive confusion. Despite his eventual need for constant care, the family decided against nursing home placement for Gramp, in large part because of restraints that might well be used there and his lifelong independent manner. Finally, one day Gramp "removed his false teeth and announced that he was no longer going to eat or drink" (Jury & Jury, 1976b, p. 57). He stated that he no longer needed his teeth, and it soon became clear that the action did not reflect confusion but, rather, resolution on his part. He continued to refuse to eat despite repeated attempts by the family to persuade him to do so. Hospitalization and the use of intravenous feeding were ruled out by the family. Gramp told his family, "I'm just going to lay here until it happens" (Jury & Jury, 1976b, p. 61). Exactly three weeks after he removed his teeth, with his family near him, he died. Gramp's obituary mentioned nothing of the role that he played in his own death, and it is unlikely that the death was certified as a suicide even though it is clear that had he continued to eat and drink Gramp would likely have lived longer.

Clinical Case Number 1.2: Mrs. S.

Mrs. S., a 78-year-old Caucasian woman, lived in her own home with an older sister. After a series of stressful events, including family members moving away and a heightening of tensions between her and her son, Mrs. S. began to complain that her throat was "too tight" and that she could no longer eat. In a period of five weeks, Mrs. S. lost 30 pounds. Physicians were consulted but all diagnoses were inconclusive. At this point, Mrs. S. began to make some indirect suicidal statements, such as "I'm going to die and it's probably just as well." She also stopped taking her medication for high blood pressure, claiming that she could not swallow.

Soon, Mrs. S.'s suicidal statements became more direct. At one point, she stated that "maybe swallowing some drain opener or cleanser would help my throat." Finally, two days after a family gathering, Mrs. S. called a daughter and said, "No one can help me. I'm going to kill myself." At this point the family consulted a psychologist. Mrs. S. was then admitted to a psychiatric unit and diagnosed as severely depressed with a strong suicidal tendency, after which psychotropic medication and psychotherapy were administered.

The development of Mrs. S.'s problems illustrates a number of issues regarding ISDB. First, she had no previous history of suicidal attempts and, as a result, the family did not readily identify her intentions until they were clearly and directly expressed. Second, her initial statements were more oriented toward death fears and wishes than suicide. Third, although there was no "major trauma" (e.g., death of a loved one, etc.) that preceded her reactions, there appears to have been an accumulation of several stressful events. Finally, as is too often the case, psychological consultation was sought only after a potential overt suicidal crisis had arisen.

Clinical Case Number 1.3: Mr. W.

Mr. W., a 76-year-old Caucasian man who was admitted to a nursing home with terminal cancer, represents another case example of ISDB. He was alert and aware of his diagnosis. Although functional assessments indicated that he was able to feed himself, Mr. W. refused to do so. Staff members interpreted this response as a possible reaction to being relocated to an institution. Mr. W. did cooperate with staff when they fed him.

Immediately after a visit from his only living family member, a son who lived several hundred miles away, Mr. W. became resistant toward being fed. He stated that "food doesn't taste good anymore. Besides I'm going to die anyway." Psychological consultation was sought and during the initial interview, Mr. W. indicated that he had taken care of all his affairs with his son and was "ready to die." He saw eating as only extending his pain and prolonging his stay in the institution.

Mr. W. accepted feeding after being assured by his physician and the nursing home staff that no extreme measures would be used to artificially extend his life. However, he was still periodically resistant and died much sooner than his prognosis had indicated.

It should be noted that, in fact, ISDB may arise in connection with relocation and has been observed in newly admitted nursing home residents. However, in this instance, Mr. W.'s reaction appears to have been more directly related to his diagnosis as being terminally ill. The pattern of ISDB progressing into more direct statements and behaviors regarding death and dying is similar to that noted in the case of Mrs. S.

It is possible that ISDB may be encountered in nursing homes and other, similar institutional settings because the nature of these safe and protected environments tends to make direct suicidal expressions difficult and tends to deny access to methods that may be used in direct suicidal behavior (see also Osgood et al., 1991). Thus, although refusal of medications or food may be prompted by confusion, psychopathology, or both, such behaviors should also be carefully considered in terms of their possible implications with regard to suicidal intent. Of course, ISDB may also be unintentional and stem from an inadequate knowledge of good health practices, from fear and confusion, or, in a strange, regimented, institutional setting, from the lack of available funds or services (e.g., adequate staff).

Survivors of Elderly Suicide

The term *survivors of suicide* refers to those who are left behind by someone who has died by suicide, and who may have to deal with considerable grief over the loss of their loved one. Characterizations of suicidal grief have been established from existing clinical evidence and experience as well as from the survivor research literature (reviews have been published by Calhoun, Selby, & Selby, 1982; Foglia, 1984; Hauser, 1987; Henley, 1984; Hiegel & Hipple, 1990; Ness & Pfeffer, 1990; van der Wal, 1989–1990). Unfortunately, this literature includes many flaws in methodology and design (McIntosh, 1987b). For example, until recently, few studies of suicide survivors have included comparison groups of individuals bereaved in connection with other causes of death (for a review, see McIntosh, 1993). For this and other reasons, characterizations and conclusions regarding the differences stemming from suicide and other losses must await further and better research evidence.

Direct comparisons have produced mixed results regarding differences in survivor grief between suicide and other causes of death. In general, many similarities have been observed, but some differences have also been identified in these investigations. Demi (1984), for example, found that suicide widows reported more guilt and resentment toward the deceased than did a survivor group of accidental and natural deaths. A study of close relatives and intimate friends showed that suicide survivors felt greater anger toward the deceased than did survivors of accidental deaths (Vargas, 1982). McIntosh and Milne's (1986) study of college students indicated that suicide survivors more often felt like killing themselves, were more ashamed, and felt more that they could have done something to prevent the death than did the survivors of natural and accidental deaths. They also more often blamed someone for the death. A qualitative study (Saunders, 1981) of widows obtained results that reflected greater rejection from friends and the husband's family among suicide survivors than those from other causes. However, no significant differences in social support were established in other studies of spouses (Pennebaker & O'Heeron, 1984) and college students (McIntosh & Milne, 1986).

A short-term longitudinal study of "primary survivors" (i.e., spouse or parents; Williams, 1986) at one week, one month, and two months after death produced few differences in physical and behavioral symptoms (e.g., sleep, appetite, activity levels, health) between suicide and nonsuicide survivors. Suicide survivors, however, more often reported major stress and emotional problems in their family in years prior to the event than did other survivors. Although no differences were found between suicide and accident survivors, Pennebaker and O'Heeron (1984) observed that the number of health problems before and after the death increased for both groups (Vargas, 1982, also found no health-related behavior differences among suicide, accident, homicide, and natural death survivors).

Using a different approach, normative data on the SCL-90 (a self-report symptom inventory) have been compared with the responses of suicide survivors by Moore (1986) and Rogers, Sheldon, Barwick, Letofsky, and Lancee (1982). Because only a single group was studied in each of these investigations (i.e., the survivors), these were not, in actuality, true comparison group studies. That is, the survivor responses were simply compared with existing norms for the standardized measure. At any rate, Moore's comparison revealed that suicide survivors showed more global distress, a greater number of clinical symptoms, and higher intensity levels in their overall symptoms. Similarly, Rogers et al. found higher scores for their suicide survivors than those established for psychiatric outpatient norms on the subscores of the SCL-90 for Somatization, Obsessive–Compulsive, and Phobic–Anxiety. Scores on virtually all dimensions of the measure were higher for suicide survivors than nonpatient norms.

No epidemiologic investigations have been published that have attempted to establish the number of elderly or other suicide survivors (e.g., McIntosh, 1989). However, a rough estimate may be made on the basis of Shneidman's (1969) suggestion that there are at least six survivors involved for each suicide. Using this as a figure to multiply by the more than 6,000 elder suicides that occur annually would result in an estimate of at least 36,000 survivors of elderly suicides each year. It has also been suggested that the survivors may themselves be at high risk for suicide and, at the least, certainly represent individuals with special needs and notable grieving problems (see Dunne, McIntosh, & Dunne-Maxim, 1987).

The emotional relationships and family kinship between the survivor and the deceased may exaggerate certain aspects of the bereavement process among some survivors while lessening it for others. At this point, we will examine the special problems related to spousal loss and how that relationship may produce important differences in relation to grief and bereavement experiences. It is important to emphasize, however, that no given survivor will necessarily experience the degree or variety of bereavement to be discussed here. Factors that may influence grief responses include the survivor's social support network, individual personality and coping abilities, emotional attachment or closeness to the deceased (e.g., Reed, 1993; Reed & Greenwald, 1991), and the ages of the deceased and the survivor. Reliance on information from spouse survivors alone is necessary because virtually no systematic studies have been published that focus on the variety of relationships that may be involved when an elderly person ends his or her life. Because spouses are the most likely survivors and are frequently themselves older adults (52% of the 6,228 elderly suicides in 1989 were married at the time of their death), they are the most representative respondents among those that have been studied to provide a preliminary survivorship picture of elderly suicides.

Among all of the stressful life events that are assessed by Holmes and Rahe's (1967) widely used Social Readjustment Rating Scale, the highest weight is assigned to life changes and the need for adaptation and readjustment following the death of a spouse. Simply put, the life of the widow or widower is greatly affected by their spouse's death and its ramifications. Widowed individuals must face many problems in addition to their grief, including loneliness, financial considerations (especially among widows), managing all household affairs, and single parenthood and care of children if the survivor is young (Stephenson, 1985).

Before proceeding to discuss how suicides may further affect survivorship and personal adjustment, it should be noted that most of the available information is based on studies of widows who have survived their husbands' deaths. Although Silverman (1972, p. 186) has contended that the experience of the widower is similar to that of the widow, there is conflicting and insufficient evidence to support that position. Indeed, on the basis of the slim evidence that we have, widowers have most typically been characterized as experiencing more difficult bereavement and adjustment problems than widows (e.g., Stephenson,

1985, p. 181; for a review, see Stroebe & Stroebe, 1983). However, there are also some research findings that question this difference and support the position that emphasizes similarities between the experiences of widowed men and women (e.g., Feinson, 1986). Because the widowed in general and suicide survivors in particular are more likely to be women (because men kill themselves at least three times as often as women; see earlier discussion), the reliance on widow-based survivor information is not totally unwarranted or nonrepresentative.

Perhaps because of the severe impact of spousal loss, there are many similarities among widows from all causes of death that have been observed and discussed (see, e.g., Silverman, 1972). A number of researchers (Barrett & Scott, 1990; Demi, 1984; Farberow, Gallagher, Gilewski, & Thompson, 1987; McNiel, Hatcher, & Reubin, 1988; Shepherd & Barraclough, 1974) have reported many more similarities than differences for specific aspects and outcomes of bereavement among surviving spouses of suicide and nonsuicide deaths. Silverman (1972) has used the case histories of three widows to illustrate such differences and similarities following the sudden deaths of their husbands resulting from a suicide, an accident, and a heart attack. The major difference that was observed in their grief experiences revolved around stigma and its ramifications. Silverman suggested that widows of all death causes may experience a degree of stigma and social discomfort, but this is particularly pronounced for suicide survivors. Associated with the stigma are guilt and blame, social isolation, embarrassment, shame, and feelings of loneliness. Barrett and Scott (1990) found that suicide survivors commonly felt embarrassed about the mode of their spouse's death and often concealed that information by stating that it was due to some other cause. Somewhat different findings were obtained by Shepherd and Barraclough (1974), who reported that some of their surviving spouses experienced stigma whereas others did not. They also emphasized that for some survivors compassion and support may indeed follow a suicide (see also Organ, 1979, p. 760).

In the only studies conducted purposely with elderly widow survivors of suicide, Farberow, Gallagher-Thompson, Gilewski, and Thompson (1992; Farberow et al., 1987, reported earlier data with the same survivors) found that compared with survivors of natural deaths and nonbereaved controls, the widows who survived suicides received less social support in their grief and for their depressive feelings following the death of their spouse. In the same study, both bereaved groups noted that a low point was reached in the social support that they had received, and especially in practical help from others, six months after the death. A particularly interesting finding was that by two years after the death, support levels had returned to what they were immediately after the death. These researchers also indicated, as might be expected, that women generally received more support than men.

A comparison between widows of suicide and nonsuicide deaths was carried out by Demi (1984), who reported that among the few differences observed were more guilt feelings and resentment among the suicide survivors. Similarly, McNiel et al. (1988) identified more guilt and blaming reactions in suicide as compared with accident survivor spouses. Suicide is typically viewed by the surviving spouse as an intentional and volitional abandonment (e.g., Cain & Fast, 1966/1972), a feeling that was also expressed by Barrett and Scott's (1990) suicide widows. The decision to commit suicide would seem to imply that the spouse could not or would not help the deceased in his or her despair or may even have contributed to the problems. In addition to searching for answers to such questions as "Why?" "What did I do?" and "What did I fail to do?," the survivor may wonder, "Was my spouse so desperate to get away from me?" (Silverman, 1972, p. 207).

The stigma surrounding suicide commonly involves blaming the spouse at the overt or covert level on the part of the community, neighbors, and especially in-laws (e.g., Cain & Fast, 1966/1972; Saunders, 1981). A suicide widow described by Silverman (1972), in contrast to accident and heart attack survivors, was neither supported nor given sympathy by her neighbors. Rather, the neighbors were described as aloof, suspicious, spreading numerous stories and gossip about her role in the husband's death, and taunting and teasing the children. In some instances, the gossip and ostracism may become so severe as to prompt a move to another community. Although this was not commonly observed in Shepherd and Barraclough's (1974) survivors, in one extreme case a spouse "felt he could not go back to the town where he had lived with a suicide because of the gossip and blame he incurred" (p. 601). The widow of the suicide victim described by Silverman (1972) moved within the year following her husband's death, and at least 5 of the 35 surviving spouses in Cain and Fast's (1966/1972) sample were "hounded out of [their] community by . . . sustained gossip, accusations, and ostracism" (p. 148).

Of course, it is not only neighbors who blame, ostracize, avoid, and fail to provide support to the bereaved spouse of a suicide. Betsy Ross (1982) commented that after her husband committed suicide, "Relatives from both families refused to attend the funeral. My family sent no flowers. My mother told neighbors not to bring food. Only 3 sympathy cards arrived" (pp. 99–100). Even in cases in which help and support is given, it may be less than that which is desired or needed by the surviving spouse. Wallace (1977) partially attributes the lack of support received by the sample of widows he studied (Wallace, 1973) to a lack of norms regarding what others should do for a suicide survivor.

A common theme in much of the literature on spouses as survivors of suicide deals with the existence of marital difficulties prior to the suicide (e.g., Silverman, 1972). In this respect, Rosenfeld and Prupas (1984, chapter 6) have written about "socially and emotionally dying marriages" (p. 53). In addition, a large number of other case examples have identified marital separations that had taken place prior to suicides (see Augenbraun & Neuringer, 1972, pp. 183–184; Demi, 1984; Ross, 1982; Wallace, 1973, 1977), where a withdrawal of emotional attachment may well have already occurred (Demi, 1984, p. 107), thus influencing the survivor's response to the death.

Among the widows interviewed by Wallace (1973, 1977), the marriages of 11 of the 12 were best described as those in which the wife was progressively required to care for the needs of a husband deteriorating as a result of physical or emotional problems (e.g., drug or alcohol addiction, tuberculosis, etc.). The escalating need for care resulted in increasing social isolation of the couple until caregiving completely dominated their lives.

Seven of the 11 wives eventually broke off their marriages and separated from their husbands within six months prior to the suicide and generally had a more favorable bereavement outcome than those who remained with their husbands. Those who said that they suspected or actually anticipated the death, as well as those who had a job prior to the death, have also been found to fare better than those who did not (Demi, 1984; Shepherd & Barraclough, 1974; Wallace, 1973).

In many cases, chronic physical and mental health problems may adversely affect a marriage and create tensions (e.g., Rosenfeld & Prupas, 1984, p. 54; Silverman, 1972), and under such circumstances, relief may certainly be felt following the death of the spouse. Organ (1979) recalled his feelings almost immediately after the suicide of his wife, who had for 12 years suffered recurrent episodes of depression: "I had the strange feeling of being three persons. One was the person in shock. The second person felt a strange sense of relief: no more psychiatrists, pills, shock therapy and hospitals. A third person witnessed the other two: 'Look at that fool weeping and yelling, and look at that other fool already experiencing relief after 12 years of sympathetic suffering'" (p. 760). However, guilt feelings may also result from the experience of relief after the death.

Finally, Silverman (1972) has noted an additional concern of the surviving widow of a suicide. When young children are involved, the surviving spouse may come to fear that one (or more) of them may be like the dead spouse with respect to suicidal potential (obviously, this may also arise if and when a sibling commits suicide). Even in the case of adult children who survive an elderly suicide, similarities with the deceased may raise fears that they too may do the same thing, and this may even operate with grandchildren who have been close to the deceased grandparent.

With respect to all of the findings mentioned above, it should be pointed out that researchers attempt to communicate their results, which are based on many participants' responses, in a number of ways, including brief summaries by listing the most important generalizations. However, these brief generalizations may be misinterpreted to mean that all survivors will exhibit similar grief and other reactions. Therefore, it should be emphasized that what is communicated involves an overview or characterization of groups of survivors, but not richly detailed information or the variety of individual and unique survivor experiences. Such information can best be provided by the survivors themselves in telling their own stories, but unfortunately, few such detailed reports have appeared in the literature. A careful reading of available personal aftermath accounts of suicide reveals that the generalities covered in this section are often confirmed as valid, but, of course, special circumstances, events, and difficulties may be involved that are not conveyed in group results (see, e.g., Alexander, 1987, 1991; Pesaresi, 1987; Ross, 1990).

The different samples of respondents and relationships represented in the few available investigations tend to make comparisons across these studies difficult. It is, of course, possible that other spouses, friends, and survivors in other relationships may have different grief experiences. Taken collectively, however, the available results suggest that there are differences between the grief reactions generated by suicide and other causes of death, but there is currently too little evidence to determine the extent and nature of these differences. To more clearly establish and understand these differences, many more investigations will be needed that directly compare various types of survivors.

A major neglected issue in dealing with the survivors of elderly suicide involves the provision of aid and support in their grieving process. Some aspects of this problem, referred to as "postvention," will be addressed in chapter 6.

The present chapter has portrayed epidemiologic and other evidence regarding the importance and variety of self-destructive behavior displayed by older adults. It is obvious that the problems are extensive and warrant more concern and attention from mental health professionals.

We now turn to a consideration of some explanations for elderly suicide, beginning in chapter 2 with the global and theoretical frameworks that have been proposed to account for elderly suicide and its motivations. Next, in chapter 3, we will present empirical literature regarding some specific factors associated with increased suicide risk among older adults.

References

Alexander, V. (1987). Living through my mother's suicide. In E. J. Dunne, J. L. McIntosh, & K. Dunne-Maxim (Eds.), *Suicide and its aftermath: Understanding and counseling the survivors* (pp. 109–117). New York: Norton.

Alexander, V. (1991). *Words I never thought to speak: Stories of life in the wake of suicide.* New York: Lexington Books.

Allen, N. (1984). Suicide statistics. In C. L. Hatton & S. M. Valente (Eds.), *Suicide: Assessment and intervention* (2nd ed., pp. 17–31). Norwalk, CT: Appleton-Century-Crofts.

Augenbraun, B., & Neuringer, C. (1972). Helping survivors with the impact of a suicide. In A. C. Cain (Ed.), *Survivors of suicide* (pp. 178–185). Springfield, IL: Charles C Thomas.

Barrett, T. W., & Scott, T. B. (1990). Suicide bereavement and recovery patterns compared with nonsuicide bereavement patterns. *Suicide and Life-Threatening Behavior, 20,* 1–15.

Bartimus, T. (1991, August 18). Misdiagnosis at heart of Bauer family tragedy [AP story]. *South Bend Tribune* (IN), pp. A10–A11.

Bettelheim, B. (1943). Individual and mass behavior in extreme situations. *Journal of Abnormal and Social Psychology, 38,* 417–452.

Bettelheim, B. (1967). *The empty fortress: Infantile autism and the birth of the self.* New York: Free Press.

Bille-Brahe, U. (1993). The role of sex and age in suicidal behavior. *Acta Psychiatrica Scandinavica, 87*(Suppl. 371), 21–27.

Bromley, D. B. (1974). *The psychology of human ageing* (2nd ed.). Baltimore: Penquin Books.

Bruno Bettelheim. (1990). In L. Mooney (Ed.), *Newsmakers: The people behind today's headlines, 1990 cumulation* (pp. 491–492). Detroit: Gale Research.

Busse, E. W. (1974). Geropsychiatry: Social dimensions. In G. J. Maletta (Ed.), *Survey report on the aging nervous system* (DHEW Publication No. [NIH] 74-296, pp. 195–225). Washington, DC: U.S. Government Printing Office.

Cain, A. C., & Fast, I. (1972). The legacy of suicide: Observations on the pathogenic impact of suicide upon marital partners. In A. C. Cain (Ed.), *Survivors of suicide* (pp. 145–154). Springfield, IL: Charles C Thomas. (Original work published 1966)

Calhoun, L. G., Selby, J. W., & Selby, L. E. (1982). The psychological aftermath of suicide: An analysis of current evidence. *Clinical Psychology Review, 2,* 409–420.

Chia, B. H. (1979). Suicide of the elderly in Singapore. *Annals of the Academy of Medicine of Singapore, 8,* 290–297.

Chynoweth, R. (1981). Suicide in the elderly. *Crisis, 2,* 106–116.

Curran, D. K. (1987). *Adolescent suicidal behavior.* New York: Hemisphere.

de Leo, D., & Diekstra, R. F. W. (1990). *Depression and suicide in late life.* Toronto: Hogrefe & Huber.

Demi, A. S. (1984). Social adjustment of widows after a sudden death: Suicide and non-suicide survivors compared. *Death Education, 8*(Suppl.), 91–111.

Diekstra, R. F. W. (1990). An international perspective on the epidemiology and prevention of suicide. In S. J. Blumenthal & D. J. Kupfer (Eds.), *Suicide over the life cycle: Risk factors, assessment, and treatment of suicidal patients* (pp. 533–569). Washington, DC: American Psychiatric Press.

Diekstra, R. F. W. (1993). The epidemiology of suicide and parasuicide. *Acta Psychiatrica Scandinavica, 87*(Suppl. 371), 9–20.

Douglas, J. D. (1967). *The social meanings of suicide.* Princeton, NJ: Princeton University Press.

Dunne, E. J., McIntosh, J. L., & Dunne-Maxim, K. (Eds.). (1987). *Suicide and its aftermath: Understanding and counseling the survivors.* New York: Norton.

Durkheim, E. (1951). *Suicide: A study in sociology* (J. A. Spaulding & G. Simpson, Trans.; G. Simpson, Ed.). New York: Free Press. (Original work published 1897)

Edmondson, B. (1991). The boomlet's still booming. *American Demographics, 13*(6), 8, 10.

Ekstein, R. (1991). Bruno Bettelheim (1903–1990). *American Psychologist, 46,* 1080.

Farberow, N. L. (Ed.). (1975). *Suicide in different cultures.* Baltimore: University Park Press.

Farberow, N. L. (1980a). Indirect self-destructive behavior: Classification and characteristics. In N. L. Farberow (Ed.), *The many faces of suicide: Indirect self-destructive behavior* (pp. 15–27). New York: McGraw-Hill.

Farberow, N. L. (Ed.). (1980b). *The many faces of suicide: Indirect self-destructive behavior.* New York: McGraw-Hill.

Farberow, N. L., Gallagher, D. E., Gilewski, M. J., & Thompson, L. W. (1987). An examination of the early impact of bereavement on psychological distress in survivors of suicide. *Gerontologist, 27,* 592–598.

Farberow, N. L., Gallagher-Thompson, D., Gilewski, M., & Thompson, L. (1992). The role of social supports in the bereavement process of surviving spouses of suicide and natural deaths. *Suicide and Life-Threatening Behavior, 22,* 107–124.

Feinson, M. C. (1986). Aging widows and widowers: Are there mental health differences? *International Journal of Aging and Human Development, 23,* 241–255.

Foglia, B. B. (1984). Survivor-victims of suicide: Review of the literature. In C. L. Hatton, & S. M. Valente (Eds.), *Suicide: Assessment and intervention* (2nd ed., pp. 149–162). Norwalk, CT: Appleton-Century-Crofts.

Ford, A. B., Rushforth, N. B., Rushforth, N., Hirsch, C. S., & Adelson, L. (1979). Violent death in a metropolitan county: II. Changing patterns in suicides (1959–1974). *American Journal of Public Health, 69,* 459–464.

Friedrich, O. (1990, March 26). Dead by his own decision. *Time,* p. 65.

Frierson, R. L. (1991). Suicide attempts by the old and the very old. *Archives of Internal Medicine, 151,* 141–144.

Gatchel, R. J., Baum, A., & Singer, J. E. (Eds.). (1982). *Handbook of psychology and health* (Vol. 1). Hillsdale, NJ: Erlbaum.

Goleman, D. (1990, March 15). Friends pondering Bettelheim death. *New York Times,* p. A24.

Hamermesh, D. S., & Soss, N. M. (1974). An economic theory of suicide. *Journal of Political Economy, 82,* 83–98.

Hauser, M. J. (1987). Special aspects of grief after a suicide. In E. J. Dunne, J. L. McIntosh, & K. Dunne-Maxim (Eds.), *Suicide and its aftermath: Understanding and counseling the survivors* (pp. 57–70). New York: Norton.

Henley, S. H. A. (1984, Summer). Bereavement following suicide: A review of the literature. *Current Psychological Research and Reviews, 3*(2), 53–61.

Hiegel, S. M., & Hipple, J. (1990). Survivors of suicide: Victims left behind: An overview. *TACD Journal, 18,* 55–67.

Holinger, P. C., & Offer, D. (1982). Prediction of adolescent suicide: A population model. *American Journal of Psychiatry, 139,* 302–307.

Holmes, T. H., & Rahe, R. H. (1967). The Social Readjustment Rating Scale. *Journal of Psychosomatic Research, 11,* 213–218.

Humphry, D. (1978). *Jean's way.* New York: Quartet Books.

Humphry, D. (1991). *Final exit: The practicalities of self-deliverance and assisted suicide for the dying.* Secaucus, NJ: Carol.

Jarvis, G. K., Boldt, M., & Butt, J. (1991). Medical examiners and manner of death. *Suicide and Life-Threatening Behavior, 21,* 115–133.

Jury, M., & Jury, D. (1976a). *Gramp.* New York: Grossman.

Jury, M., & Jury, D. (1976b, February). Gramp. *Psychology Today,* pp. 57–63.

Kastenbaum, R., & Mishara, B. L. (1971, July). Premature death and self-injurious behavior in old age. *Geriatrics, 26,* 71–81.

Kreitman, N. (1977). *Parasuicide.* New York: Wiley.

Kruijt, C. S. (1977). The suicide rate in the Western world since World War II. *Netherlands Journal of Sociology, 13,* 54–64.

Leenaars, A. A. (1988). *Suicide notes: Predictive clues and patterns.* New York: Human Sciences Press.

Lester, D. (1972). *Why people kill themselves: A summary of research findings on suicidal behavior.* Springfield, IL: Charles C Thomas.

Lester, D., & Beck, A. T. (1974). Age differences in patterns of attempted suicide. *Omega, 5,* 317–322.

Lönnqvist, J., & Achté, K. (1985). Follow-up study of the attempted suicides among the elderly in Helsinki in 1973–1979. *Crisis, 6,* 10–18.

Manton, K. G., Blazer, D. G., & Woodbury, M. A. (1987). Suicide in middle age and later life: Sex and race specific life table and cohort analyses. *Journal of Gerontology, 42,* 219–227.

Maris, R. W. (1981). *Pathways to suicide: A survey of self-destructive behaviors.* Baltimore: Johns Hopkins University Press.

Marshall, J. R. (1978). Changes in aged White male suicide: 1948–1972. *Journal of Gerontology, 33,* 763–768.

Masaryk, T. G. (1970). *Suicide and the meaning of civilization.* Chicago: University of Chicago Press. (Original work published 1881)

Matarazzo, J. D. (1980). Behavioral health and behavioral medicine: Frontiers for a new health psychology. *American Psychologist, 35,* 807–817.

McCall, P. L. (1991). Adolescent and elderly White male suicide trends: Evidence of changing well-being? *Journal of Gerontology: Social Sciences, 46,* S43–S51.

McIntire, M. S., & Angle, C. R. (1981). The taxonomy of suicide and self-poisoning: A pediatric perspective. In C. F. Wells & I. R. Stuart (Eds.), *Self-destructive behavior in children and adolescents* (pp. 224–249). New York: Van Nostrand Reinhold.

McIntosh, J. L. (1984). Components of the decline in elderly suicide: Suicide among the young-old and old-old by race and sex. *Death Education, 8*(Suppl.), 113–124.

McIntosh, J. L. (1985, November). *Suicide among minority elderly.* Paper presented at the annual meeting of the Gerontological Society of America, New Orleans, LA.

McIntosh, J. L. (1986, April). *Cross-ethnic suicide: U.S. trends and levels.* Paper presented at the annual meeting of the American Association of Suicidology, Atlanta, GA.

McIntosh, J. L. (1987a, May). *Hispanic suicide in ten U.S. states.* Paper presented at the joint meeting of the American Association of Suicidology and the International Association for Suicide Prevention, San Francisco, CA.

McIntosh, J. L. (1987b). Research, therapy, and education needs. In E. J. Dunne, J. L. McIntosh, & K. Dunne-Maxim (Eds.), *Suicide and its aftermath: Understanding and counseling the survivors* (pp. 263–277). New York: Norton.

McIntosh, J. L. (1987c). Suicide: Training and education needs with an emphasis on the elderly. *Gerontology and Geriatrics Education, 7,* 125–139.

McIntosh, J. L. (1987d). Survivors family relationships: Literature review. In E. J. Dunne, J. L. McIntosh, & K. Dunne-Maxim (Eds.), *Suicide and its aftermath: Understanding and counseling the survivors* (pp. 73–84). New York: W. W. Norton.

McIntosh, J. L. (1989, Spring). How many survivors of suicide are there? *Surviving Suicide* (newsletter published by the American Association of Suicidology), pp. 1, 4.

McIntosh, J. L. (1992a). Epidemiology of suicide in the elderly. In A. A. Leenaars, R. W. Maris, J. L. McIntosh, & J. Richman (Eds.), *Suicide and the older adult* (pp. 15–35). New York: Guilford Press.

McIntosh, J. L. (1992b). Methods of suicide. In R. W. Maris, A. L. Berman, J. T. Maltsberger, & R. I. Yufit (Eds.), *Assessment and prediction of suicide* (pp. 381–397). New York: Guilford Press.

McIntosh, J. L. (1992c). Older adults: The next suicide epidemic? *Suicide and Life-Threatening Behavior, 22,* 322–332.

McIntosh, J. L. (1992d). Suicide of the elderly. In B. Bongar (Ed.), *Suicide: Guidelines for assessment, management, and treatment* (pp. 106–124). New York: Oxford University Press.

McIntosh, J. L. (1993). Control group studies of suicide survivors: A review and critique. *Suicide and Life-Threatening Behavior, 23,* 146–161.

McIntosh, J. L., & Hubbard, R. W. (1988). Indirect self-destructive behavior among the elderly: A review with case examples. *Journal of Gerontological Social Work, 13,* 37–48.

McIntosh, J. L., Hubbard, R. W., & Santos, J. F. (1980, November). *Suicide among nonwhite elderly: 1960–1977.* Paper presented at the annual meeting of the Gerontological Society of America, San Diego, CA.

McIntosh, J. L., Hubbard, R. W., & Santos, J. F. (1981). Suicide among the elderly: A review of issues with case studies. *Journal of Gerontological Social Work, 4,* 63–74.

McIntosh, J. L., Hubbard, R. W., & Santos, J. F. (1985). Suicide facts and myths: A study of prevalence. *Death Studies, 9,* 267–281.

McIntosh, J. L., & Milne, K. L. (1986, April). *Survivors' reactions: Suicide vs. other causes.* Paper presented at the annual meeting of the American Association of Suicidology, Atlanta, GA.

McIntosh, J. L., & Santos, J. F. (1981). Suicide among minority elderly: A preliminary investigation. *Suicide and Life-Threatening Behavior, 11,* 151–166.

McIntosh, J. L., & Santos, J. F. (1982). Changing patterns in methods of suicide by race and sex. *Suicide and Life-Threatening Behavior, 12,* 221–233.

McIntosh, J. L., & Santos, J. F. (1985–1986). Methods of suicide by age: Sex and race differences among the young and old. *International Journal of Aging and Human Development, 22,* 123–139.

McNiel, D. E., Hatcher, C., & Reubin, R. (1988). Family survivors of suicide and accidental death: Consequences for widows. *Suicide and Life-Threatening Behavior, 18,* 137–148.

Meerloo, J. A. M. (1968). Hidden suicide. In H. L. P. Resnik (Ed.), *Suicidal behaviors: Diagnosis and management* (pp. 82–89). Boston: Little, Brown.

Menninger, K. (1938). *Man against himself.* New York: Harcourt, Brace & World.

Miller, J. (1991, August 22). Death in Colorado another chapter in "final exit" debate. *USA Today,* p. 8A.

Moore, S. F. (1986). After suicide: Clinical symptoms and experiences of those left behind. *Dissertation Abstracts International, 46,* 2817B. (University Microfilms No. DA 8522983)

National Center for Health Statistics. (1985). *Vital statistics of the United States, 1980, Vol. II—Mortality, Part A* (DHHS Publication No. [PHS] 85-1101). Washington, DC: U.S. Government Printing Office.

National Center for Health Statistics. (1992). Advance report of final mortality statistics, 1989. *NCHS Monthly Vital Statistics Report, 40*(8, Suppl. 2).

Nelson, F. L., & Farberow, N. L. (1977). Indirect suicide in the elderly, chronically ill patient. In K. Achté & J. Lönnqvist (Eds.), *Suicide research: Proceedings of the seminars of suicide research by Yrjo Jahnsson Foundation 1974–1977* (Supplementum 1976, pp. 125–139). Helsinki, Finland: Psychiatria Fennica.

Nelson, F. L., & Farberow, N. L. (1980). Indirect self-destructive behavior in the elderly nursing home patient. *Journal of Gerontology, 35,* 949–957.

Nelson, F. L., & Farberow, N. L. (1982). The development of an indirect self-destructive behaviour scale for use with chronically ill medical patients. *International Journal of Social Psychiatry, 28,* 5–14.

Ness, D. E., & Pfeffer, C. R. (1990). Sequelae of bereavement resulting from suicide. *American Journal of Psychiatry, 147,* 279–285.

Organ, T. (1979, August 1–8). Grief and the art of consolation: A personal testimony. *The Christian Century, 96,* 759–762.

Osgood, N. J., Brant, B. A., & Lipman, A. (1991). *Suicide among the elderly in long-term care facilities.* New York: Greenwood.

Patterson, R. D., Abrahams, R., & Baker, F. (1974, November). Preventing self-destructive behavior. *Geriatrics, 29,* 115–118, 121.

Pennebaker, J. W., & O'Heeron, R. C. (1984). Confiding in others and illness rate among spouses of suicide and accidental-death victims. *Journal of Abnormal Psychology, 93,* 473–476.

Pesaresi, J. (1987). When one of us is gone. In E. J. Dunne, J. L. McIntosh, & K. Dunne-Maxim (Eds.), *Suicide and its aftermath: Understanding and counseling the survivors* (pp. 104–108). New York: Norton.

Platt, S. (1992). Epidemiology of suicide and parasuicide. *Journal of Psychopharmacology, 6*(2, Suppl.), 291–299.

Platt, S., Bille-Brahe, U., Kerkhof, A., Schmidtke, A., Bjerke, T., Crepet, P., de Leo, D., Haring, C., Lonnqvist, J., Michel, K., Philippe, A., Pommereau, X., Querejeta, I., Salander-Renberg, E., Temesvary, B., Wasserman, D., & Faria, J. S. (1991). Parasuicide in Europe: The WHO/EURO multicentre study on parasuicide: I. Introduction and preliminary analysis for 1989. *Acta Psychiatrica Scandinavica, 85,* 97–104.

Plummer, W., Wilheim, M., & Matsumoto, N. (1990, April 2). Bruno Bettelheim had infinite patience with children, but not with the ravages of old age. *People,* pp. 51–52.

Pollinger-Haas, A., & Hendin, H. (1983). Suicide among older people: Projections for the future. *Suicide and Life-Threatening Behavior, 13,* 147–154.

Reed, M. D. (1993). Sudden death and bereavement outcomes: The impact of resources on grief symptomatology and detachment. *Suicide and Life-Threatening Behavior, 23,* 204–220.

Reed, M. D., & Greenwald, J. Y. (1991). Survivor-victim status, attachment, and sudden death bereavement. *Suicide and Life-Threatening Behavior, 21,* 385–401.

Retterstøl, N. (1993). *Suicide: A European perspective.* Cambridge, England: Cambridge University Press.

Rogers, J., Sheldon, A., Barwick, C., Letofsky, K., & Lancee, W. (1982). Help for families of suicide: Survivors Support Program. *Canadian Journal of Psychiatry, 27,* 444–449.

Rollin, B. (1985). *Last wish.* New York: Linden Press.

Rosenfeld, L., & Prupas, M. (1984). *Left alive: After a suicide death in the family.* Springfield, IL: Charles C Thomas.

Rosenwaike, I. (1985). *The extreme aged in America: A portrait of an expanding population.* Westport, CT: Greenwood.

Ross, E. B. (1982, April). After suicide: A Ray of Hope [Abstract]. In C. R. Pfeffer & J. Richman (Eds.), *Proceedings of the 15th annual meeting of the American Association of Suicidology* (pp. 99–101). Denver, CO: American Association of Suicidology.

Ross, E. B. (1990). *After suicide: A ray of hope.* Iowa City, IA: Lynn.

Ruzicka, L. T. (1976). Special subject: Suicide, 1950 to 1971. *World Health Statistics Report, 29*(7), 396–413.

Sainsbury, P., & Jenkins, J. S. (1982). The accuracy of officially reported suicide statistics for purposes of epidemiological research. *Journal of Epidemiology and Community Health, 36,* 43–48.

Saunders, J. M. (1981). A process of bereavement resolution: Uncoupled identity. *Western Journal of Nursing Research, 3,* 319–335.

Schmid, C. F., & Van Arsdol, M. D., Jr. (1955). Completed and attempted suicides: A comparative analysis. *American Sociological Review, 20,* 273–283.

Schmidtke, A., & Weinacker, B. (1991). Covariation of suicides and undetermined deaths among elderly persons: A methodological study. *Crisis, 12*(2), 44–58.

Shepherd, D. M., & Barraclough, B. M. (1974, June 15). The aftermath of suicide. *British Medical Journal, 2,* 600–603.

Shneidman, E. S. (1969). Prologue: Fifty-eight years. In E. S. Shneidman (Ed.), *On the nature of suicide* (pp. 1–30). San Francisco: Jossey-Bass.

Shneidman, E. S. (1973). *Deaths of man.* New York: Quadrangle.

Shneidman, E. S. (1985). *Definition of suicide.* New York: Wiley.

Shulman, K. (1978). Suicide and parasuicide in old age: A review. *Age and Ageing, 7,* 201–209.

Silverman, P. R. (1972). Intervention with the widow of a suicide. In A. C. Cain (Ed.), *Survivors of suicide* (pp. 186–214). Springfield, IL: Charles C Thomas.

Stenback, A. (1980). Depression and suicidal behavior in old age. In J. E. Birren & R. B. Sloane (Eds.), *Handbook of mental health and aging* (pp. 616–652). Englewood Cliffs, NJ: Prentice-Hall.

Stephenson, J. S. (1985). *Death, grief, and mourning: Individual and social realities.* New York: Free Press.

Stroebe, M. S., & Stroebe, W. (1983). Who suffers more? Sex differences in health risks of the widowed. *Psychological Bulletin, 93,* 279–301.

Tousignant, M., & Mishara, B. L. (1981). Suicide and culture: A review of the literature (1969–1980). *Transcultural Psychiatric Research Review, 18,* 5–32.

U.S. Bureau of the Census. (1990a). Marital status and living arrangements: March 1989. *Current Population Reports,* Series P-20, No. 445.

U.S. Bureau of the Census. (1990b). United States population estimates, by age, sex, race, and Hispanic origin: 1989. *Current Population Reports,* Series P-25, No. 1057.

van der Wal, J. (1989–1990). The aftermath of suicide: A review of empirical evidence. *Omega, 20,* 149–171.

Vargas, L. A. (1982). *Bereavement in the four modes of death in Whites, Blacks, and Hispanics.* Unpublished doctoral dissertation, University of Nebraska.

Wallace, S. (1973). *After suicide.* New York: Wiley.

Wallace, S. E. (1977). On the atypicality of suicide bereavement. In B. L. Danto & A. H. Kutscher (Eds.), *Suicide and bereavement* (pp. 44–53). New York: MSS Information Corporation.

Walsh, D., Cullen, A., Cullivan, R., & O'Donnell, B. (1990). Do statistics lie? Suicide in Kildaire—and in Ireland. *Psychological Medicine, 20,* 867–871.

Weissman, M. M. (1974). The epidemiology of suicide attempts, 1960 to 1971. *Archives of General Psychiatry, 30,* 737–746.

Wexler, L., Weissman, M. M., & Kasl, S. V. (1978). Suicide attempts 1970–1975: Updating a United States study and comparisons with international trends. *British Journal of Psychiatry, 132,* 180–185.

Williams, M. (1986, April). *Comparing responses of sudden death survivors.* Paper presented at the annual meeting of the American Association of Suicidology, Atlanta, GA.

Wolff, K. (1970). Observations on depression and suicide in the geriatric patient. In K. Wolff (Ed.), *Patterns of self-destruction: Depression and suicide* (pp. 33–42). Springfield, IL: Charles C Thomas.

World Health Organization. (1991). *World health statistics annual 1990.* Geneva: Author.

2

Theories of Suicide

S uicide theories are intended to help us understand why individuals or groups of individuals commit suicide or are at high risk of self-destructive acts. Since Durkheim's 1897 (1897/1951) treatise, theories of suicidal behavior have been almost exclusively unidisciplinary. That is, with few exceptions, it has been sociologists who have focused on the societal forces that are associated with or predispose those at high suicide risk in populations. In comparison, psychologists and psychiatrists have emphasized individual internal characteristics and forces, biological researchers have focused on neurotransmitters as well as genetic and biological correlates, and sociobiologists have provided explanations on the basis of species survival and the genetic pool. So far, no overarching, unifying, or multidimensional theory of suicide has emerged.

This situation is somewhat analogous to John G. Saxe's poem describing a group of blind men who each encountered a different anatomical part of an elephant (Saxe, 1878, "The Blind Men and the Elephant," pp. 135–136). When asked to characterize the animal, each responded on the basis of his own unique perception. The blind man who touched the trunk likened the elephant to a snake. Another, who happened upon the leg, said that elephants resembled trees; the tail provided the impression of a rope; and so forth. Each characterization was correct to some extent, but also incorrect in that the blind men only described an aspect rather than the totality of an elephant. Similarly, suicidologists have been influenced by their particular orientation and discipline in their theoretical efforts that provide only partial explanations as to why suicide occurs. What is needed is an integrative theory or an integration of theories to expand and enlighten our understanding of the many complex aspects of suicidal behavior more effectively.

The task of integrative theorizing is beyond the scope of this book (for a thorough discussion of theoretical problems related to suicidal behavior, see Maris, 1981, chapter 11). However, in this chapter we will briefly review the major theoretical positions in the field, with special emphasis on the issue of how geriatric suicide is dealt with by each.

Sociological Theories

Durkheim

Emile Durkheim (1897/1951) advanced the prototypical sociological framework of suicidal behavior. According to Thompson (1982), Durkheim "wanted to demonstrate and establish sociology's scientific status by providing a sociological explanation of that seemingly most individual of acts—suicide" (p. 109). In doing this, he delineated three major types of suicide on the basis of the sociological forces that produced them. Furthermore, he briefly noted a fourth type that he regarded as minor in importance. Although Durkheim's is the oldest theory, along with several more recent variations it continues to generate contemporary sociological research (see, e.g., McIntosh, 1985, chapter 4).

Durkheim's typology differentiates between the causes of suicide produced by circumstances of integration and regulation within society. He used official statistics to support his contention that these social forces resulted in the levels of suicide that were observed within a culture. *Egoistic suicide*, the first type, occurs when the individual lacks adequate integration into society and also lacks, or has weak, integration into the family. Those persons who are not involved in society and its institutions (such as religion, marriage and family, etc.) are not constricted by their rules, including those that regulate, and often prohibit, suicide. Instead, they have only their own rules of conduct to regulate their behavior, and may act in terms of their own private interests. As Durkheim (1897/1951) stated, in egoism, "the individual ego asserts itself to excess in the face of the social ego and at its expense. . . ." He further defined egoism as "the special type of suicide springing from excessive individualism" (p. 209).

In contrast, *altruistic suicide,* a second type, results from insufficient individuation and, therefore, excessive integration into society. In such circumstances, the behavior of the individual, which is "almost completely absorbed" (p. 221) into the social group, is largely determined by the customs and commandments of the society. Such a person may commit suicide as a sacrifice for, or to benefit the larger, collective or cultural good. Death in such cases is the result of duty; "sacrifice then is imposed by society for social ends" (p. 220).

The third major type Durkheim proposed was referred to as *anomic suicide. Anomie* is produced by insufficient societal regulation on the individual, so that the person lacks "normative" behavior. Under normal circumstances societal regulation helps to provide a sense of equilibrium and limits for the individual. When there are changes in the situation of the individual or of the culture (e.g., economy, government, widowhood, divorce), usually of an abrupt nature, the equilibrium is disrupted and a state of deregulation exists. Under such circumstances, the anomic individual is left without clear norms to guide or regulate behavior. Both egoistic and anomic suicide "spring from society's insufficient presence in individuals. . . . In egoistic suicide it is deficient in truly collective activity. . . . In anomic suicide, society's influence is lacking in the basically individual passions, thus leaving them without a check-rein" (p. 258). The close potential relationship of these two forms of suicide were such that Durkheim observed their frequent joint appearance in the same individual (e.g., p. 288).

Durkheim (p. 276) only briefly noted, in a footnote, a fourth type that was the opposite of anomic suicide and, therefore, the result of excessive regulation of the individual by society. He felt that this form of suicide occurred in "persons with futures pitilessly blocked and passions violently choked by oppressive discipline." Such suicide might occur, for instance, in slaves. Although Durkheim felt that this type of suicide was of "little contemporary importance and examples are so hard to find," some contemporary authors (e.g., Peck, 1980–1981) have suggested that, in actuality, it may be more common in present society than in Durkheim's time.

Elderly suicide in Durkheim's theory

Both egoistic and anomic forms of suicide occur, often concurrently, in older adulthood. There are several factors that may produce the conditions that Durkheim associated with high suicide risk. First, *lessened integration* may result when older adults lose significant others and their support through death and lessened active participation in social groups. Fewer contacts with one's support network and society in general may result from a variety of reasons, including the residential mobility of younger members of society along with the relative lack of mobility among the elderly. Reduced social contacts may also be created by the everyday limitations on the mobility of older adults within their own communities.

Other aspects of egoism are predictable on the basis of the *disengagement process,* a prominent social theory of aging. Disengagement theory suggests that older adults will be most satisfied in their elderly years by relinquishing or becoming less involved in their social roles and in society. At the same time, it posits that disengagement is initiated by society and is mutually beneficial to the person as well as to society. One form of disengagement would involve retirement and its relinquishing of the roles that are associated with work. Although Cummings and Henry (1961) proposed that there are benefits to the individual and society resulting from mutual disengagement, it may also be a factor in producing egoism and, thereby, may increase the risk of suicide among older adults. As will be noted in chapter 3, the role of retirement as a factor in suicide is unclear. Some argue that it results in increased risk (e.g., Miller,

1979), whereas others contend that no such increases are involved (e.g., Atchley, 1980).

Another factor conducive to the development of egoism in older adulthood involves *social isolation*. Older adults are those most likely to be living alone (U.S. Bureau of the Census, 1992) and, therefore, at high risk for such isolation. The smaller size of elderly households may also be a contributing influence. Lessened contact with and involvement in family and other social relationships are, by definition, aspects of social isolation, and because of this, Durkheim would have predicted an increase in suicide risk. Research reviewed by Trout (1980) has, in fact, shown that social isolation is associated with higher levels of suicide, and Gardner, Bahn, and Mack (1964) have similarly found this to be the case among older persons.

Multiple factors that may produce anomie among older adults have also been identified in the gerontological literature, particularly with respect to the *loss of roles*. Old age has been characterized as involving a "roleless role" (e.g., Atchley, 1985, p. 164), a notion that implies that the norms that may be available to guide behavior are unclear or lacking. In addition, some people in the field (e.g., Blau, 1956) have suggested that cumulative role loss may influence elderly suicide, because it appears as a reaction more to a total life situation than to any single factor. Multiple role losses, of course, may also include those associated with retirement, loss of job, and widowhood.

For the current cohort of elderly men, retirement produces, along with other changes, a potential loss of self-definition because men most often identify with their job roles as a source of self-definition. With retirement and the loss of this role definition, the elderly man may experience feelings similar to those often seen in adolescence, so that in both cases a crisis may exist surrounding issues of identity (e.g., Erikson, 1963). Older and adolescent males may be uncertain about self as well as what behaviors are appropriate and expected of them (i.e., anomie).

Widowhood could be referred to as "domestic anomie." With the loss of a marital partner through death, longtime roles become nonfunctional and leave the widow or widower without clearly established rules of behavior (e.g., Berardo, 1992). In the process, other social roles may also be altered, as, for instance, in social groups where couples are involved. The widowed individual must operate without his or her partner in social and other settings, and after many years or a lifetime of such companionship, the appropriate actions for a newly single individual may be unknown or perhaps seem strange or uncomfortable.

The amount of change in roles and the resulting necessity for adaptation may vary with age, gender, race, and other factors, and the forces that tend to produce anomie or egoism will therefore likely vary as well. For instance, widowers have often been observed to experience greater difficulty than widows in coping with the loss of their spouse (e.g., Stroebe & Stroebe, 1983; however, not all research findings agree, e.g., Feinson, 1986). The loss may result in greater feelings of both anomie and egoism as their roles change abruptly along with their social relationships and contacts. Similarly, elderly White men, more often than their non-White counterparts, have been found to experience the changes in their roles and the pressures to adapt that are associated with retirement (e.g., McIntosh & Santos, 1981; Seiden, 1981). Thus, the more dramatic losses in status (as well as finances) would likely produce greater egoism in White than non-White elderly men. Non-White elderly men are generally more likely to be found in lower status and lower paying occupations, so that their adaptation to retirement may require less extreme adaptations to status and economic changes. In addition, it is the White man who is most likely to base self-definition on his job, so that its loss might more often lead to anomie for him than for non-White elderly males.

Although scholars writing about suicide in old age have not usually discussed it, *altruistic suicide* was common in the past and probably still occurs. In ancient eras and in primitive societies, it was apparently common for older adults who could no longer hunt or otherwise contribute to the group to leave and subsequently die of exposure to the elements or by other causes (e.g., Alvarez, 1972; Durkheim, 1897/1951, chapter 4). The intent, of course, was to avoid being a burden and to conserve resources for contributing members of the group or those who would be more effective in determining its future (i.e., the young). Thus, dying by ones's own hand or actions was the duty and expectation of the older adult under such circumstances.

In contemporary society, this type of suicide is often considered inappropriate, antiquated, and nonexistent. However, similar actions among older adults who do not wish to exhaust or drain the economic and other resources of their families, or who wish not to be an undue burden, may be viewed as a present-day form of altruistic suicide. In effect, they choose death by suicide and may feel obligated to do so to limit their dependence and avoid the strain on family resources. (This topic will be considered further in chapter 6.)

Other Social Theories

Sociologists over the years have debated the merits of Durkheim's theory, but in fact, nearly every social theory of suicide "owes Durkheim's study a considerable intellectual debt" (Collette, Webb, & Smith, 1979). One such theoretical position proposes that Durkheim's four suicide types are reducible to a single modern category (e.g., Johnson, 1965). The primary focus of that argument has been that there have been few modern examples of either altruistic or fatalistic suicide. In addition, egoistic and anomic suicide are the same, both conceptually and by virtue of the fact that they occur together, so that from a conceptual standpoint, egoism's lack of integration produces at the same time a lack of regulation (i.e., anomie).

Among the oldest of such reductionistic views of Durkheim's position is that of Gibbs and Martin (1964). These authors suggested that the key element in suicide is *status integration*. In defining this concept in a more precise fashion than Durkheim had done, Gibbs and Martin postulated that suicide rates would vary inversely with the degree of status integration in the population. It was proposed that status integration was reflected in the stability and durability of social relationships (marital, parental, labor force, etc.). Of course, it should be pointed out that there are great difficulties in establishing a single measure of status that can encompass all statuses of all individuals in a population. Research by a number of investigators over time has varied in the support that it has provided for status integration as a predictor of the suicide rates in populations (e.g., Gibbs, 1982; Gibbs & Martin, 1981; Schalkwyk, Lazer, & Cumming, 1979; Stafford & Gibbs, 1985). As previously noted in connection with Durkheim's position, the elderly are often less integrated and lose roles in the course of their older years, so that both of these developments might be expected to be associated with increased suicidal risk.

One major theoretical departure from Durkheim was advanced by Henry and Short (1954). Their predictions of suicide involved populations or societies, and they used the psychological construct of *frustration–aggression* proposed by Dollard, Doob, Miller, Mowrer, and Sears (1939) as a basic concept. Thus, suicide, like homicide, is one form of aggressive behavior (turned inward rather than outward). Henry and Short contended that when the environment frustrates the individual by blocking or thwarting an approach to a goal, aggressive behavior may result. To test their hypothesis, they suggested that business cycles (i.e., economic forces) would differentially influence high and low status groups and, thus, their suicide rates as well.

Henry and Short (1954) posited that business cycles also produce differential rewards and statuses among individuals and that frustrations result from failure to maintain a rising or constant status. They presented data that were interpreted to reflect an increase in suicide during business depressions, a decline in times of prosperity, and a higher correlation between rates and business cycles for higher than for lower status groups. It was suggested that high-status groups would lose status relative to low-status groups in times of business depressions, but that low-status groups would lose status relative to high groups during business prosperity. Finally, these researchers proposed that suicide occurs primarily in high-status groups, whereas homicide is found mainly among low-status groups.

Interestingly enough, however, Henry and Short acknowledged that the lower status associated with older adulthood represents an exception to their position. In other words, the lower status of the elderly should be associated with lower suicide rates compared with the higher status of younger and middle-aged adults. To deal with this contradiction, Henry and Short (1954, pp. 72–80) postulated the existence of an unknown second variable (in addition to status) that operates in connection with older persons. One such factor that they proposed to provide consistency in their model's predictions was the degree of involvement in cathectic relationships, particularly those with parents. Thus, the strength of the relational system is weak for the elderly, and Henry and Short suggested the possibility (along with others) that this produces higher suicide rates for the old compared with the young and middle-aged.

A final extension of Durkheim's theoretical position was proposed by Nolan (1979), who suggested that the notion of "role distance" advanced in 1961 by Goffman could be usefully employed within Durkheim's conceptual system. In fact, Nolan argued that this concept is a sociological explanation of what might usually be thought of as a psychological concept, namely, that of self. As he explained, suicide may emerge as a response when the more permanent self of the individual is incongruent with the self that is mandated to the individual by society. However, in fact, both selves are socially determined, with the more permanent self resulting from the social forces to which the individual has been exposed during his or her lifetime (psychologists have also discussed the existence of different selves; e.g., James, 1893, Chapter X; Rogers, 1951).

The dissonance between selves might be demonstrated when the person is compelled or forced to behave in a fashion that is inconsistent with the permanent self. In other words, "an individual 'breaks role'. . . [when] what he is doing is not what he *is*" (Nolan, 1979, p. 99) and the pressure to behave in keeping with the imposed self rather than the more permanent self creates "role distance." An interesting aspect of this notion is that "the rejection of one self is only a means of preserving another" (p. 102), so that when the individual acts in accordance with coercion, the more permanent self is essentially destroyed while the socially imposed self is maintained. On the other hand, to preserve the permanent self would require "destruction" of the coercive self. Thus, embracing a role in the extreme can also be destructive, just as Durkheim had suggested in his concept of altruistic suicide.

This notion of role distance as a possible influence in elderly suicide might also be applied to those circumstances in which the individual's long-established self and its accompanying behavior are threatened by life situations. For example, an older adult, after a lifetime of independent living, may, as a result of health or economic circumstances, be forced into dependence on others. Such a traumatic change might result in suicidal thoughts and behavior. The case of "Gramp" in chapter 1 (Public Case Number 1.3), for instance, could be interpreted in this way to explain the removal of his false teeth and refusal of food. This independent coal miner's organic brain disorder had placed him in a situation of extreme dependence that was in sharp conflict with his long-established "self." Apparently, he finally reached a point at which he refused to behave in a way that was required by his current life situation. In the same way, some cases of "rational suicide" (to be discussed further in chapter 6) can be interpreted in terms of attempts to avoid the destruction of the permanent self. This destruction can occur if the individual carries out behaviors that are consistent with an imposed self that results from either social pressure or physical health circumstances, for example. Suicide in such cases serves to maintain the integrity of the permanent self until death rather than allow it to cease to exist when the person is forced to embrace the new self by behaving in a fashion consistent with physical or social realities. This is, in fact, a line of reasoning used by some researchers for rational suicide (e.g., Prado, 1990).

Psychological Theories

Freud and Psychoanalytic Theory

Although Freud wrote no formal publication specifically about suicide, his writings contain several theoretical notions that may be used to explain it. Perhaps the best synthesis of these ideas was presented by Litman (1967). He noted that Freud suggested that suicide was multiply determined rather than the result of any single factor, so that he regarded it as a complex behavior, involving complicated, nonunitary psychological factors and more. For Freud to understand suicide, it was essential that it be part of a basic human instinct or tendency toward aggression and destruction. That is, he regarded suicide as one manifestation of the human death instinct, which he called the *thanatos* (as opposed to the *eros,* or life instinct); in suicide, the death instinct somehow manages to overcome the powerful life instinct.

The second major explanation of suicide by Freud was considerably more complex and based on the notion that the individual who commits suicide feels aggressively toward others but, instead of carrying out any overt action, actually expresses the aggression inwardly toward the self. This inwardly directed murderous impulse derives from what Litman (1967) has called a "splitting of the ego." In other words, the ego arises and develops largely as a result of our identifications with others. Identification involves the incorporation of our experiences and perceptions involving these other individuals into distinct, separate, and permanent components of the ego, thus resulting in a splitting. For instance, suicide may be related to the guilt one feels over death wishes about others, especially parents, with whom there is also much identification. These guilt feelings and the resultant suicidal wishes may occur when the loved one (i.e., love object), toward whom the death wishes have been directed, actually dies. Freud (1917/1963) described the obsessional self-reproach of the melancholic individual as actually reproach against a dead loved object that has "shifted on to the patient's own ego" (p. 169). Freud (1920/1955) further summarized his thoughts as follows: "Probably no one finds the mental energy required to kill himself unless, in the first place, in doing so he is at the same time killing an object with whom he has identified himself, and, in the second place, is turning against himself a death-wish which had been directed against someone else" (p. 162).

Other psychoanalytic writers have accepted Freud's concept of "retroflexed murder" as an explanation of suicide (e.g., Freud, 1917/1963, p. 173) but have suggested other patterns, including suicide as a reunion with a lost loved one, as a rebirth, and as a self-punishment (Hendin, 1963/1968; Klopfer, 1961; Meissner, 1977; Litman, 1967, noted that Freud also recognized that there were other patterns of suicide and that suicide was multiply determined). Kilpatrick (1948/1968, p. 155, according to Horney's theory of neurosis) proposed that suicide is the result of "accumulated self-contempt" in which self-pride is restored by the suicide act. In other cases, this self-hatred may be coupled with strained social relationships, and the suicide provides self-annihilation and, at the same time, inflicts suffering on those with whom interpersonal problems may exist. It is interesting to note that suicide intended to inflict pain on others and to exact revenge was common among primitive peoples (e.g., Alvarez, 1972, chapter 1; Colt, 1991, chapter 2).

Menninger (1938) divided Freud's concept of murder of and by the self into three components, which he labeled the wish to kill, the wish to be killed, and the wish to die. Individual cases of suicide, however, may involve one of these elements more strongly than the others. The wish to kill involves Freud's idea of primary aggressiveness and destructiveness turned inward, thus achieving a displaced murder. The wish to be killed refers to the desire to be punished or to suffer that occurs as a result of guilt feelings and conscience for real or imagined transgressions of various kinds. These transgressions can include Freud's notion of death wishes directed toward others such as the parents. The third component, the wish to die, is best understood as a manifestation of the death instinct becoming more powerful than the life instinct and putting an immediate end to the person's existence.

Alfred Adler, a member of the original psychoanalytic group who later broke away, described suicide in more social terms than did Freud. The individual cannot be considered separate from his or her social context. For Adler (e.g., 1937/1968), suicide was a solution that an individual makes to an "urgent problem" when he or she is at the end of their limited connectedness with society. All behavior requires social connectedness to be successful, but the suicidal individual lacks the level of "social interest" necessary to produce an adaptive solution. Suicide, in fact, may be regarded as a form of dramatic communication with others in the social environment. The suicide conveys a message intended to hurt or manipulate others and, also, to make clear the loss that these survivors contributed to with the suicide's death so that an element of revenge is obvious (e.g., Ansbacher, 1968). Ansbacher (1961) also noted that a common aspect of suicide is social uselessness, which is the lack of contribution, and even liability, to society by the individual.

From a cognitive context, however, Adler (as described by Ansbacher, 1961) believed that suicidal individuals have common characteristics. In addition to hurting oneself to hurt others, as noted above, these include a "pampered life style" (p. 207) in which there is dependence and reliance on others for wish fulfillment, with expectations that outcomes in life will be favorable. Suicidal individuals are also self-centered but feel inferior. The act of suicide is a vain attempt to gain superiority through control of life and death.

Although the notion that certain personality traits or characteristics might be associated with suicidal behavior has generally stimulated little interest, Kastenbaum and Aisenberg (1972, especially pp. 280–284) have been an exception in suggesting a Basic Suicidal Personality (BSP) that is clearly rooted in psychoanalytic theory. Although this notion was mentioned briefly in chapter 1 in connection with future trends in elderly suicide, a more complete discussion of this concept will be provided here. Kastenbaum and Aisenberg suggested that "all individuals possessed of this kind of basic personality would have in common certain pathological attributes or potentially lethal 'flaws'" (p. 280). Although they admitted that inherited factors might play a role, they suggested that early childhood experiences are mostly likely of primary importance in producing the BSP. They emphasized child-rearing practices and events and, particularly, social actions that separate mother and child; early rejection, deprivation, or separation; "psychological absence" of the parents; and the absence of any satisfactory parental substitutes. Among the characteristics produced by these conditions are low self-esteem, insecurity, hostility, anxiety, and guilt.

Kastenbaum and Aisenberg have hypothesized that people who possess the BSP as a result of these and other early experiences may develop "flaws" that predispose them to suicide by increasing their sensitivity and problems under conditions such as object loss, failure, and rejection. In addition, coping mechanisms for dealing with everyday problems will be poorly developed, so that such persons would also be predisposed to failure. These authors further speculated that these flawed individuals may be thought of as making up a potential "suicidal pool": a group of vulnerable individuals among whom the majority of suicides will occur. The amount of individual and societal stress to which they have been exposed and the impact that it has had on them will influence how many will actually commit suicide.

Finally, two other scholars have advanced what are referred to as developmental theories of suicide (Draper, 1976; Leonard, 1967). Although there are some differences in the theoretical formulations proposed by each, both authors have suggested that suicide results from problems surrounding the process of differentiation from and importance of the mother as a love object. Those for whom this process of differentiation and identification is disrupted, such as through abandonment or rejection in the young years, may develop a weakness or vulnerability to suicide under subsequent life stresses and losses.

Elderly suicide and psychoanalytic theory

Although few of the theorists mentioned above have specifically focused on elderly suicide, there are, in fact, some aspects of psychoanalytic theory that do have relevance to this problem in older adults. Achté (1988) has contended that the greater likelihood of a lethal outcome when the elderly attempt suicide, along with their use of more lethal methods than other age groups (see chapter 1), is the result of "a profound death wish" (p. 55). Relatedly, Farberow and Shneidman (1957) classified over 600 suicide notes, using Menninger's (1938) triad of wishes to kill, be killed, and die, with the notes being grouped by age into young, middle-aged, and old (60+ years of age). The results of the classification showed that themes relating to the wish to kill and be killed were highest among the youngest group and lowest among the oldest (for the former theme, 31% of the young compared with only 11% of the old notes; for the latter theme, 27% compared with 16%, respectively). The wish to die, on the other hand, was significantly higher among the elderly, being represented in 57% of the notes (compared with only 23% of the young; as might be expected, the middle-aged were intermediate for all themes). From these results, it appears that guilt and self-blame are low in the elderly but that themes related to despair as well as emotional and physical tiredness are common in this group.

As Achté (1988) concluded, these results could be interpreted as indicating an overwhelming death instinct and suggesting that the many losses associated with older adulthood provide the basis for poorly resolved loss and incomplete mourning that might be associated with suicide. Similarly, physical and social changes can undermine self-esteem in old age and also create difficulties in establishing object relationships. Older persons may also experience anxiety, insecurity, and hopelessness that may make death seem attractive "to achieve peace, [and] to free oneself from inner evil" (p. 64).

Suicide may be seen by an elderly person as a way of reuniting with a dead loved one, perhaps a spouse. It might also be regarded, in this sense, as a way of dealing with personal feelings of responsibility or guilt about a loved one's death. This may be particularly true when the death had a protracted course that was emotionally exhausting or economically draining.

Kastenbaum and Aisenberg's (1972) theory might be used to explain the higher risk of suicide in old age. Among those vulnerable individuals who survive to older adulthood, larger numbers might be expected to commit suicide because of the greater stresses that commonly accompany the later periods of life (i.e., losses, health and economic problems, etc.). Similarly, developmental theories (Draper, 1976; Leonard, 1967, chapter 7) would argue that those individuals that are vulnerable to suicide because of difficulties early in life are more likely to experience problems in older adulthood. If such a person feels inadequate and unworthy of the love of their significant other (a person serving as a transference mother object) because of physical age changes, or with the loss of important persons in their lives, suicide risk may increase.

Another concept that has its roots in psychiatry and the psychoanalytic tradition is particularly relevant to suicide in older adulthood. Butler (1968) has proposed that a natural, inevitable event in old age involves a life review. This review process entails an evaluation that will, if positive, aid the person in preparing for the end of life and death.

Butler's concept is similar to that of Erikson's (1963) final stage of psychosocial development. For Erikson, the general crisis of late life involves ego integrity as opposed to despair. It is a time in which the person evaluates his or her own life to determine whether it has been meaningful and worthwhile or, perhaps, a self-absorbed one in which the main concern was on self-interests rather than those of others and society. If the person decides that their life has been meaningful and worthwhile, they would achieve ego integrity and would not fear death. Conversely, a decision that one's life was not meaningful may produce despair and anxiety in connection with death and life's end, particularly if there is the realization that the time remaining to reconcile and reverse this evaluation is short. Whereas Erikson did not address suicide in terms of the negative evaluation of one's life in late adulthood, Butler did suggest that suicide was one possible outcome of a negative life review.

Nonpsychoanalytic Psychological Theory

Behavioral theory. Traditional psychological learning/behavioral theories, as well as cognitive models, have been used to understand and prevent suicidal behaviors. Although cognitive models are discussed in more detail in chapter 5, the basic features of these systems will be presented here.

Jeger (1979) has briefly noted that behavioral theories do not discuss suicidal individuals as much as the overt aspects of suicidal behaviors. The assumption is that suicide, like all other behavior, is learned and can be unlearned according to the principles of learning that are well established. Therefore, suicide can result from habits and learned associations (see, e.g., Frederick & Resnick, 1971), reinforcement of such behaviors, or the lack of reinforcement of other, more appropriate and adaptive behaviors (as in operant learning). It may also occur as a result of imitation or modeling (including those in the media; see, e.g., Phillips & Carstensen, 1988; Stack, 1990), as in observational or social learning. Each of these assumptions about suicidal actions carries with it the possibility or implication of therapeutic intervention. Viewed in this way, older adult suicide would not be essentially different than that at any other age and, therefore, would be subject to the same principles for unlearning.

In addition to traditional learning theory, cognitive theory has had a major impact on the conceptualization and treatment of the suicidal individual. Leenaars (1990) described the basic features of the cognitive–behavioral approach as typified by the work of Aaron Beck and his colleagues (e.g., Beck, Rush, Shaw, & Emery, 1979). This model includes a conceptualization of depression and emphasizes the strong relationship between suicide and depression. Beck and his colleagues have repeatedly shown in empirical studies that hopelessness is a mediating link between suicide and depression, so that hopelessness alone "appears to be the critical factor in suicide" (Leenaars, 1990, p. 162). Other components of the cognitive–behavioral model emphasize negative views and expectations of the future, the outside world, others, and the self; the existence of errors in and distortions of cognitions; and the desire by the suicidal person to escape the suffering brought about by these factors.

Another application of the cognitive–behavioral model has involved the use of Seligman's (1975) learned helplessness theory of depression. In this conceptualization individuals, through past experiences, come to believe that their own responses or behaviors do not produce reinforcement (i.e., there is noncontingency of outcomes on behavior). In other words, they believe that they are unable to effect changes in their environment or obtain the reinforcement that they seek by their personal actions. Thus, these individuals remain passive and do not respond, even in circumstances in which their behavior could effect change. Depression is one possible outcome in this scenario, and because of the strong relationship between depression and suicide, suicide may also follow. A "reformulated" learned helplessness model of depression (e.g., Abramson, Seligman, & Teasdale, 1978) also introduces attribution processes to improve predictions as to when depression will occur. Thus, individuals will most likely become depressed when they expect the consistent absence of a contingency relationship between their behavior and its outcome to be recurrent or long-lived, global (occurring in a broad range of situations), and external (determined outside the self). In both cognitive–behavioral and learned helplessness settings, as in traditional behavioral models, the age of the individual is largely irrelevant. However, the attribution concept that is used in the reformulated learned helplessness theory of depression has been referred to as "internal–external" and is similar to Rotter's (1966) concept of internal–external locus of control. Boor (1979) has found this attributional dimension to be closely related to suicide rates, especially for the elderly.

Personal construct theory. A nonbehavioral cognitive formulation of suicide derived from Kelly's (1955) personal construct theory has been elaborated by several authors (e.g., Hughes & Neimeyer, 1990; Neimeyer, 1983; Stefan & Von, 1985). Kelly has suggested that all people evaluate, analyze, and form hypotheses about the events that occur around and involve them, in order to understand their meaning. He identifies the cognitive entity resulting from these hypotheses, and their refinement following additional experiences, as the construct. According to Hughes and Neimeyer (1990), "suicidal behavior becomes more likely if this cycle [of construct formation and refinement] is disrupted in one of two ways; when the future appears totally predictable, and one's hypotheses prove redundant; or when the future appears totally unpredictable, and one's hypotheses are no longer effective" (p. 5). In the first case, the person views the future as already certain, hopeless, totally negative, and unescapable, and the authors labeled this "depressive fatalism," with a likely outcome being a highly lethal, premeditated suicidal act. In the second case, individuals feel helpless, desperate, and anxious because of the total uncertainty of their circumstances and life space. The only way to regain any degree of certainty or avoid further negative experiences is to end their life, in what Neimeyer (1983) identified as an "anxious suicide." The outcome in this case is typically an impulsive but infrequently lethal attempt at suicide.

From Kelly's (1961) viewpoint, these two circumstances are "mere suicide," and he also described another form (see also Stefan & Von, 1985): In the "dedicated act," the suicide prevents the person from abandoning his or her core construct system and the meaning it gives to life. Continuing to live would result in destruction of the self and of the self's system, so that, rather than permit this to occur, the individual chooses to die. In making this choice, the core system remains unaltered (even though the individual is dead). The crucial question in this scenario is what the suicidal behavior is expected to accomplish (or avoid) for the individual at the time of its occurrence.

Neimeyer (1983) has described the cognitive and attributional characteristics of the suicidal person as involving constriction and disorganization of constructs and the construct system, the anticipation of failure, emotional distancing from others, and the tendency to view the self negatively and events as dichotomous (i.e., the tendency to explain events in extremes, e.g., success or failure). These elements are much the same as those described by other cognitive and cognitive behavioral theorists and researchers, but here they are applied in somewhat different ways in connection with the core theoretical concepts. Although no specific discussion of elderly suicide has been provided by any of the personal construct theory authors, it may be assumed that any of the types of suicide could occur, although not exclusively, in old age. The changes, losses, demands for coping, and so on involved in the later years could conceivably produce any of the types of suicide described here.

Cubic model of suicide and commonalities. Shneidman (1985, 1987) has suggested two concepts to explain the occurrence of suicidal behavior as well as the common features of suicidal individuals. To aid in understanding the factors that may lead to suicide, Shneidman (1987) proposed a cubic (i.e., three-dimensional) model that represents three components of suicide: press, pain, and perturbation (see Figure 1). *Press* refers to the events in life that are important to the individual and influence thoughts, behavior, feelings, and so forth. There are both positive (i.e., good) and negative (i.e., harmful) presses in life, but it is the negative type that predisposes to suicide.

"*Pain* refers to psychological pain resulting from thwarted psychological needs" (1987, p. 174), whereas *perturbation* refers to the degree to which the person is upset. In Shneidman's model, each of these dimensions may vary from low to high levels of pain and perturbation and positive to negative press. It is his contention that only those individuals who are in the

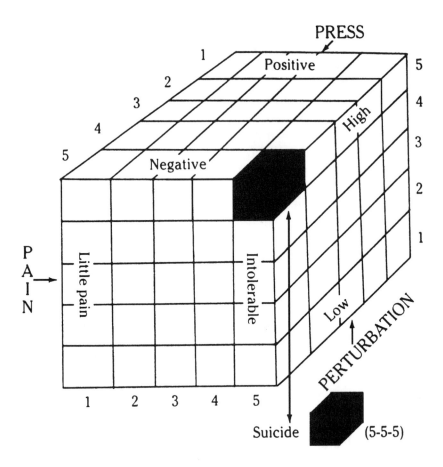

Figure 1. Shneidman's (1987) cubic model of suicide.

single cube position, on this 125-cubelet model, that represents the maximum levels of perturbation, intolerable pain, and negative press commit suicide. Although the three factors interact, Shneidman believes that pain is central in importance and that its reduction is the key to preventing suicide. Thus, demographic and other factors (such as age) are more peripheral, except for their influence on psychological pain.

In addition to this general conceptual model of suicide, Shneidman (1985, 1987) has incorporated these three dimensions into a larger set of commonalities that characterize suicidal individuals. On the basis of his extensive clinical experience, he has identified the most frequently occurring (i.e., common) psychological features of suicidal persons (see Table 1).

For Shneidman, the common stimulus in suicide is the intolerable psychological pain that is the prominent factor in the cubic model, and this pain results from the common stressor, frustrated psychological needs. The individual seeks "cessation," or complete stoppage, of painful consciousness, but not

---

Table 1

Shneidman's Ten Commonalities of Suicide

I.	The common purpose of suicide is to seek a solution.
II.	The common goal of suicide is the cessation of consciousness.
III.	The common stimulus in suicide is intolerable psychological pain.
IV.	The common stressor in suicide is frustrated psychological needs.
V.	The common emotion in suicide is hopelessness–helplessness.
VI.	The common cognitive state in suicide is ambivalence.
VII.	The common perceptual state in suicide is constriction.
VIII.	The common action in suicide is egression.
IX.	The common interpersonal act in suicide is communication of intention.
X.	The common consistency in suicide is with lifelong coping patterns.

Note. From Shneidman (1987, p. 167), as adapted from Shneidman (1985).

death per se. There may be a feeling that circumstances are hopeless and that the individual is personally helpless to effect any change. At the same time, there may be some ambivalence, in wanting to live but not being able to see a way to continue under conditions of intolerable and unrelenting pain. The person may be able to see only a restricted number of the possible solutions (i.e., constriction), wish to escape the pain, and even communicate a suicidal intention to those around him or her in a number of ways (see chapter 6).

Finally, Shneidman has suggested that there is a lifelong pattern of coping that "predicts" that suicide will eventually occur. This is also the major feature in the "suicidal careers" that have been studied and elaborated by Maris (1981). Menninger (1938) has also noted that "we are frequently able to see the steady progression of self-destructive tendencies first appearing long before the consummation of the critical act" (p. 73). Finally, Clark (1993) extrapolated from psychological autopsies of elderly suicides to theorize a "lifelong character fault" in these cases. This involves an inability to adapt to the aging process and lies hidden until "triggered" by sufficient stressors in old age. The possibility of an early identification of such a lifelong pattern provides hope and potential for both prevention and early intervention in the suicide process.

Most recently, Shneidman (1993) has underscored the prominence of psychological pain by coining the term *psychache*. In fact, on the basis of his extensive experience in the field, he has proposed that the most significant overall statement is that *"Suicide is caused by psychache"* (p. 145) that is perceived as intolerable. He contends that other explanations are unable to predict or explain suicide adequately because they ignore this central variable. In this connection, Shneidman has not abandoned his cubic model or commonalities but, rather, wishes to focus attention on the most important potential factor for understanding and preventing suicide.

In his cubic model and elsewhere, Shneidman (personal communication, May 1988) has contended that the commonalities of suicide are the same regardless of the individual's age. These common features involve similar processes and potential targets for preventive and interventive measures for those of all ages. In his 1985 book, Shneidman discussed the therapeutic possibilities for suicide prevention in connection with each commonality. For example, on the basis of his cubic model, he emphasized that a key in preventing suicide is to lessen the psychological pain of the individual and that the reduction need not necessarily be great. However, the reduction must be sufficient for the pain to become tolerable in terms of the individual's own coping abilities. This would be true for the older adult or the young person, depending on individual differences and unique backgrounds. To effect this diminution of pain, Shneidman (1993) has emphasized that efforts should be focused on identifying and meeting the frustrated psychological needs of the individual.

Biological Theories

Research evidence regarding biological aspects of suicide have primarily emphasized the possible genetic factors and neurotransmitter substances that may be involved (for a review, see Roy, 1992). It should be noted that much of this literature and research overlaps with and shares common conceptualizations with that on depression.

Genetic Factors

Genetic research that includes studies of twins, adoptions, and families has consistently produced an impressive body of evidence that strongly supports the role of genetic factors in depression (e.g., Wesner & Winokur, 1990). However, the exact nature of that genetic component has not yet been established, and the extent to which interactions with environmental factors may influence the outcome has not been determined.

Similar to the studies of depression, research on family pedigrees (e.g., Egeland & Sussex, 1985), twins (e.g., Roy, Segal, Centerwall, & Robinette, 1991), and adoptions (e.g., Schulsinger, Kety, Rosenthal, & Wender, 1979) have also supported the notion that suicide tends to run in families; however, the interpretation of the possible relationship remains controversial.

For instance, Roy (1986) reviewed the genetic evidence and suggested three possible explanations for family histories of suicide:

> First, the genetic factors in suicide may be the genetic transmission of psychiatric disorders per se—particularly affective disorders. Second, . . . there may be a genetic factor for suicide that is additive to psychiatric disorders and this genetic factor may be related to the control of impulsive behavior. Third, a family member who has committed suicide may serve as a role model for a disturbed individual. (pp. 667–668)

Roy et al.'s (1991) study of twins was unable to provide an answer as to whether there is an independent genetic component specifically for suicide. However, the research did produce evidence in support of a predisposition for psychiatric disorders that, in turn, were associated with suicide.

Biochemical Factors

Biological studies of suicide involving biochemical compounds are in general accord with the research and theories on biology and depression (e.g., Golden & Janowsky, 1990; Maris, 1986; van Praag, 1986). Although a number of compounds and substances have been investigated, the most convincing primary evidence generally has had to do with neurotransmitters. It should be pointed out, however, that the currently available research on biology and suicide is fraught with methodological and other problems (e.g., Motto, 1986; Motto & Reus, 1991; Stanley, Stanley, Traskman-Bendz, Mann, & Meyendorff, 1986) and therefore should be viewed with caution. As for depression, the well-known neurotransmitters such as serotonin have been implicated in the case of the young as well as the elderly (e.g., Jones et al., 1990).

Although the potential for identifying biological markers of suicide is great, the evidence is far from conclusive. This area of research continues to be actively pursued because of the obvious preventive implications that the data will have if such a marker or markers can ultimately be discovered and identification of those at risk for suicide can be improved. The investigations to date have been far too small in number to provide reliable results and have involved no serious efforts to include demographic variables such as age. Therefore, any firm conclusions regarding the role of biochemical factors in influencing suicide in the elderly would certainly be premature at this time (Rifai, Reynolds, & Mann, 1992). However, some researchers (Winchel, Stanley, & Stanley, 1990) feel that the evidence for a "serotonin–suicide connection" and its implications for treatment are sufficiently compelling to warrant special attention. They suggest that the possible development of pharmacologic therapy that intervenes by altering the serotonergic system has promise for some suicidal individuals.

Sociobiological Theory

DeCatanzaro (1980, 1981, 1986, 1991) has advanced a theory of suicide that is based on the tenets of sociobiology, which attempts to integrate biological and particularly evolutionary notions into the social sciences. In his earliest formulations, deCatanzaro (1980, 1981) suggested a model wherein "suicide should be tolerated by evolution when it has no effect on the gene pool" (1980, p. 265). According to this model, those who promote their genes, particularly through reproduction, have developed coping abilities or have resources that enhance coping, whereas those who do not cope are less likely to be actively involved in reproduction.

All of this would appear to hold true for the depressed, those in poor health, the terminally ill, the elderly, those under stress, and those who feel hopeless about their future. However, suicide is also more common in the unmarried (i.e., the single, divorced, separated, and widowed) than in those who are married, and among the socially isolated. Reproduction is one way to advance one's genes, but a second way is through relationships with relatives. Particularly, those who are "without contact with kin . . . would be incapable of behaving to improve their [kin's] inclusive fitness, advancing their genes as they exist in relatives" (deCatanzaro, 1980, p. 270) by contributing to the general welfare of these relatives.

The sociobiology model further suggests that there may be less ecological and societal pressure to prevent suicide in the groups of individuals identified above (i.e., the depressed, elderly, etc.) because their deaths would not represent any significant loss to the gene pool that was not already present as a result of their lack of gene promotion. By contrast, suicides among those who are well adapted would not be tolerated by society because their death would have a detrimental impact on the genetic pool. Therefore, there is ecological pressure to prevent their suicides and they "have a reason to live."

For the elderly in particular, suicide is more likely to be tolerated because they are likely to be beyond reproductive age or to engage infrequently in reproduction, and may also be less able to engage in activities that promote the welfare of their off-spring and other kin. DeCatanzaro (1980, p. 271) observed that even gender differences in geriatric suicide may be understood in terms of this model, so that differing societal roles and expec-tations for elderly men and women may produce differences in their "reproductive strategies and nurturance of offspring."

In his more recent works, deCatanzaro (1986, 1991) has devel-oped a mathematical model of "instincts of self-preservation" (and also its opposite, self-destruction) that incorporates and expands his earlier ideas. This model takes into account the reproductive potential of the individual and kin, a component for contributions and burdensomeness, and a weighting for the genetic relatedness of kin (i.e., a "potential reproductive incre-ment," 1986, p. 88) that is based on the kinship relation to the individual. Thus, self-preservation will be high when the person is highly involved in reproducing and there are many contacts with and support of kin. The most recent version of the model (deCatanzaro, 1991) also includes formulae for determining the self-preservation of cohorts.

The sociobiological theory also incorporates the expectation that suicide will be high in those who are dependent on their kin or who bring shame on them by their actions. Thus, older adults who feel that they are a burden on family would be at higher risk for suicide. This would also seem to have been true of the elderly in earlier and more primitive cultures when they could no longer hunt or handle needed duties and responsibilities. Such individuals may often have left the group voluntarily to die from exposure or hunger, or they might even have requested that a family member kill them (e.g., Alvarez, 1972, presented historical accounts of such behavior among Native American tribes). Alternatively, those old who were dependent, but who possessed important knowledge or skills, might have had special value to the family and group and, therefore, would not have felt compelled to take such drastic action (deCatanzaro, 1991, p. 24).

DeCatanzaro has noted that geographic mobility and the pace of change in contemporary society have tended to reduce the regular contacts with kin and to provide fewer geographically close persons with whom kinship ties of various kinds are possible. As a result, there may be fewer opportunities for "socially productive behavior" to be maintained and thereby justify survival. Technological advances have also provided access to swift and efficient means of death for which there exists no biological preparedness or evolutionary adaptation (see also Lorenz, 1963, especially chapter 13). The same has been noted for the pace of change in general. Coping tends to break down or become inadequate without evolutionary adaptation, thereby producing pathology and self-destruction.

Obviously, much more research based on the implications of this model is needed. However, it does represent one of the first serious and promising attempts to expand theoretical explanations of suicide into biological realms.

Other Theoretical Explanations

In addition to the social, psychological, and biological theories of suicide that have already been reviewed, a number of somewhat more focused and specialized theories have also been advanced, and some of these will be covered in this section.

Hamermesh and Soss (1974) have taken a dramatically different approach to suicide than did Henry and Short (1954) in the latter's economic-based theory. They began by admitting that although the majority of suicides cannot be reduced to economic factors, in some particular cases such factors may be a significant influence. This position is cited here because age plays a prominent role in its conceptualization. Simply stated, these authors posited that for any given individual, a determination of "utility" can be derived by subtracting the "cost" of keeping one's self alive at a bare, subsistence level from one's current and available resources. The resources, of course, will vary as a function of the person's age and income at a given period in their lifetime so that when the costs equal (or exceed) the resources, the lifetime utility would equal zero.

Also included in Hamermesh and Soss's (1974) determination of the likelihood of suicide is the assumption that each individual has some expectation of their maximum attainable age, the probability that they will reach that age given that they have survived to their current age, and their "taste for living, or conversely, . . . distaste for suicide" (p. 85). The authors further assumed that the taste for living will differ by cohort and be determined at the time of the birth of the cohort. In short, it was proposed that the person will commit suicide when the net sum of their lifetime utility and taste for living equals zero. Thus, income distribution and tastes for or against suicide are primary factors in determining the number of suicides that will occur in a particular population.

Hamermesh and Soss (1974) presented statistical evidence that their theory-based explanation is consistent with the increase of suicide rates with age and the decrease in rates with increases in income. They further argued that their theory would predict the decreases in suicides among older adults as well as those nearing retirement age since World War II, on the basis of the fact that income from all sources has risen in that time period while the rates of suicide have decreased. Overall, increased income during this time has also reduced some of the earlier variability in income levels within groups nearing and reaching retirement, especially when this is combined with the introduction and expansion of Social Security benefits for the elderly. In summary, these researchers argued, as noted in chapter 1, that economic factors have been an important contributor to the decline in elderly suicide rates since the 1930s.

In an essentially cognitive/psychological vein, Buchanan (1991) has suggested that the key determiner in suicide is whether the individual can find meaning in life. The evaluation of meaningfulness by the individual will have an important impact on his or her thoughts, feelings, and actions. This position, of course, is based on some of the same cognitive literature that was cited earlier, with a focus on the feelings and cognitions surrounding hopelessness and depression. This position "suggests that the individual who is still able to determine a meaning in life will choose to continue living, even though they may accept or welcome death" (p. 346). This conception helps us to understand the strong will to live in some older adults who have experienced losses, physical health problems, pain, and perhaps many "exit events" that might be conducive to suicide in others.

Nelson (1980) has advanced a psychosocial theory in which the social and subjective value of the individual are the factors that lead toward or away from suicidal behavior. He proposed that people have social value or utility to the degree that they are needed or integrated into social groups and communities. This assessment might be based on the economic utility of the person, the marketability of their skills or attributes, or their affective importance to others in a group. Nelson also argued that the value of social utility has generally decreased as society undergoes rapid technological change and has become more heavily populated, complex, urbanized, and depersonalized.

At the same time, Nelson (1980) suggested that society's overall lack of need or concern for the individual in and of itself is not sufficient for the person to become suicidal. The subjective value that the person perceives that he or she has, which is called hedonistic value, may allow that individual to feel happy and find high life satisfaction despite their low social utility. In somewhat the same vein as Buchanan's (1991) emphasis on meaning in life, a given person may be able to find adequate pleasure in living even in the face of illness, social isolation, or other problems and losses. According to Nelson, "what may be pleasurable for one person may be boring or painful to another. Thus, one's particular developmental history, biological endowment, and personal expectations would tend to influence one's hedonistic utility somewhat independent of one's objective life situation" (p. 128). In general, however, Nelson feels that changes in one type of utility will be associated with similar changes in another (i.e., a positive relationship).

Nelson gave no examples or cases to support or illustrate his choice of social and subjective utility, but older adults may be viewed as one of the groups most likely to experience lessened social utility. If a positive relationship exists between social and subjective utility, then those who are least able to cope with rapid changes and multiple losses and who may not be well integrated into social groups may be expected to demonstrate low levels of social utility. Their awareness of this apparent lessened value to society may produce feelings of uselessness, obsolescence, and being a burden on others. Suicide would be one possible solution to this dilemma, particularly if the individual finds it difficult to maintain an adequate level of satisfaction in his or her life (and, thus, personal subjective utility). In the case of the elderly, like any other group, they do not generally commit suicide in spite of the fact that almost all older adults experience many changes, problems, losses, and so forth that may lower social utility and would be expected to influence hedonistic utility. The relative infrequency of suicide in the elderly (as in all age groups) would suggest that Nelson's "exception" of the individual who is happy despite declines in social utility may actually represent the norm more than the exception.

One of the most elaborate "mixed-factors" theories of suicide was advanced by Farber (1968), who discussed the societal surroundings of the individual and the person's resulting probability of suicide. One of several formulae that he provided (pp. 74–75) suggests that the psychological component of suicide is a function of the "Vulnerability in the Personality and the degree of certain Deprivations" as well as hope, one's sense of competence, and the degree of "Threat to acceptable life conditions." According to Farber, the social–environmental component of suicide includes societal demands for competence and interpersonal giving, societal tolerance of suicide, the degree of hope for the future within the society, and the availability of assistance in the environment ("succorance"). Although precise measures of these variables were not provided, the formulation did identify both individual and social variables that may contribute to suicidal acts.

Farber specifically discussed geriatric suicide, where older persons may have a number of physical, psychological, and social contributors to the loss and lack of hope (pp. 102–103). His prescriptions for alleviation of the problems included welfare states, cultural attitude changes toward death to facilitate acceptance rather than avoidance, the development of useful roles for the elderly, and medical advances for diseases that seemed hopeless and for the treatment of pain. These prescribed improvements would each attack one or more of the psychological and social components that he conceived as being related to suicide.

A final theoretical model that considers several factors is the Overlap Model of Blumenthal and Kupfer (as described in Blumenthal, 1990). These authors suggested that five risk factor domains help to understand suicidal behavior. The five domains are biochemistry, family history and genetics, psychiatric disorders, personality traits and disorders, and psychosocial life events and chronic medical illness. To make the model more concrete, Blumenthal and Kupfer envisioned these five spheres as overlapping Venn diagrams, with the sectors and intersections representing levels of vulnerability. In particular, the existence of more than one of these factors in the same individual increases the risk of or vulnerability to suicidal behavior (e.g., psychiatric disorder as well as poor social supports in the psychosocial dimension). Blumenthal (1990) argued that this model can be used to understand and make clinical judgments across the life span. Although the specifics of this argument are largely lacking, it was suggested that the high rates in old age "may reflect an accumulation of risk factors as the individual ages" (p. 700) and the lack of readily available interventions for this group. A difficulty here, which exists for many other approaches as well, is that the model would likely predict far greater suicidal behavior in older adults than actually exists because of the very accumulation of risk factors that accompany normal aging. There is too little specific knowledge about older adults in each of these domains to make the model useful. The potential for such an approach, however, is compelling and may hold great promise as basic evidence about elderly suicide grows and expands to include all of the domains of this model.

In summary, a number of theoretical positions have been proposed that, in whole or in part, attempt to deal with suicide in general and with geriatric suicide in particular. None of these, however, are sufficiently comprehensive to deal with the broad scope and complexity of suicidal behavior across the life span. In addition, none are able to predict with any degree of accuracy which older person will be most likely to commit suicide. Although many of the current conceptualizations provide a general framework that may be helpful in interpreting some of the available facts, no single theory fares well in predicting or explaining the differences and complexities encountered from one case to the next. This is certainly true in relation to the case studies that are described in this book, where some aspects are relevant and explainable within a given theoretical position and others are not. Clearly, much remains to be done to develop and expand the empirical base of information on suicidal behavior and thus make possible improvement in the scope and sophistication of suicide theory.

References

Abramson, L. Y., Seligman, M. E. P., & Teasdale, J. D. (1978). Learned helplessness in humans: Critique and reformulation. *Journal of Abnormal Psychology, 87,* 49–74.

Achté, K. (1988). Suicidal tendencies in the elderly. *Suicide and Life-Threatening Behavior, 18,* 55–64.

Adler, A. (1968). Suicide. In J. P. Gibbs (Ed.), *Suicide* (pp. 146–150). New York: Harper & Row. (Original work published 1937)

Alvarez, A. (1972). *The savage god: A study of suicide.* New York: Random House.

Ansbacher, H. L. (1961). Suicide: The Adlerian point of view. In N. L. Farberow & E. S. Shneidman (Eds.), *The cry for help* (pp. 204–219). New York: McGraw-Hill.

Ansbacher, H. L. (1968). Adler and the 1910 Vienna symposium on suicide. *Journal of Individual Psychology, 24,* 181–192.

Atchley, R. C. (1980). Aging and suicide: Reflections on the quality of life? In S. G. Haynes & M. Feinleib (Eds.), *Second conference on the epidemiology of aging* (NIH Publication No. 80-969, pp. 141–158). Washington, DC: U.S. Government Printing Office.

Atchley, R. C. (1985). *Social forces and aging: An introduction to social gerontology* (4th ed.). Belmont, CA: Wadsworth.

Beck, A. T., Rush, A. J., Shaw, B., & Emery, G. (1979). *Cognitive therapy of depression.* New York: Guilford Press.

Berardo, F. M. (1992). Widowhood. In E. F. Borgatta & M. L. Borgatta (Eds.), *Encyclopedia of sociology* (Vol. 4, pp. 2250–2253). New York: Macmillan.

Blau, Z. S. (1956). Changes in status and age identification. *American Sociological Review, 21,* 198–203.

Blumenthal, S. J. (1990). An overview and synopsis of risk factors, assessment, and treatment of suicidal patients over the life cycle. In S. J. Blumenthal & D. J. Kupfer (Eds.), *Suicide over the life cycle: Risk factors, assessment, and treatment of suicidal patients* (pp. 685–733). Washington, DC: American Psychiatric Press.

Boor, M. (1979). Anomie and United States suicide rates, 1973–1976. *Journal of Clinical Psychology, 35,* 703–706.

Buchanan, D. M. (1991). Suicide: A conceptual model for an avoidable death. *Archives of Psychiatric Nursing, 5,* 341–349.

Butler, R. N. (1968). The life review: An interpretation of reminiscence in the aged. In B. L. Neugarten (Ed.), *Middle age and aging* (pp. 486–496). Chicago: University of Chicago Press.

Clark, D. C. (1993). Narcissistic crises of aging and suicidal despair. *Suicide and Life-Threatening Behavior, 23,* 21–26.

Collette, J., Webb, S. D., & Smith, D. L. (1979). Suicide, alcoholism and types of social integration: Clarification of a theoretical legacy. *Sociology and Social Research, 63,* 699–721.

Colt, G. H. (1991). *The enigma of suicide.* New York: Summit.

Cummings, E., & Henry, W. E. (1961). *Growing old: The process of disengagement.* New York: Basic Books.

deCatanzaro, D. (1980). Human suicide: A biological perspective. *Behavioral and Brain Sciences, 3,* 265–290.

deCatanzaro, D. (1981). *Suicide and self-damaging behavior: A sociobiological perspective.* New York: Academic Press.

deCatanzaro, D. (1986). A mathematical model of evolutionary pressures regulating self-preservation and self-destruction. In R. W. Maris (Ed.), *Biology of suicide* (pp. 84–99). New York: Guilford Press.

deCatanzaro, D. (1991). Evolutionary limits to self-preservation. *Ethology and Sociobiology, 12,* 13–28.

Dollard, J., Doob, L. W., Miller, N. E., Mowrer, O. H., & Sears, R. F. (1939). *Frustration and aggression.* New Haven, CT: Yale University Press.

Draper, E. (1976). A developmental theory of suicide. *Comprehensive Psychiatry, 17,* 63–80.

Durkheim, E. (1951). *Suicide: A study in sociology* (J. A. Spaulding & G. Simpson, Trans.; G. Simpson, Ed.). New York: Free Press. (Original work published 1897)

Egeland, J. A., & Sussex, J. N. (1985). Suicide and family loadings for affective disorders. *Journal of the American Medical Association, 254,* 915–918.

Erikson, E. H. (1963). *Childhood and society* (2nd rev. ed.). New York: Norton.

Farber, M. L. (1968). *Theory of suicide.* New York: Funk & Wagnalls.

Farberow, N. L., & Shneidman, E. S. (1957). Suicide and age. In E. S. Shneidman & N. L. Farberow (Eds.), *Clues to suicide* (pp. 41–49). New York: McGraw-Hill.

Feinson, M. C. (1986). Aging widows and widowers: Are there mental health differences? *International Journal of Aging and Human Development, 23,* 241–255.

Frederick, C. J., & Resnik, H. L. P. (1971). How suicidal behaviors are learned. *American Journal of Psychotherapy, 25,* 37–55.

Freud, S. (1955). The psychogenesis of a case of homosexuality in a woman. In J. Strachey (Ed. & Trans.), *The standard edition of the complete psychological works of Sigmund Freud* (Vol. 18, pp. 147–172). London: Hogarth Press. (Original work published 1920)

Freud, S. (1963). Mourning and melancholia. In P. Rieff (Ed.), *General psychological theory: Papers on metapsychology* (pp. 164–179). New York: Collier. (Original work published 1917)

Gardner, E. A., Bahn, A. K., & Mack, M. (1964). Suicide and psychiatric care in the aging. *Archives of General Psychiatry, 10,* 547–553.

Gibbs, J. P. (1982). Testing a theory of status integration and suicide rates. *American Sociological Review, 47,* 227–237.

Gibbs, J. P., & Martin, W. T. (1964). *Status integration and suicide.* Eugene: University of Oregon Press.

Gibbs, J. P., & Martin, W. T. (1981). Still another look at status integration and suicide. *Social Forces, 59,* 815–823.

Goffman, E. (1961). *Encounters.* New York: Bobbs-Merrill.

Golden, R. N., & Janowsky, D. S. (1990). Biological theories of depression. In B. B. Wolman & G. Stricker (Eds.), *Depressive disorders: Facts, theories, and treatment methods* (pp. 3–21). New York: Wiley.

Hamermesh, D. S., & Soss, N. M. (1974). An economic theory of suicide. *Journal of Political Economy, 28,* 83–98.

Hendin, H. (1968). The psychodynamics of suicide. In J. P. Gibbs (Ed.), *Suicide* (pp. 133–146). New York: Harper & Row. (Original work published 1963)

Henry, A. F., & Short, J. F., Jr. (1954). *Suicide and homicide: Some economic, sociological and psychological aspects of aggression.* New York: Free Press.

Hughes, S. L., & Neimeyer, R. A. (1990). A cognitive model of suicidal behavior. In D. Lester (Ed.), *Current concepts of suicide* (pp. 1–28). Philadelphia: Charles Press.

James, W. (1893). *The principles of psychology* (Vol. 1). New York: Holt.

Jeger, A. M. (1979). Behavior theories and their application. In L. D. Hankoff & B. Einsidler (Eds.), *Suicide: Theory and clinical aspects* (pp. 179–199). Littleton, MA: PSG Publishing.

Johnson, B. D. (1965). Durkheim's one cause of suicide. *American Sociological Review, 30,* 875–886.

Jones, J. S., Stanley, B., Mann, J. J., Frances, A. J., Guido, J. R., Traskman-Bendz, L., Winchel, R., Brown, R. P., & Stanley, M. (1990). CSF 5-HIAA and HVA concentrations in elderly depressed patients who attempted suicide. *American Journal of Psychiatry, 147,* 1225–1227.

Kastenbaum, R., & Aisenberg, R. (1972). *The psychology of death.* New York: Springer.

Kelly, G. A. (1955). *The psychology of personal constructs.* New York: Norton.

Kelly, G. A. (1961). Suicide: The personal construct point of view. In N. L. Farberow & E. S. Shneidman (Eds.), *The cry for help* (pp. 255–280). New York: McGraw-Hill.

Kilpatrick, E. (1968). A psychoanalytic understanding of suicide. In J. P. Gibbs (Ed.), *Suicide* (pp. 151–169). New York: Harper & Row. (Original work published 1948)

Klopfer, B. (1961). Suicide: The Jungian point of view. In N. L. Farberow & E. S. Shneidman (Eds.), *The cry for help* (pp. 193–203). New York: McGraw-Hill.

Leenaars, A. A. (1990). Psychological perspectives on suicide. In D. Lester (Ed.), *Current concepts of suicide* (pp. 159–167). Philadelphia: Charles Press.

Leonard, C. V. (1967). *Understanding and preventing suicide.* Springfield, IL: Charles C Thomas.

Litman, R. E. (1967). Sigmund Freud on suicide. In E. S. Shneidman (Ed.), *Essays on self-destruction* (pp. 324–344). New York: Science House.

Lorenz, K. (1963). *On aggression.* New York: Bantam Books.

Maris, R. W. (1981). *Pathways to suicide: A survey of self-destructive behaviors.* Baltimore: Johns Hopkins University Press.

Maris, R. W. (Ed.). (1986). *Biology of suicide.* New York: Guilford Press.

McIntosh, J. L. (1985). *Research on suicide: A bibliography.* Westport, CT: Greenwood Press.

McIntosh, J. L., & Santos, J. F. (1981). Suicide among minority elderly: A preliminary investigation. *Suicide and Life-Threatening Behavior, 11,* 151–166.

Meissner, W. W. (1977). Psychoanalytic notes on suicide. *International Journal of Psychoanalytic Psychotherapy, 6,* 415–447.

Menninger, K. (1938). *Man against himself.* New York: Harcourt, Brace & World.

Miller, M. (1979). *Suicide after sixty: The final alternative.* New York: Springer.

Motto, J. A. (1986). Clinical considerations of biological correlates of suicide. In R. Maris (Ed.), *Biology of suicide* (pp. 1–20). New York: Guilford Press.

Motto, J. A., & Reus, V. I. (1991). Biological correlates of suicide across the life span. In A. A. Leenaars (Ed.), *Life-span perspectives of suicide: Time-lines in the suicide process* (pp. 171–186). New York: Plenum Press.

Neimeyer, R. A. (1983). Toward a personal construct conceptualization of depression and suicide. *Death Studies, 7,* 127–173.

Nelson, F. L. (1980). Social and hedonistic utility: A conceptual model of self-destructive behavior. *Crisis, 1,* 125–133.

Nolan, P. D. (1979). "Role distance" is suicide: A cumulative development in theory. *Sociology and Social Research, 64,* 99–104.

Peck, D. L. (1980–1981). Towards a theory of suicide: The case for modern fatalism. *Omega, 11,* 1–14.

Phillips, D. P., & Cartensen, L. L. (1988). The effect of suicide stories on various demographic groups, 1968–1985. *Suicide and Life-Threatening Behavior, 18,* 100–114.

Prado, C. G. (1990). *The last choice: Preemptive suicide in advanced age.* Westport, CT: Greenwood Press.

Rifai, A. H., Reynolds, C. F., & Mann, J. J. (1992). Biology of elderly suicide. In A. A. Leenaars, R. Maris, J. L. McIntosh, & J. Richman (Eds.), *Suicide and the older adult* (pp. 48–61). New York: Guilford Press.

Rogers, C. (1951). *Client-centered therapy.* Boston: Houghton-Mifflin.

Rotter, J. B. (1966). Generalized expectancies for internal versus external control of reinforcement. *Psychological Monographs, 80*(1, Whole No. 609).

Roy, A. (1986). Genetic factors in suicide. *Psychopharmacology Bulletin, 22,* 666–668.

Roy, A. (1992). Genetics, biology, and suicide in the family. In R. W. Maris, A. L. Berman, J. T. Maltsberger, & R. I. Yufit (Eds.), *Assessment and prediction of suicide* (pp. 574–588). New York: Guilford Press.

Roy, A., Segal, N. L., Centerwall, B. S., & Robinette, D. (1991). Suicide in twins. *Archives of General Psychiatry, 48,* 29–32.

Saxe, J. G. (1878). *The poems of John Godfrey Saxe* (complete ed.). Boston: Osgood.

Schalkwyk, J., Lazer, C., & Cumming, E. (1979). Another look at status integration and suicide. *Social Forces, 57,* 1063–1080.

Schulsinger, R., Kety, S., Rosenthal, D., & Wender, P. (1979). A family study of suicide. In M. Schou & E. Stromgren (Eds.), *Origin, prevention, and treatment of affective disorders* (pp. 277–287). New York: Academic Press.

Seiden, R. H. (1981). Mellowing with age: Factors influencing the nonwhite suicide rate. *International Journal of Aging and Human Development, 13,* 265–284.

Seligman, M. E. P. (1975). *Helplessness: On depression, development, and death.* San Francisco: Freeman.

Shneidman, E. S. (1985). *Definition of suicide.* New York: Wiley.

Shneidman, E. S. (1987). A psychological approach to suicide. In G. R. VandenBos & B. K. Bryant (Eds.), *Cataclysms, crises, and catastrophes: Psychology in action* (pp. 151–183). Washington, DC: American Psychological Association.

Shneidman, E. S. (1993). Suicide as psychache. *Journal of Nervous and Mental Disease, 181,* 145–147.

Stack, S. (1990). Audience receptiveness, the media, and aged suicide, 1968–1980. *Journal of Aging Studies, 4,* 195–209.

Stafford, M. C., & Gibbs, J. P. (1985). A major problem with the theory of status integration and suicide. *Social Forces, 63,* 643–660.

Stanley, M., Stanley, B., Traskman-Bendz, L., Mann, J. J., & Meyendorff, E. (1986). Neurochemical findings in suicide completers and suicide attempters. In R. Maris (Ed.), *Biology of suicide* (pp. 204–218). New York: Guilford Press.

Stefan, C., & Von, J. (1985). Suicide. In E. Button (Ed.), *Personal construct theory and mental health: Theory, research and practice* (pp. 132–152). Cambridge, MA: Brookline Books.

Stroebe, M. S., & Stroebe, W. (1983). Who suffers more? Sex differences in health risks of the widowed. *Psychological Bulletin, 93,* 279–301.

Thompson, K. (1982). *Emile Durkheim.* Chichester, England: Ellis Horwood Limited.

Trout, D. L. (1980). The role of social isolation in suicide. *Suicide and Life-Threatening Behavior, 10,* 10–23.

U.S. Bureau of the Census. (1992). Sixty-five plus in America. *Current Population Reports* (Special Studies, P23-178). Washington, DC: U.S. Government Printing Office.

van Praag, H. M. (1986). Biological suicide research: Outcome and limitations. *Biological Psychiatry, 21,* 1305–1323.

Wesner, R. B., & Winokur, G. (1990). Genetics of affective disorders. In B. B. Wolman & G. Stricker (Eds.), *Depressive disorders: Facts, theories, and treatment methods* (pp. 125–146). New York: Wiley.

Winchel, R. M., Stanley, B., & Stanley, M. (1990). Biochemical aspects of suicide. In S. J. Blumenthal & D. J. Kupfer (Eds.), *Suicide over the life cycle: Risk factors, assessment, and treatment of suicidal patients* (pp. 97–126). Washington, DC: American Psychiatric Press.

Chapter

3

Special High-Risk Factors in Suicide Among Older Adults

A number of high-risk factors have been discussed in the previous chapters with respect to suicide in late life. Each of those to be elaborated here has been noted briefly in chapter 1 or 2. In chapter 1, our intent was to provide the reader with basic demographic features of the suicidal elderly. In that regard, we introduced several of the topics that we will enlarge upon here and conveyed their primary relationship with suicidal incidence. In this chapter, we will give special attention to a selected number of those risk factors that are particularly important in late life, by expanding the coverage and reviewing the literature for each. These factors can be divided in terms of those involving losses and exit events (including retirement, social isolation, and widowhood), and those involving mental and physical pathology (including physical illness and pain as well as terminal illness, psychopathology, Alzheimer's Disease and other organic brain disorders, and alcoholism). Finally, we will review two additional issues that deserve special attention: nursing home and other institutional suicides, and murder–suicide and suicide pacts.

Losses and Exit Events

Retirement

Retirement is an event that has the potential for bringing about profound life changes and the need for major adjustment on the part of the older adult. Some of the changes associated with retirement are as follows: income loss; lessened financial and emotional security and independence; the loss of work roles; feelings of obsolescence, uselessness, rejection, abandonment, being a burden, and having no place or purpose; loss of power, prestige, status, self-esteem, control, and direction in one's life; and increases in social isolation with the loss of occupational relationship ties. Individual adaptation to these changes is likely to be influenced by factors such as personality and long-standing coping styles, flexibility in dealing with role change, social support, economic resources, health, and psychological and monetary preparation for retirement.

With the long list of potentially negative aspects of retirement, it is not surprising that the event and period of retirement have been suggested by some authors as possible factors in elderly suicide in general, and particularly in male and White male elderly suicide. Miller (1978, 1979) argued that retirement and its consequences were major factors in the White, elderly male suicides that he studied. Among this group in particular, the Protestant work ethic and the definition of self that is achieved through one's work may combine to produce a major life crisis when they are lost by retiring. The lack of planning for retirement and the lack of focus in life that followed were mentioned prominently in a number of the cases that he investigated. Blau (1956) has also argued that cumulative role loss from work and family can produce a significant negative impact in association with a larger number of other lost social roles. Similarly, Rachlis (1970) discussed the importance of the accumulation of losses in older adulthood.

Other investigators have also emphasized retirement as a factor in elderly suicides. Sainsbury (1962) suggested that *loss* of employment was important as a predisposing factor in young and middle-aged suicides, whereas the *lack* of employment was more important in elderly suicides. However, Shepherd and Barraclough (1980) did not find that suicides were more likely to occur among the retired in their study that included 75 completed suicides of various ages along with 150 matched controls. They did observe that among the controls retirement appeared to follow a more gradual pattern, as compared with the more abrupt and complete retirement that was characteristic of suicides. In addition, the age at full retirement was significantly younger for suicides than for the controls. This implies that it may not be retirement per se but, rather, the timing and abruptness of retirement that may determine the extent of negative impact.

Peretti and Wilson (1978–1979) attempted to investigate Durkheim's concepts of anomie and egoism (see chapter 2) as influences on suicide contemplation among retirees, through interviews of 140 Chicago residents of a retirement hotel for the aged. The group was divided on the basis of the voluntary or involuntary nature of their retirement, as well as their emotional stability (an indicator of anomie) and involvement in interpersonal relationships (indicating egoism). Regardless of the voluntary or involuntary nature of their retirement, those who were involved in a variety of interpersonal relations, as well as those with a high degree of emotional stability, appeared to contemplate suicide infrequently. The authors suggested that these two factors were more important in predicting the contemplation of suicide than was the voluntary nature of retirement. However, they also found that those who retired involuntarily tended to show more anomie and egoism than did those who retired voluntarily. Anomie in particular was strongly associated with more frequent contemplation of suicide.

On the other hand, Atchley (1980) argued that retirement has no significant effect on male suicide rates because there are no significant increases in rates immediately after or at the age of retirement. Of course, it is possible that on an individual level suicides are affected by retirement, with the process of retirement being highly individual and predictive and, therefore, more consistent with Shepherd and Barraclough's (1980) conclusions noted earlier. This individual and variable pattern would tend to show effects across an extended span of time, so that suicides would be spread over a period of later life as other factors combine and interact with retirement to precipitate individual suicides. Atchley (1985, pp. 194–196) has himself theorized about a honeymoon period in retirement, with its euphoria for some retirees, and later phases of retirement where disenchantment and even depression may occur. Atchley suggested that there is no universal timing of retirement and thus no chronological age at which any of these particular phases occur. Because retirements do not all occur at any single age, this would contribute to the variability of suicides across older ages.

In a discussion of the changes in suicide rates in Europe since World War II, and particularly the declines in elderly suicide rates over that time period, Kruijt (1977) suggested that changing attitudes toward retirement may have been a contributing factor to those results. The change in attitudes was thought to involve the view that retirement is a welcomed life period rather than one of frustration and loss. This explanation should be considered and subjected to further investigation.

Social Isolation and Widowhood

As noted in chapter 2, older adults lose significant others for a number of reasons, including death; the mobility of the general population and the relative lack of mobility among older adults, which may, in turn, result in emotional as well as physical distance; and the loss of occupational relationships that are associated with retirement. Lower risk of suicide has been found to be associated with larger numbers of meaningful social and interpersonal relationships and involvements (Bock, 1972; Bock & Webber, 1972a). As indicated in chapter 1, married older persons have been found to be at much lower risk of suicide than the single, widowed, or divorced. However, Bock and Webber (1972b) have also found that the strength of the larger relational system may be more important as a suicide deterrent than marital status per se.

The elderly are those members of the population that are most likely to be living alone. However, social isolation is more than simply living alone. Those who are isolated from society in any number of ways, not just those who live alone, tend to be at higher risk for suicide (for a review, see Trout, 1980). One aspect of this isolation involves the loss of the individual's support network, and suicidal elderly have been found to have fewer resources and supports (Farberow & Moriwaki, 1975; Gardner, Bahn, & Mack, 1964), to have less contact with friends and relatives, and to be more socially isolated (Gardner et al., 1964) than the young. Elderly suicide completers (Jarvis & Boldt, 1980; Sainsbury, 1963) and attempters (Lester & Beck, 1974) more often tend to live alone than do their younger counterparts. Cahn (1966) has also cited the loneliness of elderly suicide attempters who had been admitted to a psychiatric facility as a major factor in their behavior. Relatedly, Frierson (1991) found that solitary living arrangements were characteristic of older adult attempters who were subsequently given psychiatric evaluations. Dodge and Austin (1990) have provided evidence that the three-generation family of elderly Japanese may help to prevent egoism and ultimately reduce isolation and elderly suicides. Proudfoot and Wright (1972) have pointed out that an unfortunate consequence of social isolation and the likelihood of living alone is that there is less chance that older adults who attempt suicide will be discovered and rescued before their attempt results in a fatal outcome.

Other Factors and Special Issues

Physical Illness

The chronic and frequently debilitating diseases that many older adults face often have deleterious effects on their quality of life and, therefore, on their reasons for living (Fawcett, 1972). As mobility, energy level, and strength decline, opportunities for previously pleasurable events and activities are likely to be lost. Leisure activities tend to be reduced in coping with arthritic joints and deterioration of the visual system. Rising medical costs can severely limit travel and shopping, and problems with ambulation or incontinence may result in an individual being essentially homebound. Although many of the diseases associated with aging can be medically managed, and the associated deterioration sometimes slowed, their impact on an individual's perceived quality of life is still likely to be great. Increased suicide risk has consistently been observed and reported among those with physical illness (Dorpat, Anderson, & Ripley, 1968; Fawcett, 1972; Rao, 1990).

Health factors have been repeatedly found to be issues more often in the suicide completions of older adults than for either the young or middle-aged (e.g., Chynoweth, 1981; Conwell, Rotenberg, & Caine, 1990; Darbonne, 1969; Jarvis & Boldt, 1980; Kwan, 1988; Sainsbury, 1962, 1963). The same has been true in comparing older to younger attempters (e.g., Kontaxakis, Christodoulou, Mavreas, & Havaki-Kontaxaki, 1988; Lester & Beck, 1974; Lyness, Conwell, & Nelson, 1992; Sendbuehler & Goldstein, 1977; although Dorpat et al., 1968, found no differences). Rich, Warsradt, Nemiroff, Fowler, and Young (1991) observed illnesses as the major stressors in suicides of the old-old (80 years of age and above) especially. Among completers, physical illness has more often been identified as a contributing factor in the suicides of men than in those of women. Chia (1979), for instance, found illness in 80% of older male suicides but in only 33% of elderly female suicides in Singapore. Chynoweth (1981) also observed illness as a contributing factor in the suicides of 64% of elderly male and 46% of elderly female Australians. As proposed above, illness may have an impact by threatening employment, producing greater isolation and loneliness (Dorpat et al., 1968), and potentially reducing independence and control.

The relationship between depression and physical health is also strong (e.g., Butler & Lewis, 1982, p. 73). In attempting to interpret the relationship between suicide and physical illness, it is difficult to determine whether the depressive–suicidal tendencies were a preexisting condition exacerbated by the illness or a co-morbid condition that emerged along with the health problems.

Pain and suicide. The chronic pain that accompanies some diseases in later life may also lead to increased levels of depression and feelings of helplessness and hopelessness. Although chronic pain can be effectively managed and controlled in most cases, it may not be possible to totally alleviate it, and therefore, it may require some adaptation and acceptance on the part of the older client. Thus, it is critical to assess the patient's medical problem in terms of the degree of dysfunction in activities of daily living and the degree of disruption of pleasurable activities that the problem has created so that the clinician can ascertain the overall severity and impact of the condition.

The pain that accompanies many chronic and acute disorders may play a particularly important role in the suicide–illness relationship (e.g., Breitbart, 1990, pp. 404–405; Fishbain, Goldberg, Rosomoff, & Rosomoff, 1991), as seen, for example, in the case of Wanda Bauer in chapter 1 (Public Case Number 1.2). An understanding of the concept of suffering and of subjective and psychological experience of pain, as opposed to nociception, the neurological sensation of pain, is helpful in this regard (Fordyce, 1990). Feeling as though the pain will never cease and that no medical intervention will alleviate it sufficiently are common depressive thoughts that have led to suicidal behavior in some individuals. The poet Emily Dickinson portrayed the qualities of pain and the impact that it has on the individual in her insightful poem "The Mystery of Pain" (Dickinson, 1890/1955, pp. 501–502):

> Pain—has an Element of Blank—
> It cannot recollect
> When it began—or if there were
> A time when it was not—
>
> It has no Future—but itself—
> Its Infinite realms contain
> Its Past—enlightened to perceive
> New Periods—of Pain.[1]

Shneidman's (1993a, 1993b) focus on intolerable psychological pain, which may be produced or made intolerable by physical pain, has particular relevance here. It should also be noted

---

[1]Reprinted by permission of the publishers and the Trustees of Amherst College from The Poems of Emily Dickinson, Thomas H. Johnson, ed., Cambridge, Mass.: The Belknap Press of Harvard University Press, Copyright © 1951, 1955, 1979, 1983 by the President and Fellows of Harvard College.

that most experts in the field of pain management maintain that almost any pain can be significantly reduced or eliminated through proper analgesic therapy. (This issue will be reconsidered in chapter 6.)

A number of specific illnesses and conditions have been studied in relation to suicidal acts, including multiple sclerosis (e.g., Stenager et al., 1992), epilepsy (e.g., Barraclough, 1981; Batzel & Dodrill, 1986), and kidney problems that required chronic hemodialysis (e.g., Dubovsky, 1978). Horton-Deutsch, Clark, and Farran (1992) conducted psychological autopsies of elderly suicides and found several cases of men for whom chronic dyspnea (i.e., labored or difficult breathing) was the chief complaint. However, most attention has been focused on terminal illnesses, particularly those related to cancer.

Terminal illness and cancer. When controversies arise in connection with the right to suicide, rational suicide, or physician-assisted suicide (see chapter 6), those most often identified are the terminally ill and especially those in their advanced years. Siegel and Tuckel (1984–1985) have pointed out that cancer patients provide the prototypical case for the right to end one's life (e.g., Public Case Number 3.1). Unfortunately, it is unknown how frequently terminally ill individuals contemplate or commit suicide (Saunders & Valente, 1988), but it is assumed that they are at high risk because of pain, despair, and the hopelessness of and wish to escape their condition. Siegel and Tuckel have reviewed the available literature on the topic and concluded that contrary to expectations, suicide rates for cancer patients were not higher than those for the population as a whole or those without cancer. However, a number of additional studies have found increased risk for cancer patients, and some specific tumor sites have been found to produce higher suicide rates than others (e.g., Allebeck, Bolund, & Ringbäck, 1989). Of course, it should be kept in mind that clinical assessments of risk by medical personnel may differ from those used in research studies (e.g., Breitbart, 1990). However, although the research findings of risk have been mixed, the general conclusion has emerged that few cancer patients commit suicide (e.g., Bolund, 1985a), particularly in hospital settings (e.g.,. Bolund,

1985b; Filiberti, Ripamonti, Saita, De Conno, & Maino, 1991; Hietanen & Lönnqvist, 1991).

An important aspect of suicide risk in relation to cancer and other terminal conditions has to do with how patients feel about their illness, their fears about it (Danto, 1981), even if they do not actually have cancer (e.g., Conwell, Caine, & Olsen, 1990; G. K. Murphy, 1977), and especially the coexistence of depression with the illness (Brown, Henteleff, Barakat, & Rowe, 1986). Massie and Holland (1988) concluded that vulnerability to suicide among cancer patients was likely to be elevated in connection with

> prognosis or advanced stages of illness, with a prior psychiatric history . . . a history of previous attempts or a family history of suicide. In addition, the recent death of friends or spouse, few social supports, depression, particularly when hopelessness is a key feature, poorly controlled pain, delirium, and recently having been given information about a grave prognosis are significant risk factors. (p. 6)

Public Case Number 3.1: Ida Rollin

Ida Rollin represents a case of suicide in which physical illness was the primary factor. In her early 70s in 1981, Ida was an active, seemingly healthy older woman. She was widowed following a successful and happy marriage of 43 years, and several years earlier had entered into a close friendship with a widowed man. Although neither seemed interested in marriage, the relationship was obviously an emotionally satisfying one. She had one child, a daughter, Betty, with whom there was an extremely close attachment and intertwining of lives. Ida's life and dying process were described in Betty's book *Last Wish* (Rollin, 1985).

Following her 72-year-old husband's death from a heart attack, Ida took piano lessons, learned bridge, folk danced, and joined a theatrical group. As was true throughout her life, in these activities she made friends easily, with her natural affinity as an excellent listener. The friendships and acquaintances that she made tended to be close, to the extent that she often "adopted" others. She was an active, flexible, optimistic older adult who felt high life satisfaction and was financially secure.

Ida had lived a good life. She was the first American-born child of Eastern European immigrants to the United States who had settled in the Bronx. She was an intelligent, self-assured, and determined individual who had graduated from college with the intention of becoming a teacher. Over the years, she taught occasionally, but in 1929 when she graduated, there were no jobs for teachers. However, she did secure a position in the personnel department of a Manhattan hospital. She married in her early twenties and took a better paying, and what proved to be a long-term, job in a construction company office. She and her husband saved and invested well, and she helped her husband start his own wholesale hardware business.

Their lives and that of their daughter flourished through adulthood and into their old age. Her bout with cancer and subsequent death began with a stomach ache. When the pain persisted after two weeks, she made an appointment to be examined by her internist and was referred to a gynecologist. A complete hysterectomy was performed, during which malignant ovarian cancer was found.

Chemotherapy was initiated to treat the cancer, and Ida's body reacted violently to the treatment. As expected, she lost her hair, and her physical reactions to the multiple drugs she was given made the treatments particularly difficult for her. She had to endure constant vomiting and nausea as well as weakness and disruption of activities most of the week following weekend-long hospitalization for the therapy itself. Her dread of the next treatment was extreme, but she responded well to the regimen of treatments, and after their completion her life, energy, weight, and hair returned to normal levels. This trend continued for most of a year, until after Ida's 75th birthday.

The problems started again with stomach pain that would not go away, and medical examination revealed a recurrence of her cancer. Surgery was not deemed possible, so chemotherapy was again initiated in an attempt to shrink the tumor and stop the pain that it was producing. Although Ida described the therapy as "torture," she consented to go along with it as her only hope. She experienced almost constant pain that was worse than before, found walking to be difficult, and was bedridden often with the pain.

The family sought a second medical opinion, and the recommendation was for even more vigorous and frequent chemotherapy.

Following the second round of chemotherapy treatments, Ida finally showed some alleviation in her pain symptoms, but they remained chronic in nature, even with medication. Eating and drinking made her feel sick and caused her to vomit. She also had trouble first with bowel movements, and then with diarrhea followed by dehydration. Subsequently, she was rehospitalized for the dehydration and responded well to treatment so that she felt some pain relief. However, this turnaround proved to be simply one of the ups that would be followed by even worse downs. Although the pain was reduced, she also experienced extreme bowel control problems that troubled her greatly. She became too weak to undergo further chemotherapy treatments and had trouble keeping anything down that she had eaten.

Through all of Ida's experience, Betty and her husband were greatly affected. As Betty described it, the disease had "taken over" her mother's life as well as her own. She said that "disease may score a direct hit on only one member of a family, but shrapnel tears the flesh of the others. And as I had learned, there was no quick way out of the war zone" (Rollin, 1985, p. 129). Another period of dehydration and rehospitalization made it clear that this cycle of events was likely to be repeated for Ida for the rest of her life. Her request to die and be relieved of the pain became more insistent and persistent, and the family was told that she would probably live only for several months. This diagnosis brought mixed emotions, but mostly psychological pain and anguish for Ida and her family.

Betty, a television correspondent and journalist, contacted the local hospice in the hope that her mother might find help and treatment there in her terminal state. However, there was only one home care hospice in New York City, and it had a long waiting list, so hospice care was not a feasible option. The slow, tortured course of Ida's cancer led her to ask Betty's assistance in helping her to die. This was troubling for Betty and her husband as they discussed and pondered the request then decided to gather information about how to help someone die. They obtained books with some information and made many phone calls to doctors, pharmacists, and others that they felt might be sympathetic to Ida's situation and offer sound advice, but they were mostly met with noncooperative responses.

Betty and her husband felt it likely that Ida would decide not to kill herself once she had all of the relevant information that they wanted to provide. They hoped that simply having the option would be enough to relieve the suffering she felt. When Ida could eat without vomiting, she wanted to kill herself before she might not be able to keep the drugs needed to kill her down long enough to be effective. After more frustration and dead ends in her search for assistance, Betty got information from a physician outside of the United States. He provided precise information about specific drugs, procedures, and steps that Betty requested, but only after questioning Betty at length about her mother's state of mind, depression, illness, treatments, and so forth.

The beginning of the end occurred for Ida when she was scheduled to be released from the hospital after her most recent improvement. Armed with the knowledge of what drugs she would need in addition to those she already possessed, she asked her physician to prescribe the most crucial medication by telling him that she was experiencing anxiety and sleeplessness that were unrelieved by her present medications. On release from the hospital, days of preparation began with Ida putting her affairs in order and becoming more resolved in her decision to die. Although she still had frequent intense pain, her mood was sufficiently cheery so that Betty suggested that for the first time in quite a while, her mother seemed like herself. Once again she appeared to be in control of her life.

Betty and her mother discussed their plans and upcoming actions repeatedly, and it was clear that Ida knew what she was doing and that she wanted to do it. When the time for the planned death came, Betty was with Ida as she took the drugs. At this time, she said, "I want you to know that I am a happy woman. . . . No one has been more blessed than I. I've had a wonderful life. I've had everything that is important to me. I have given love and I have received it. No one is more grateful" (Rollin, 1985, p. 235). After exchanges of "I love you," Betty left and Ida died in her sleep during the next few hours. Ten years later, Betty Rollin (1992) wrote that "watching her die was like watching her go over a prison wall. Life for her had become a trap. . . . she was grateful to escape. And my husband and I were grateful that she made it" (p. 32).

This case portrays the psychological pain that can accompany unrelieved physical pain and a terminal illness. Feelings of helplessness and particularly hopelessness, discussed so prominently by theorists in connection with the impact of terminal illness (to be elaborated further in chapter 4), are an obvious problem to be considered in geriatric suicides. There are, of course, many ethical issues associated with physician-assisted suicide (see chapter 6), and numerous others that are created when family members are involved. Concerns about legal ramifications were prominent among Ida's family members throughout the last weeks of her life. Cases such as Wanda Bauer's (Public Case Number 1.2) have made criminal prosecution an obvious possibility in such circumstances.

Psychological Factors

Depression will be covered in depth in chapters 4 and 5 as the leading psychological factor associated with suicide among the aged. It should be noted that anxiety is also a prominent factor in this age group and that agitated depression has been seen by some clinicians as a salient feature in depressed elderly persons. Disorders such as schizophrenia and bipolar disorder typically occur earlier in adulthood and rarely, if ever, emerge initially in later life. These disorders both carry a high suicidal risk within younger age groups, but their influence on suicide in old age appears to be minimal.

Although alcohol consumption generally decreases with age, the dangers of suicidal behavior resulting from the combination of alcohol and depression appear to hold both for older adults and for younger age groups (e.g., Hirschfeld & Davidson, 1988, pp. 316–325). Alcoholism is a self-limiting disorder, in that most alcoholics die before they reach old age, so that alcohol and other substance use and abuse tend to occur less often among suicides (Abel & Zeidenberg, 1985; Conwell, Rotenberg, & Caine, 1990) and attempted suicides (Lyness et al., 1992) with increasing age. However, those chronic alcoholics who do survive into old age typically demonstrate increased health problems along with poverty and familial rejection, which, in turn, may lead to increased levels of alcohol consumption, depression, and, ultimately, self-destructive behavior. Late-onset alcoholics, incidentally, who do not meet the criteria for alcoholism until the later years of life, appear to account for no more than one third of the elderly alcoholic population.

Again, when depression is present along with drinking that seems to be a maladaptive coping mechanism for losses such as retirement and death of a spouse, increased suicide risk must be considered, as it would be at any age. In fact, although alcohol abuse may less often be seen in connection with geriatric suicides, Lyness et al. (1992, p. 323) pointed out that this fact alone ignores a number of other important issues that may be involved in suicide risks among elderly alcoholics. This group must indeed be regarded as being at high risk, and Osgood (1992b, chapter 5) appropriately pointed out that the connection between alcohol and suicide in old age has been ignored and may be stronger than others have suggested. Finally, two subgroups about which very little is known are those who abuse alcohol as an analgesic (Hubbard & Carrol, 1992) and recovering alcoholics who return to drinking in old age after years of abstinence.

G. E. Murphy (1992) reported the results of a study of alcoholics who committed suicide. Although suicides over age 45 (and only one above age 60) were included in his sample, his findings implicated seven risk factors for suicide in alcoholics. The interrelationships that predicted suicide included the following in addition to current alcohol abuse: major affective disorder, little or no social support, unemployment, threatened or actual affectional loss within six weeks, serious medical problems, living alone, and talking about or threatening suicide. As can be seen, many of these factors are more likely among the older adult population. The combination of drinking and depression therefore becomes particularly important in the context of several of these other risk factors. Murphy's research findings indicate that the presence of four or more of these factors was highly predictive of suicide—identifying four fifths of the highest risk cases. The clinical implication is to assess the presence and level of each of these factors regularly and take appropriate measures to combat not only drinking, but depression and other existing factors as well. Murphy also noted that many of these conditions are cumulative and occur over a period of time, leading to even greater possibilities for interactions among the factors. This observation has special significance for the elderly, who often have chronic health conditions, are unemployed, and have lost significant others.

Organic Brain Syndromes/Alzheimer's Disease. Despite recent public attention to Alzheimer's Disease (e.g., "Alzheimer's Disease," 1992), little scrutiny of possible relationships between Alzheimer's and suicide has appeared in the literature. A few studies (Batchelor & Napier, 1953; Kiørboe, 1951; Sendbuehler & Goldstein, 1977) have indicated organic brain syndromes in association with nonfatal suicide attempts in old age. These researchers have also indicated, however, that organic brain syndromes are infrequently mentioned as a precursor to suicide. Sendbuehler and Goldstein (1977) suggested that organic disorders tend to reduce the effectiveness of successful completion of suicide attempts, because of confusion and "clouding of the sensorium." They specifically identified interference with coordination, planning, determination, and awareness of reality as aspects that tended to reduce the fatal outcomes. Kiørboe (1951) also added physical weakness that might accompany mental impairment among demented patients as a factor in nonfatal outcomes.

In a study of geriatricians' attitudes toward assisted suicide of demented patients (Watts, Howell, & Priefer, 1992), it was found that 66% would not assist in a demented patient's suicide even if current restrictions on such actions were eased (only 21% said they would even consider it for competent dementia patients;

although "competent" was not defined, it might be expected to involve an early case of Alzheimer's who expresses a wish to die, a wish made early and verbally expressed to others, or the existence of a living will; e.g., see Battin, 1992). However, it is interesting that many of these same geriatricians (41%) said that if they themselves were diagnosed with dementia, they would personally consider suicide as an option. Thus, it appears that there is widespread uncertainty and mixed attitudes toward suicide and its appropriateness for those patients with organic brain disorders.

A number of cases of Alzheimer's suicides have been reported. In chapter 1, the case of Gramp (Public Case Number 1.3), who had Alzheimer's, was described in detail. The actress Angie Dickinson has discussed the progress of Alzheimer's disease and her own terror in watching the disorder slowly ravage her sister. She stated that "I have told my daughter that if I get it [Alzheimer's], I will off myself. I will kill myself" (Greene, 1990). Similarly, another actress, Shelley Fabares, told a *Redbook* interviewer that her mother had stated that if she ever had Alzheimer's Disease, she would kill herself. Fabares suggested that by the time her mother was diagnosed, however, she could not remember the promise ("Alzheimer's Made Her Mom Forget," 1990). Margo and Finkel (1990) presented a case history of a patient with early dementia who was depressed and denied suicidal ideation but only weeks later committed suicide. The authors identified the patient's distress over the deterioration of cognitive functioning as a major factor in the suicide. A much more publicized case, of course, occurred in 1990 when Dr. Jack Kevorkian was involved in his first assisted suicide, that of Janet Adkins, who was in the early stages of Alzheimer's Disease.

Public Case Number 3.2: Janet Adkins

By all accounts, 54-year-old Janet Adkins of Portland, Oregon wanted to die before the Alzheimer's diagnosis was followed by debilitation and the loss of those things she loved in life.

Adkins was an active grandmother, wife, and former English teacher who avidly enjoyed music, tennis, hiking, and mountain climbing. She was described by her husband Ronald as a person who always wanted to be in control, and even before her Alzheimer's diagnosis she was a member of the Hemlock Society, suggesting that she wanted control over her death as well. Three years before her death she had begun to notice memory problems, particularly for long-known piano music. Later, her ability to read music began to decline as well. The diagnosis of Alzheimer's was made a year before her death, and her husband recalled how devastated she was at the news, commenting that "her mind was her life" (Egan, 1990, p. A15). She wanted to commit suicide almost immediately after the diagnosis, but following discussions with her clergy and family she postponed her actions. However, she remained determined to die before the disease destroyed her mind.

Jane read an article in *Newsweek* about Dr. Jack Kevorkian's interest in physician-assisted suicide and saw him on a "Donahue" television program. She contacted Kevorkian and arranged to fly the 2,000 miles from their home to Michigan to further discuss her use of his "suicide machine."

Although perhaps a year or more remained before she would suffer severe symptoms from Alzheimer's, on June 4, 1990, Janet Adkins joined Dr. Kevorkian in his Volkswagen van and drove to a suburban Detroit campsite. In the back of the van the doctor's machine, consisting of bottles of saline, thiopental sodium to produce unconsciousness, and potassium chloride to cause death, was ready. Dr. Kevorkian inserted an intravenous needle into Janet's arm and after thanking the doctor, she pushed a button that started the machine and ended her life a few minutes later. Autopsy verified her diagnosis of Alzheimer's Disease (Beck et al., 1990; Egan, 1990; Martinez, 1990; Robinson, 1990; Vento, 1991; Walmer & DeSimone, 1990).

Although Michigan had no law against assisted suicide, in early December of 1990 Dr. Kevorkian was charged with murder for his involvement in helping Adkins commit suicide. However, a Michigan judge dismissed the charges later that same month (Clancy, 1990; Howlett, 1990; see also Public Case Number 6.2).

The tragedy of Alzheimer's Disease (and other irreversible organic brain conditions) has become well known, and much research is underway to help us understand and identify treatments and, eventually, possible cures for the disorder. Ironically, at the same time that Janet Adkins's assisted suicide made the headlines, the findings of a group of Alzheimer's researchers also appeared in the national news that described their work on a spinal fluid test that might provide early detection of the disorder (Sperling, 1990). The medical as well as ethical implications of earlier identification for those who may eventually have the disease are obviously great.

In the survey of geriatricians by Watts et al. (1992), the respondents felt strongly (66%) that Janet Adkins's suicide was not justified. Post (1990) presented arguments against "senicide" (the killing of the old) on the basis that the present and future growth of the elderly population is expected to produce an increasingly large number of individuals with severe dementia. The "justification" of senicide in terms, for example, of the cost to society and families for the care of the demented elderly can be answered by philosophical counterarguments such as "the negative message [it conveys] to all those older persons who are dependent on others" (p. 717). This issue will be addressed further in chapter 6 in the context of rational and physician-assisted suicide (see also Battin, 1992; Moody, 1992; Thomasma, 1992).

Nursing Homes and Institutions

A generally neglected topic with respect to elderly suicide involves the older adult population that resides in nursing homes and other institutional settings. This is a potentially important elderly subgroup on the basis of their increasing number as part of a growing population of older adults. Concern for this group also seems warranted because of the prevalence of major depressive disorder and other problems among nursing home residents. The numbers are significant, and there is strong evidence that most of those in need of mental health services do not receive them (Borson, Liptzin, Nininger, & Rabins, 1987; Burns et al., 1993; Rovner et al., 1991). A study of nursing home elderly by Rovner et al. (1991) indicated that the likelihood of death from all causes within a year increased by 59% where there was a diagnosis of major affective disorder. Relatedly, Cohen-Mansfield and Marx (1993) found that depression tended to be associated with the presence of greater levels of pain in nursing home residents as well as the existence of more medical diagnoses and the poorer quality of residents' social networks.

Several early studies have provided evidence of suicidal behavior among institutionalized older adults. As noted in chapter 1, Kastenbaum and Mishara (1971) conducted an early investigation of institutionalized elderly and found that self-injurious behavior occurred during a one-week report period among sizable proportions of both male and female residents. Nelson and Farberow (1980) also looked at indirect self-destructive behavior (ISDB; see chapter 1) among 99 chronically ill elderly men in a Veterans Administration (VA) nursing home over a 13-month period. It was found that those diagnosed with diabetes mellitus had the highest incidence of ISDB. Additionally, ISDB was positively and significantly related to the experience of major loss, cognitive confusion, dissatisfaction with life and hospital treatment programs, infrequent contact with family and friends, and limited possibilities of discharge. Finally, Nelson and Farberow observed a significant positive relationship between ISDB and the absence of religious commitment. This latter relationship had been obtained by Nelson (1977) in other research that involved a separate seven-day observance of 58 intensive care elderly VA patients with chronic illnesses.

The only available early investigation that presented data for overt suicidal behavior (i.e., suicide attempts and completions) in institutionalized elderly was reported by Kiørboe (1951). He looked at all cases of suicide (14 men) and "the most serious" attempts (11 men and 10 women) in a Copenhagen institution over a 16-year period. Nearly all of the individuals had been in the institution for over 3 years. For both groups, there was the presence of physical health problems that most often were accompanied by depression and acute pain appearing as a factor in the completed suicides. All but 2 of the cases demonstrated mental illness, with alcoholism being a factor in 5 of the 14 completers but none of the attempters. Unlike elderly suicides in general, marital or financial problems or loneliness did not often appear to be part of the motivation for the self-destructive behavior.

An important factor noted by Kiørboe (1951) that differentiated the two groups was dementia, in that none of the completers showed symptoms of dementia but 11 of the 21 attempters did. Kiørboe suggested that "a debilitated constitution may aggravate an existing dementia and provoke an attempt at suicide, which is seldom successful because of mental and physical weakness" (p. 235). One implication of this investigation is that those at risk for suicide completions and attempts in institutions may represent different groups of elderly individuals.

In recent years, the institutionalized elderly have again been investigated in connection with suicidal and related behavior. Osgood, Brant, and Lipman (1991; reported as well in Brant & Osgood, 1990, Osgood, 1992a, and Osgood & Brant, 1990) received 463 returned questionnaires from 1,080 mailings to a national random sample of long-term care facility administrators. The results indicated that the mean age of the residents of those facilities that returned the questionnaires was 65 years, with 78% of them over age 65. This exploratory and groundbreaking survey questioned the administrators as to whether there had been any suicide deaths, suicide attempts, ISDB (see chapter 1), or deaths from ISDB in their facilities during the past two years. The researchers compared facilities in which deaths had occurred with those in which there were none, and they also made site visits to four locations and collected detailed information about these facilities and the deaths that occurred there.

Long-term care residents generally have limited access to highly lethal methods of suicide, and in addition, the occurrence of suicide deaths is likely to be underreported by administrators for obvious reasons. Osgood and her colleagues found that nearly 20% of the administrators reported suicidal behaviors by their residents during the two-year period that the questionnaire covered. Specifically, they reported that 294 residents (1% of the sample's residents) had displayed some form of suicidal act during that time period. Not surprisingly, the most common reports involved ISDB. Overall, among those who engaged in suicidal behaviors, 80% used indirect methods, which most often included refusals to eat, drink, or take medications; of all those who carried out such behavior (overt and indirect), 20% died.

In the Osgood et al. study, overt suicidal behavior occurred at rates slightly lower than those for the elderly at the national level and were markedly higher for men than for women. The highest overall demographic risk profile involved White, old-old (75+ years), and male persons. The young-old (60–74 years) dominated the reports of overt suicidal acts, whereas ISDB and fatal outcomes were more typical of the old-old group. Osgood et al. also considered the influence of institutional characteristics and found that suicidal acts were more common in facilities with high staff turnover and large resident populations and in "religious or other" facilities (vs. public and private).

In an investigation of New York City skilled nursing and health-related facilities over a six-year period, Abrams, Young, Holt, and Alexopoulos (1988) could identify only six suicides among residents age 70 and above, and this risk level was considerably lower than that for the same-age population in New York City. The mean age of the deaths was almost 85 years, and they involved three men and three women, with two each using hanging, jumping, and drug overdose methods. Thus, it appears, as the authors noted, that nursing home residence does not afford complete protection against suicide.

In another study, Loebel and his colleagues (Loebel, Loebel, Dager, Centerwall, & Reay, 1991) investigated the degree to which anticipation of nursing home placement might precipitate suicide. Among 60 suicides age 65 and above in King County, Washington in a single year, information regarding the reasons for the self-destructive acts was available in 18 cases. This information was obtained from suicide notes or verbal comments to informants who communicated the details to officials as part of the death investigation. Of the 18 cases, 8 indicated that the anticipation of or recent nursing home placement was the significant factor leading to their suicidal act. This motivation was the one most commonly mentioned and was particularly observed among those persons who were married at the time of their suicide. The researchers cautioned, however, that although 14% of the 60 suicides provided this reason, the figure could well be higher because motivations were not readily apparent for over two thirds of the sample. Alexopoulos (1991) also reported a case of a 76-year-old woman who committed suicide in which the relocation to a nursing home was felt to be a possible contributing factor. As Bettelheim's case in chapter 1 (Public Case Number 1.1) demonstrates, residents of nursing homes may commit suicide in overt or indirect ways, and such cases show that institutionalization may well be a contributing factor. In addition, the threat or anticipation of admission to a nursing home might also increase the risk of suicide attempts or suicide.

Murder–Suicide/Suicide Pacts/Double Suicides

Another ignored aspect of self-destructive behavior among the elderly involves the concurrent deaths of two older adults, such as a married couple, by suicide. This might also be viewed as murder–suicide, because at times one member of the couple "kills" the other and then kills him- or herself. However, in virtually all of the few studies that are available on murder–suicide, the individuals were younger and the suicides appeared to follow an aggressive act of murder, usually of a spouse or other partner (e.g., Copeland, 1985; Marzuk, Tardiff, & Hirsch, 1992; Rosenbaum, 1990; West, 1967). In the case of the elderly, however, the act is often more properly classified as either a dyadic death or a dual suicide/suicide pact. In all such cases, the male partner is the one most likely to kill himself after taking the life of his loved one or other relative, who is most often a woman.

Cavan (1926/1965) specifically discussed situations where there is murder–suicide with an altruistic motive. In these cases, the person that eventually commits suicide first kills another person who is perceived to be totally dependent on him or her or would suffer without his or her continued presence and assistance. Berman (1979) has classified such cases as "dependent–protective" (p. 22), and Marzuk et al. (1992, p. 3181) simply referred to them as "spousal murder–suicide (declining health)." Although these cases did not involve older adults, this sort of situation may well occur with an elderly couple where the wife or husband is physically ill or has a condition such as Alzheimer's Disease and relies entirely on the spouse for survival and care. If and when the spouse becomes despondent or ill, he or she may perform what they believe to be a mercy killing before taking his or her own life. In the case of a demented spouse, the deaths might more properly be regarded as murder–suicide because consent and agreement are not involved. However, where both partners are lucid and not cognitively impaired, there may be a suicide pact in which one partner agrees to "kill" the other before committing suicide. In other cases, both partners may commit suicide at the same time, either separately or together (such as a case of carbon monoxide poisoning in the same automobile/garage). Although Young, Rich, and Fowler (1984) have suggested that older married couples were most likely to be involved in double suicides or suicide pacts in the United States, Vijayakumar and Thilothammal (1993) have found that older couples are infrequently involved in such arrangements in India.

Although some anecdotal reports of double suicides have appeared, few formal investigations of the phenomenon have been published. For example, a nonsuccessful suicide pact by the actor Robert Young and his wife was made public in early 1991. The Youngs, both in their early 80s, planned to commit suicide together by carbon monoxide poisoning, but as it turned out, their car's battery was dead so that their attempt failed. The couple reported the attempt to police, and afterwards Mr. Young apparently entered a facility for psychiatric observation. The wife was said to have indicated that their actions had occurred after drinking, but other details were unavailable ("Sad Suicide Pact," 1991).

There have been no published reports of the incidence of dual/dyadic suicides. The available evidence is based on extremely small samples and rarely deals with the problem among older adults. Overall, it has been suggested that such suicide occurs infrequently and that there is no way of knowing if these acts have become more common. It should be pointed out, however, that this problem could potentially become more prominent in the future with the growing number of older adults in the United States and other countries.

Public Case Number 3.3: Henry and Elizabeth Van Dusen

Dr. Henry Van Dusen and his wife Elizabeth had long debated the issue of euthanasia and suicide with their family and friends, so their advocacy of active and passive
euthanasia was well known, as was their membership in the
Euthanasia Society. Dr. Van Dusen was president of Union
Theological Seminary from 1945 until his retirement in 1963.
Not only was he known as an educational leader, but even
following his retirement he continued to be regarded as an
eminent Presbyterian religious leader.

Following his retirement Dr. Van Dusen continued his writing and public speaking activities. Then, in 1970, he suffered
a stroke that reportedly did not cause him great pain and al-
lowed him to walk, but only with the help of a cane. The
most frustrating and agonizing result of the stroke, however, was the effect that it had on his speech. Van Dusen
was famous for his vigor, intensity, and verbal articulation,
and the stroke left his speech "largely incomprehensible"
("Good Death?," 1975, p. 83). He had contemplated suicide
after the stroke, but friends related that this violated his principles regarding euthanasia, so he had resolved to adapt to
his infirmities. His wife Elizabeth's declining physical condition was apparently the significant factor, in combination
with his own problems, that changed his mind and made
their suicide act acceptable. Elizabeth, who was an active individual, had undergone two hip operations and suffered
from a severe arthritic condition that was becoming progressively worse. Cousins (1975) described their circumstances
in a mostly negative way, suggesting that "in recent years,
they had become increasingly ill, requiring almost continual
medical care. Their infirmities were worsening, and they realized they would soon become completely dependent for
even the most elementary needs and functions" (p. 4).

The Van Dusens, Henry age 77 and Elizabeth 80, initiated
a suicide pact and swallowed overdoses of sleeping pills in
their New Jersey home. Elizabeth died from the overdose,
but Dr. Van Dusen vomited and did not die. He was given
treatment at a local clinic and for a time showed some improvement, but 15 days after Elizabeth's death, he died of a
heart attack in the clinic.

At Elizabeth's funeral, the cause of death and the suicide pact were openly discussed. Friends had known of their plans, but not until Henry's death did public discussion take place, despite clear evidence that the couple wished for the facts to be known. They had also left a brief letter to explain their actions.

Although some accounts have suggested that the Van Dusens had been depressed, most of the available information suggests that such was not the case and that the only factor was their health. Their concerns led to a decision to commit suicide that was consistent with their publicly declared attitudes toward dying, and their note made it clear that they considered neither despair nor pain to be the reason for their suicides. They wrote that "we are both increasingly weak and unwell and who would want to die in a nursing home?" Although their lives had been happy, their current physical debilities did not allow them to do what they wished to do. Their action was taken as an affirmation of their strong belief in free will. The note further elaborated on their beliefs in stating that "nowadays, it is difficult to die. We feel that this way we are taking will become more usual and acceptable as the years pass" (Briggs, 1975a, 1975b; Cousins, 1975; "Good Death?," 1975).

In chapter 6, the debate on the right to die and rational suicide will be further discussed.

References

Abel, E. L., & Zeidenberg, P. (1985). Age, alcohol and violent death: A postmortem study. *Journal of Studies on Alcohol, 46,* 228–231.

Abrams, R. C., Young, R. C., Holt, J. H., & Alexopoulos, G. S. (1988). Suicide in New York City nursing homes: 1980–1986 [Letter to the editor]. *American Journal of Psychiatry, 145,* 1487.

Alexopoulos, G. S. (1991). Psychological autopsy of an elderly suicide. *International Journal of Geriatric Psychiatry, 6,* 45–50.

Allebeck, P., Bolund, C., & Ringbäck, G. (1989). Increased suicide rate in cancer patients: A cohort study based on the Swedish Cancer–Environment Register. *Journal of Clinical Epidemiology, 42,* 611–616.

Alzheimer's disease. (1992, July 24). *CQ Researcher*, 2(Whole No. 27), pp. 617–640.

Alzheimer's made her mom forget suicide pledge. (1990, November 13). *South Bend Tribune* (IN), p. C12.

Atchley, R. C. (1980). Aging and suicide: Reflections on the quality of life? In S. G. Haynes & M. Feinleib (Eds.), *Second conference on the epidemiology of aging* (NIH Publication No. 80-969, pp. 141–158). Washington, DC: U.S. Government Printing Office.

Atchley, R. C. (1985). *Social forces and aging: An introduction to social gerontology* (4th ed.). Belmont, CA: Wadsworth.

Barraclough, B. (1981). Suicide and epilepsy. In E. H. Reynolds & M. R. Trimble (Eds.), *Epilepsy and psychiatry* (pp. 72–76). New York: Churchill Livingstone.

Batchelor, I. R. C., & Napier, M. B. (1953). Attempted suicide in old age. *British Medical Journal, 2,* 1186–1190.

Battin, M. P. (1992). Euthanasia in Alzheimer's disease? In R. H. Binstock, S. G. Post, & P. J. Whitehouse (Eds.), *Dementia and aging: Ethics, values, and policy choices* (pp. 118–137). Baltimore: Johns Hopkins University Press.

Batzel, L. W., & Dodrill, C. B. (1986). Emotional and intellectual correlates of unsuccessful suicide attempts in people with epilepsy. *Journal of Clinical Psychology, 42,* 699–702.

Beck, M., Springen, K., Murr, A., Beachy, L., Hager, M., Washington, F., & Boss, S. (1990, June 18). The doctor's suicide van. *Newsweek*, pp. 46–47, 49.

Berman, A. L. (1979). Dyadic death: Murder–suicide. *Suicide and Life-Threatening Behavior, 9,* 15–23.

Blau, Z. S. (1956). Changes in status and age identification. *American Sociological Review, 21,* 198–203.

Bock, E. W. (1972). Aging and suicide: The significance of marital, kinship, and alternative relations. *Family Coordinator, 21,* 71–79.

Bock, E. W., & Webber, I. L. (1972a). Social status and relational systems of elderly suicides: A reexamination of the Henry–Short thesis. *Life-Threatening Behavior, 2,* 144–159.

Bock, E. W., & Webber, I. L. (1972b). Suicide among the elderly: Isolating widowhood and mitigating alternatives. *Journal of Marriage and the Family, 34,* 24–31.

Bolund, C. (1985a). Suicide and cancer: I. Demographic and social characteristics of cancer patients who committed suicide in Sweden, 1973–1976. *Journal of Psychosocial Oncology, 3,* 17–30.

Bolund, C. (1985b). Suicide and cancer: II. Medical and care factors in suicides by cancer patients in Sweden, 1973–1976. *Journal of Psychosocial Oncology, 3,* 31–52.

Borson, S., Liptzin, B., Nininger, J., & Rabins, P. (1987). Psychiatry and the nursing home. *American Journal of Psychiatry, 144,* 1412–1418.

Brant, B. A., & Osgood, N. J. (1990). The suicidal patient in long-term care institutions. *Journal of Gerontological Nursing, 16*(2), 15–18.

Breitbart, W. (1990). Cancer pain and suicide. *Advances in Pain Research and Therapy, 16,* 399–412.

Briggs, K. A. (1975a, February 25). Suicide pact preceded deaths of Dr. Van Dusen and his wife. *New York Times,* pp. 1, 43.

Briggs, K. A. (1975b). The Van Dusens' decision. *The Christian Century, 92,* 276–277.

Brown, J. R., Henteleff, P., Barakat, S., & Rowe, C. J. (1986). Is it normal for terminally ill patients to desire death? *American Journal of Psychiatry, 143,* 208–211.

Burns, B. J., Wagner, H. R., Taube, J. E., Magaziner, J., Permutt, T., & Landerman, L. R. (1993). Mental health service use by the elderly in nursing homes. *American Journal of Public Health, 83,* 331–337.

Butler, R. N., & Lewis, M. I. (1982). *Aging and mental health: Positive psychosocial and biomedical approaches* (3rd ed.). St. Louis: Mosby.

Cahn, L. A. (1966). Suicide and attempted suicide in old age. *Proceedings: Seventh international congress of gerontology* (pp. 43–45). Vienna: Wiener Medizinischen Akademie.

Cavan, R. S. (1965). *Suicide.* New York: Russell & Russell. (Original work published 1926)

Chia, B. H. (1979). Suicide and the generation gap. *Life-Threatening Behavior, 2,* 194–208.

Chynoweth, R. (1981). Suicide in the elderly. *Crisis, 2,* 106–116.

Clancy, P. (1990, December 4). Doctor charged in suicide case. *USA Today,* p. 2A.

Cohen-Mansfield, J., & Marx, M. S. (1993). Pain and depression in the nursing home: Corroborating results. *Journal of Gerontology: Psychological Sciences, 48,* P96–P97.

Conwell, Y., Caine, E. D., & Olsen, K. (1990). Suicide and cancer in late life. *Hospital and Community Psychiatry, 41,* 1334–1339.

Conwell, Y., Rotenberg, M., & Caine, E. D. (1990). Completed suicide at age 50 and over. *Journal of the American Geriatrics Society, 38,* 640–644.

Copeland, A. R. (1985). Dyadic death—Revisited. *Journal of the Forensic Science Society, 25,* 181–188.

Cousins, N. (1975, June 14). The right to die [Editorial]. *Saturday Review,* p. 4.

Danto, B. L. (1981). Suicide among cancer patients. In S. E. Wallace & A. Eser (Eds.), *Suicide and euthanasia: The rights of personhood* (pp. 26–35). Knoxville: University of Tennessee Press.

Darbonne, A. R. (1969). Suicide and age: A suicide note analysis. *Journal of Consulting and Clinical Psychology, 33,* 46–50.

Dickinson, E. (1955). The mystery of pain. In T. H. Johnson (Ed.), *The poems of Emily Dickinson* (Vol. II, pp. 501–502). Cambridge, MA: Belknap Press and Harvard University Press. (Original work published 1890)

Dodge, H. H., & Austin, R. L. (1990). Household structure and elderly Japanese female suicide. *Family Perspective, 24,* 83–97.

Dorpat, T. L., Anderson, W. F., & Ripley, H. S. (1968). The relationship of physical illness to suicide. In H. L. P. Resnik (Ed.), *Suicidal behaviors: Diagnosis and management* (pp. 209–219). Boston: Little, Brown.

Dubovsky, S. L. (1978). Averting suicide in terminally ill patients. *Psychosomatics, 19,* 113–115.

Egan, T. (1990, June 7). No easy answers in suicide-machine dispute: Adkins' family and friends believe she knew exactly what she was doing. *South Bend Tribune* (IN), pp. A1, A15.

Farberow, N. L., & Moriwaki, S. Y. (1975). Self-destructive crises in the older person. *Gerontologist, 15,* 333–337.

Fawcett, J. (1972). Suicidal depression and physical illness. *Journal of the American Medical Association, 219,* 1303–1306.

Filiberti, A., Ripamonti, C., Saita, L., De Conno, F., & Maino, E. (1991). Frequency of suicide by cancer at the National Center Institute of Milan over 1986–90. *Annals of Oncology, 2,* 610.

Fishbain, D. A., Goldberg, M., Rosomoff, R. S., & Rosomoff, H. (1991). Completed suicide in chronic pain. *Clinical Journal of Pain, 7,* 29–36.

Fordyce, W. E. (1990). Learned pain: Pain as behavior. In J. J. Bonica (Ed.), *The management of pain* (Vol. 1, 2nd ed., pp. 291–299). Philadelphia: Lean & Febiger.

Frierson, R. L. (1991). Suicide attempts by the old and the very old. *Archives of Internal Medicine, 151,* 141–144.

Gardner, E. A., Bahn, A. K., & Mack, M. (1964). Suicide and psychiatric care in the aging. *Archives of General Psychiatry, 10,* 547–553.

Good death? (1975, March 10). *Time,* pp. 83–84.

Greene, M. (1990, April 4). Actress pleads for Alzheimer victims. *USA Today,* p. 2A.

Hietanen, P., & Lönnqvist, J. (1991). Cancer and suicide. *Annals of Oncology, 2,* 19–23.

Hirschfeld, R. M. A., & Davidson, L. (1988). Risk factors for suicide. In A. J. Frances & R. E. Hales (Eds.), *American Psychiatric Press review of psychiatry* (Vol. 7, pp. 307–333). Washington, DC: American Psychiatric Press.

Horton-Deutsch, S. L., Clark, D. C., & Farran, C. J. (1992). Chronic dyspnea and suicide in elderly men. *Hospital and Community Psychiatry, 43,* 1198–1203.

Howlett, D. (1990, December 14–16). "Suicide doctor" cleared. *USA Today,* p. 1A.

Hubbard, R. W., & Carrol, E. N. (1992). Alcohol use and patients with chronic pain: A pain clinic perspective. *Alcoholism Treatment Quarterly, 9,* 93–97.

Jarvis, G. K., & Boldt, M. (1980). Suicide in the later years. *Essence, 4,* 144–158.

Kastenbaum, R., & Mishara, B. L. (1971, July). Premature death and self-injurious behavior in old age. *Geriatrics, 26,* 71–81.

Kiørboe, E. (1951). Suicide and attempted suicide among old people. *Journal of Gerontology, 6,* 233–236.

Kontaxakis, V. P., Christodoulou, G. N., Mavreas, V. G., & Havaki-Kontaxaki, B. J. (1988). Attempted suicide in psychiatric outpatients with concurrent physical illness. *Psychotherapy and Psychosomatics, 50,* 201–206.

Kruijt, C. S. (1977). The suicide rate in the Western world since World War II. *Netherlands Journal of Sociology, 13*, 54–64.

Kwan, A. Y.-H. (1988). Suicide among the elderly: Hong Kong. *Journal of Applied Gerontology, 7*, 248–259.

Lester, D., & Beck, A. T. (1974). Age differences in patterns of attempted suicide. *Omega, 5*, 317–322.

Loebel, J. P., Loebel, J. S., Dager, S. R., Centerwall, B. S., & Reay, D. T. (1991). Anticipation of nursing home placement may be a precipitant of suicide among the elderly. *Journal of the American Geriatrics Society, 39*, 407–408.

Lyness, J. M., Conwell, Y., & Nelson, J. C. (1992). Suicide attempts in elderly psychiatric inpatients. *Journal of the American Geriatrics Society, 40*, 320–324.

Margo, G. M., & Finkel, J. A. (1990). Early dementia as a risk factor for suicide. *Hospital and Community Psychiatry, 41*, 676–678.

Martinez, J. (1990, June 6). Suicide machine triggers ethics debate. *South Bend Tribune* (IN), pp. A1, A15.

Marzuk, P. M., Tardiff, K., & Hirsch, C. S. (1992). The epidemiology of murder–suicide. *Journal of the American Medical Association, 267*, 3179–3183.

Massie, M. J., & Holland, J. C. (1988). Assessment and management of the cancer patient with depression. *Advances in Psychosomatic Medicine, 18*, 1–12.

Miller, M. (1978). Geriatric suicide: The Arizona study. *Gerontologist, 18*, 488–495.

Miller, M. (1979). *Suicide after sixty: The final alternative.* New York: Springer.

Moody, H. R. (1992). A critical view of ethical dilemmas in dementia. In R. H. Binstock, S. G. Post, & P. J. Whitehouse (Eds.), *Dementia and aging: Ethics, values, and policy choices* (pp. 86–100). Baltimore: Johns Hopkins University Press.

Murphy, G. E. (1992). *Suicide in alcoholism.* New York: Oxford University Press.

Murphy, G. K. (1977). Cancer and the coroner. *Journal of the American Medical Association, 237*, 786–788.

Nelson, F. L. (1977). Religiosity and self-destructive crises in the institutionalized elderly. *Suicide and Life-Threatening Behavior, 7*, 67–74.

Nelson, F. L., & Farberow, N. L. (1980). Indirect self-destructive behavior in the elderly nursing home patient. *Journal of Gerontology, 35*, 949–957.

Osgood, N. J. (1992a). Environmental factors in suicide in long-term care facilities. *Suicide and Life-Threatening Behavior, 22*, 98–106.

Osgood, N. J. (1992b). *Suicide in later life: Recognizing the warning signs.* New York: Lexington Books.

Osgood, N. J., & Brant, B. A. (1990). Suicidal behavior in long-term care facilities. *Suicide and Life-Threatening Behavior, 20*, 113–122.

Osgood, N. J., Brant, B. A., & Lipman, A. (1991). *Suicide among the elderly in long-term care facilities.* New York: Greenwood.

Peretti, P. O., & Wilson, C. (1978–1979). Contemplated suicide among voluntary and involuntary retirees. *Omega, 9*, 193–201.

Post, S. G. (1990). Severely demented elderly people: A case against senicide. *Journal of the American Geriatrics Society, 38,* 715–718.

Proudfoot, A. T., & Wright, N. (1972). The physical consequences of self-poisoning by the elderly. *Gerontologia Clinica, 14,* 24–31.

Rao, A. V. (1990). Physical illness, pain, and suicidal behavior. *Crisis, 11,* 48–56.

Rachlis, D. (1970, Fall). Suicide and loss adjustment in the aging. *Bulletin of Suicidology,* No. 7, pp. 23–26.

Rich, C. L., Warsradt, G. M., Nemiroff, R. A., Fowler, R. C., & Young, D. (1991). Suicide, stressors, and the life cycle. *American Journal of Psychiatry, 148,* 524–527.

Robinson, B. (1990, Winter). Questions of life and death: No easy answers. *Ageing International, 17*(2), 27–35.

Rollin, B. (1985). *Last wish.* New York: Linden Press.

Rollin, B. (1992, July). If you love her, help her die. *Redbook,* pp. 32, 34.

Rosenbaum, M. (1990). The role of depression in couples involved in murder–suicide and homicide. *American Journal of Psychiatry, 147,* 1036–1039.

Rovner, B. W., German, P. S., Brant, L. J., Clark, R., Burton, L., & Folstein, M. F. (1991). Depression and mortality in nursing homes. *Journal of the American Medical Association, 265,* 993–996.

Sad suicide pact. (1991, January 21). *South Bend Tribune* (IN), p. B12.

Sainsbury, P. (1962). Suicide in the middle and later years. In H. T. Blumenthal (Ed.), *Aging around the world: Medical and clinical aspects of aging* (pp. 97–105). New York: Columbia University Press.

Sainsbury, P. (1963). Social and epidemiological aspects of suicide with special reference to the aged. In R. H. Williams, C. Tibbitts, & W. Donahue (Eds.), *Processes of aging: Social and psychological perspectives* (Vol. 2, pp. 153–175). New York: Atherton Press.

Saunders, J. M., & Valente, S. M. (1988). Cancer and suicide. *Oncology Nursing Forum, 15,* 575–581.

Sendbuehler, J. M., & Goldstein, S. (1977). Attempted suicide among the aged. *Journal of the American Geriatrics Society, 25,* 244–248.

Shepherd, D. M., & Barraclough, B. M. (1980). Work and suicide: An empirical investigation. *British Journal of Psychiatry, 136,* 469–478.

Shneidman, E. S. (1993a). Suicide as psychache. *Journal of Nervous and Mental Disease, 181,* 147–149.

Shneidman, E. S. (1993b). *Suicide as psychache: A clinical approach to self-destructive behavior.* Northvale, NJ: Jason Aronson.

Siegel, K., & Tuckel, P. (1984–1985). Rational suicide and the terminally ill cancer patient. *Omega, 15,* 263–269.

Sperling, D. (1990, June 6). Alzheimer's test promising. *USA Today,* p. 1.

Stenager, E. N., Stenager, E., Koch-Henriksen, N., Brønnum-Hansen, H., Hyllested, K., Jensen, K., & Bille-Brahe, U. (1992). Suicide and multiple sclerosis: An epidemiological investigation. *Journal of Neurology, Neurosurgery, and Psychiatry, 55,* 542–545.

Thomasma, D. C. (1992). Mercy killing of elderly people with dementia: A counter-proposal. In R. H. Binstock, S. G. Post, & P. J. Whitehouse

(Eds.), *Dementia and aging: Ethics, values, and policy choices* (pp. 101–117). Baltimore: Johns Hopkins University Press.

Trout, D. L. (1980). The role of social isolation in suicide. *Suicide and Life-Threatening Behavior, 10,* 10–23.

Vento, M. (1991, November 24). Kevorkian states his defense of assisted suicide: He believes intensely in right of patients to choose death. *South Bend Tribune* (IN), p. G2.

Vijayakumar, L., & Thilothammal, N. (1993). Suicide pacts. *Crisis, 14,* 43–46.

Walmer, T., & DeSimone, B. (1990, June 8). "She believed in a dignified death." *USA Today,* p. 6A.

Watts, D. T., Howell, T., & Priefer, B. A. (1992). Geriatricians' attitudes toward assisting suicide of dementia patients. *Journal of the American Geriatrics Society, 40,* 878–885.

West, D. J. (1967). *Murder followed by suicide.* Cambridge, MA: Harvard University Press.

Young, D., Rich, C. L., & Fowler, R. C. (1984). Double suicides: Four modal cases. *Journal of Clinical Psychiatry, 45,* 470–472.

4

Clinical Approaches to
Depressed and Suicidal Elders

Clinical techniques for dealing with the suicidal elderly will vary with the orientation of the therapist and the resources of the patient. Recently, there has been a growing emphasis on cognitive–behavioral approaches for the assessment and treatment of depression and suicide in later life, and this orientation will be covered in detail in this chapter. Figure 1 illustrates the cognitive–behavioral model that we will use in this chapter. Although we emphasize the cognitive–behavioral model in this book, we must note that psychodynamic, client-centered, group, and family interventions have also been used in treating the suicidal elderly (e.g., Richman, 1993). Psychiatric methods, especially the use of antidepressant medications and electroconvulsive therapy, have also been used. Some of these other therapeutic modes will be discussed briefly later in this chapter.

The cognitive–behavioral approach to working with the older suicidal patient combines an emphasis on irrational thoughts and inappropriate attributions with the importance of behavioral patterns such as learned helplessness and a lack of reinforcements, especially those of a social nature. For example, the increasing social isolation brought about by the death of a spouse or other loved one that many older adults face is viewed as a precipitator of depression in that it reduces available social reinforcements. From a cognitive perspective, irrational and catastrophic thoughts regarding the feeling of being a burden to

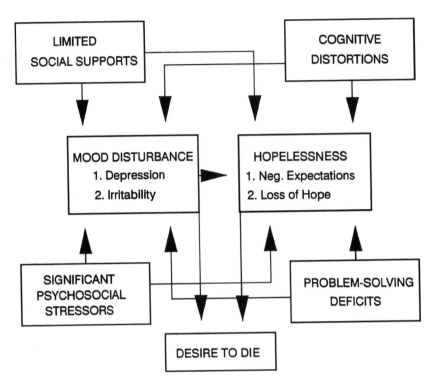

Figure 1. Evaluation of suicide potential using a cognitive–behavioral approach.

family, or the overestimation of physical health problems, may also contribute to the depressive spiral.

As shown in the first part of Figure 1, four basic factors (significant psychosocial stressors, limited social supports, cognitive distortions, and problem-solving deficits) have been found to be related to the two central conditions of mood disturbance and hopelessness. The coexistence of mood disturbance and feelings of hopelessness is thought to result in a desire to die. Whenever the desire to die is present, the clinician is advised to explore the intensity of such suicidal ideation in a thorough manner (see Figure 1, second part). This involves the identification and evaluation of an existing suicide plan, the possession or avail-

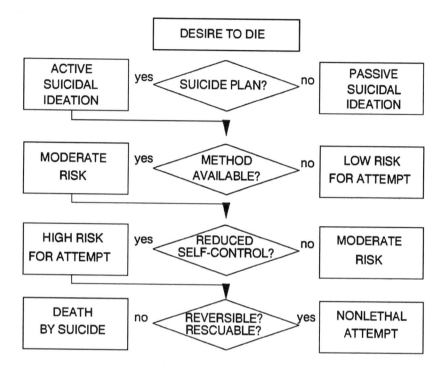

Figure 1. (*continued*)

ability of the planned methods, and any indication of reduced impulse control (intoxication, psychotic characteristics, previous suicide attempts). Finally, an assessment must be made of the avoidance of possible suicidal behavior and the probability of recovery once the attempt is initiated. In this way, the clinician can evaluate the client's suicide potential in an efficient and comprehensive manner.

For the elderly, an evaluation of suicide potential along the dimensions listed above should also take into account psychosocial problems of aging and the aged and an understanding of personality, motivation, and stress in the later years. As will be indicated in this and other chapters, suicidal risk in the elderly may be reflected in certain ways that differ subtly from younger age groups. For example, comments about death are often made in a more "matter-of-fact" manner by older persons than by younger adults. As a result, thoughts of suicide may be presented in a less dramatic and more concrete or straightforward way by the suicidal elderly. It should also be pointed out that because of the increasing number of aged persons living alone, reversibility and rescue may be more problematic.

This and the following chapter will focus on a cognitive–behavioral approach to suicide, with an emphasis on the aspects that are unique to geriatric patients. Case studies are provided to illustrate the application of cognitive–behavioral principles in the assessment and treatment of elderly suicidal persons. Before examining these latter topics, however, it is important, first, to consider the professional in the social context in which treatment occurs and, then, to highlight some of the special characteristics of suicidal behavior among older persons. This chapter will conclude with brief considerations of treatment modalities for suicidal individuals other than the cognitive–behavioral approach.

The Suicidal Elderly and the Profession of Psychology

A frequently ignored factor contributing to the problem of elderly suicide is that older adults do not regularly seek out mental health services, and, when they do, it is unlikely that they will be treated by a provider who has training in geropsychology (Santos & VandenBos, 1982). Thus, psychology as a profession must improve the identification and referral mechanisms for suicidal older persons and increase the number of qualified therapists that are available to meet their needs.

The gap between needed and available geriatric mental health services has important clinical implications. When psychologists do encounter suicidal older persons, they may be seeing them at a much later stage in the development of the problem than with younger suicidal patients. In other words, the act may be more imminent and the intervention may need to be more immediate. Behaviorally, this may be reflected in more detailed suicide plans and preparations (e.g., Morgan, 1989), including estate planning as well as funeral and burial arrangements on the part of the elderly client. Morgan (1989) also noted that older adults may have an "enhanced degree of comfort with the idea of suicide" (p. 245) that can increase risk.

The importance of developing linkages between community mental health centers and local aging programs has been stressed by several authors (e.g., Kethley & Ehrlich, 1990). The high suicide rates among the elderly provide a clear mandate for careful case finding and more effective service delivery programs targeting the elderly population. Model programs that have been developed to respond to the mental health needs of the aged will be discussed in chapter 6.

The training of psychologists and geropsychologists in particular with regard to suicide needs to be considered in terms of the amount of attention that self-destructive behavior currently receives in classrooms and clinical training sites (McIntosh, 1987). As with other areas in geriatrics, superimposing a coverage of the unique aspects of elderly suicide on a strong core of training in general suicidology seems to be an appropriate approach to improve training (Santos & Hubbard, 1990). Obviously, inadequate knowledge about this problem area among clinicians can be lethal for older clients and overwhelming for service providers. Therapists who are inadequately trained in geropsychology may be confused by the complexities presented in many cases of elderly suicide. Multiple and chronic medical conditions, problems of polypharmacy, impaired sensory processes, and minor memory impairments may all combine to complicate the detection of depression and suicidality in the older patient.

Among the first issues that the therapist must keep in mind with elderly clients is their own fears, attitudes, and beliefs regarding older adults, aging, and old age and any tendency to have negative perceptions and distorted expectations about aging and the aged. The therapist must confront issues of ageism and accompanying aspects of transference and countertransference (Butler, Lewis, & Sunderland, 1991; Morgan, 1989). Cohen (1990) suggested that changes in memory, cognitive processes, sleep patterns, and sexual capacity should not be summarily dismissed as concomitants of the aging process and should instead be investigated as possible signals of mental disorder. Those who view depression as a normal aspect of the aging process (e.g., "If I were in his shoes, I'd drink and cry a lot too") or as a natural consequence of aging (e.g., "The patient's BDI [Beck Depression Inventory] is elevated but not unusual given his age") may be prone to misdiagnose depression and frequently to apply inadequate interventions as well. At an extreme, this type of "ageism" can lead to the conclusion that suicide in old age is a reasonable and, perhaps, inevitable response to a miserable stage of life. Professionals who hold such biased views are less likely to diagnose depression in the aged correctly and to screen for suicide risk (see also Arbore, 1990).

Factors such as those discussed above suggest that countertransference may need to be closely monitored in dealing with the suicidal older adult. For example, the therapist's own fears regarding aging and infirmity may be heightened during treatment. Even more striking is the possibility that issues regarding the therapist's relationship with his or her aging parents, or grief regarding the loss of a parent, may further complicate the ongoing therapeutic relationship. In another area, Maltsberger (1991) cautioned the therapist to be aware of countertransference and the accompanying helplessness produced by the older adult client who "complains incessantly, when he sits uncommunicatively for long periods, or when he rejects interpretations and interventions over and over" (pp. 232–233). Finally, the therapist's personal value system regarding suicidal behavior may be challenged, particularly when confronted with clients such as a rational 80-year-old who opts for death-enhancing alternatives in refusing surgery or being medically noncompliant rather than selecting those interventions aimed at extending life (see, e.g., Kahn, 1990).

General Therapeutic Principles in Working With the Elderly

A number of authors have identified several characteristics of the elderly population that have importance for accurate clinical assessments and appropriate interventions (e.g., Cohen, 1990). Chief among these is that today's cohort of persons age 65 and over bring with them a certain set of experiences and attitudes toward mental health and mental health professionals. Many older individuals grew up in an era when mental illness was regarded as a characterological problem that required institutionalization. In addition, the probability of recovery from "mental illness" was poor, pharmacological intervention was primitive or largely unknown, and outpatient treatment was minimal. As a result, many of today's elderly persons have never been to a psychologist, have never taken a course in psychology, and tend to pride themselves in having been able to cope and to adjust to psychological problems throughout their lives without any professional assistance. This means that more socialization to the acceptability of therapy is often necessary with older patients. This process should include attention to information and details such as cost, length, scheduling of therapy (transportation, for example, may be a problem), and assurances regarding confidentiality. The process of therapy also needs to be discussed with such clients. For instance, if a patient–therapist collaboration model is to be used, this may come as a surprise to older adults who are more accustomed to being passive recipients in health care interventions. The development of rapport should take into account the client's history and perspective regarding his or her past accomplishments, failures, and critical events.

Additional factors that should be taken into account may include increased economic concerns among older patients that may lead to resistance to long-term treatment or a tendency toward premature termination. It is also important to be aware that older persons tend to engage in life reviews, which are most often a healthy form of reminiscence. However, clinicians should be aware of the possibility that this process may turn into self-deprecating rumination in a depressed elderly client.

A further complication is posed by the fact that many of the losses encountered by older clients, such as forced retirement or widowhood, represent roles and relationships that may be impossible to replace in any satisfactory fashion. This has led some to propose that loss acceptance in the elderly is a natural process, whereas others have emphasized loss transcendence or behaviors that are directed toward finding new ways to meet old needs (Hubbard, 1992).

Several practical issues arise when conducting therapy with or making assessments of suicide potential in older adults. The therapist must be mindful of such issues as quicker fatiguability among older adults and various sensory and other physical changes associated with the aging process (e.g., hearing deficits, visual changes, etc.; Butler et al., 1991). It is recommended (e.g., Butler et al., 1991; Morgan, 1989; Osgood, 1985) that clinicians take special care in establishing trust and a sense of safety among elderly clients in the therapy setting. Addressing elderly clients respectfully (i.e., by using the designations "Mr." or "Mrs." rather than using their first names alone) may be a more sensitive issue in therapy. Therapists should also consider the importance and significance of touch in therapeutic settings, as well as the need for patience and a possibly slower pace. Butler et al. (1991) suggested the active inclusion of the older adult to the largest degree possible in decisions about his or her own mental health care.

Hopelessness, Suicide, and the Aged

Hopelessness has received a great deal of attention as a moderating variable between depression and suicide (Alloy, Abramson, Metalsky, & Hartledge, 1988). Beck and his colleagues (Beck, Brown, Berchick, Stewart, & Steer, 1990; Beck, Steer, Kovacs, & Garrison, 1985) have stressed its importance from the perspective of cognitive therapy, in which hopelessness is viewed as a set of cognitions and expectancies that can influence the occurrence of negative life events. Essentially, the cognitive schemata take the form of negative expectations or pessimism about future outcomes and events, and result in a loss of motivation and negative feelings about the future. Stable, global attributions regarding life events are also viewed as a critical part of the hopelessness concept. A weak positive relationship between hopelessness and age has been noted (Greene, 1981; Hill, Gallagher, Thompson, & Ishida, 1988). In terms of clinical measurement, the Hopelessness Scale (Beck, Weissman, Lester, & Trexler, 1974) has been found to be a valid and reliable instrument with older patients.

The clinician needs to be aware that some elderly clients feel as though their physical and psychological pain will never improve (i.e., hopelessness) and that they are powerless in terms of making any significant changes in their lives (i.e., helplessness). Clients with these attitudes may see suicide as a viable alternative. Additionally, if it is concluded on the part of the client (or the therapist) that their problems are an inevitable part of their aging and old age, they will view them as global, stable events that are beyond control. The irrational thought that says, "All my problems are due to old age and there is nothing that can be done about them" needs to be confronted and countered by cognitive–behavioral interventions.

Hopelessness may be related to larger numbers of losses and threats for the elderly as compared with younger age groups. The multicausal nature of suicide in old age and the many problematic life circumstances that may be present for the older adult often lead individuals to feel that their situation is hopeless and that they are personally helpless to effect any improvement. Many older adults face chronic health problems, social exit events, such as retirement and widowhood, and other negative life events, including financial concerns, institutionalization of the spouse, and shrinkage of peer support systems because of illness and death. These, in turn, may heighten their feelings of hopelessness. The role of health perceptions as a predictive variable for elderly suicidal ideation was identified by Hill et al. (1988). Although a great deal of research in this field still needs to be done, it seems clear that hopelessness should be considered an important and relevant factor in the relationship between depression and suicide and should be carefully assessed and treated in elderly patients.

Unique Aspects of Elder Suicide

In general, the clinician can expect to find more similarities than differences in psychological disorders between younger and older clients. However, the differences that do exist are often subtle and critical to effective treatment. There appear to be a number of factors that are unique in their relationship to suicide in the later years of life. First, suicidal intent may frequently be present along with a number of coexisting physical and mental disorders such as chronic pain, terminal disease, and deficits in cognitive, perceptual, and motor skills. Dementia, along with conflict over physical dependency, abnormal grief reactions, or alcohol dependence, may intensify the wish to die. At the extreme, the interaction of these factors may result in what has been called "failure to thrive," as demonstrated in the unexplained death of an elderly person in the absence of life-threatening illness or behavior. It is also possible that treatment for one of these symptoms may serve to enhance suicidal intent by increasing physical pain or psychological discomfort, or mask such intent by diverting the attention of family and health care professionals away from the communication of suicidal intent.

Another special feature associated with older adults is the atypical presentation of depression. Depression may be masked by vague physical decline or multiple somatic complaints, and an additional complication relates to the misdiagnosis of depression as dementia (i.e., pseudodementia). This makes it important to carefully assess potential symptoms of dementia to ensure that the symptoms are not in reality the result of depressive rather than organic disorder (Cohen, 1990; Morgan, 1989).

Not only are older adults more likely to use violent methods such as handguns or hanging (see chapter 1), they are also more physically vulnerable to the trauma that they inflict. Thus, an important factor contributing to the high suicide completion rate in the elderly as compared with their younger counterparts may be their lack of functional reserve to withstand or recover from physical injury. In other words, physical insult to an already compromised physical system increases the likelihood of death. The possibility that the use of more violent methods may also reflect a greater intent on the part of older suicide attempters cannot be ignored. Elderly persons who demonstrate suicidal ideation are typically very serious in their intent and are less likely to be ambivalent in their desire to die.

To add to this already complicated picture, because of their social isolation, the older suicide attempter is less likely to be found in a short period of time after an attempt. Thus, social isolation may contribute both to depression and suicidal ideation and to the efficacy of the attempt (Gove & Hughes, 1980). The shrinkage of reference groups and dispersion of family members that often occur along with the aging process clearly create significant barriers to treatment.

Table 1 lists some of the salient aspects of elderly suicide that may be compared to those of younger adults. Although there is little research and hard data related to the comparisons listed in Table 1, clinical experience suggests that elderly and younger suicidal adults differ on a variety of predisposing variables and precipitating events. Demographic and clinical data indicate that the typical elderly suicidal patient will be a White man over 65, socially isolated, physically ill, and bereaved and that, if an attempt occurs, it is likely to be fatal.

If any single characteristic distinguishes younger from older suicide attempters, it is the incidence of physical illness during the later years of life and its subsequent impact on mood and self-destructive behavior (see chapter 3). Terminal illnesses that impede autonomy and involve chronic pain may serve to stimulate suicidal intent. Under such circumstances, the older person may decide that the quality of his or her remaining years will be unacceptable and that suicide, therefore, offers a more acceptable alternative. Although such decisions are sometimes referred to as rational suicide, they may be driven more by feelings than by facts. In such cases, a problem-solving approach that includes a consideration of all possible alternatives and outcomes is likely to be absent (see chapter 6). The impact of disease on the client's independence and economic state should be assessed when physical illnesses are also present in depressed individuals. Other critical factors that should be given attention in the evaluation include level of pain, the client's beliefs about the course and trajectory of the illness, and their view of its impact on the current and future quality of life.

The client's expectations concerning health care and institutionalization also need to be examined closely. Even relatively minor health problems may generate catastrophic thinking in the older adult who sees them as leading to nursing home placement, loss of independence, or a slow and painful death. Contributing to such misperceptions may be personal experiences

Table 1

Comparison of Younger Adults and the Elderly on Variables Relevant to Suicidal Behavior

Domain	Adults	Elderly
Method of attempt	Drug overdose	Gunshot wound
Marital status	Divorced	Widowed
Physical health	Stable	Deteriorating
Acute stressors	Divorce	Bereavement
Chronic stressors	Limited finances	Health problems and social isolation
Complications	Varied	Physically vulnerable
Setting of attempt	Home	Home alone
Frequency of indirect self-destructive behavior	Occasional	Common
Alcohol abuse	Occasional	Occasional
Cognitive focus	Future	Past
Social supports	Variable	Diminishing
Predominant diagnosis	Depression	Depression
Problem-solving deficits	Common	Common

with a spouse or friends in which a relatively minor health problem or brief hospitalization preceded institutionalization or death. This is increasingly relevant now that new regulations on hospital stays are leading to the placement of acute patients in nursing homes. For example, older persons recovering from hip surgery may be particularly despondent when they learn that their recuperation will involve placement in a long-term care facility. This is especially true if they associate such placement with loss of home, independence, or life and fear that their brief stay will become a permanent one.

Physical illness can also create or increase social isolation and limit access to reinforcements associated with pleasant activities and social relationships. Being ill may not only be depressing in and of itself, but may also contribute to depression by the limitations it imposes. Long-term illness in particular often requires the use of medications that may influence mood and also provide an accessible suicide method (Benson & Brodie, 1975).

Another set of predisposing factors in elderly suicide is the increase in chronic physical and emotional problems that many older adults may encounter. Chronic stressors may also develop acute phases, such as periodic increased levels of arthritic pain or an anniversary reaction during the course of the grieving process. All of these possibilities underscore the importance of evaluating suicidal risk periodically rather than solely on a one-time or intake basis.

In addition to suicidal acts that result in death, there are those behaviors that indirectly enhance the probability of death occurring. Such indirect self-destructive behavior (ISDB; see chapter 1) would include refusing medication or food, rejecting hospitalization or surgery, or failing to alter illness-related behaviors such as smoking or alcohol use. However, identifying such patterns as intentional acts with suicidal intent can be complicated. On the one hand, individuals suffering from dementia may refuse medication or food because of confusion, hallucinations, or delusions. On the other hand, the refusal may reflect a free choice made by a competent older adult who has decided that the quality of his or her remaining years will not be worth the effort to maintain them.

When ISDB takes the form of smoking or drug or alcohol consumption, interventions relevant to addiction should be implemented. Although the person may not have a prior history of addiction and may not score high in this respect on screening instruments, the choice of a drug over life provides strong evidence for a diagnosis of addiction. Refusing medical treatment or medication may involve cognitive distortions in which acceptance of treatment is seen as actually being life threatening (e.g., "If you want to stay healthy, don't go to doctors and stay out of hospitals," "Most of my friends died when they went to a hospital, after their doctors sent them there"). From this perspective, ISDB may be viewed as a form of avoidance behavior that is based in part on an irrational belief system (e.g., "Medical treatment makes things worse") that needs to be challenged for survival.

The assessment of ISDB requires a thorough knowledge of the patient's cognitive status in order to determine the level of intention (e.g., did they fail to take their medication because of a memory deficit), awareness (e.g., did they understand the recommendations made by the physician), and competence (are they capable of making a rational choice not to pursue medical treatment). Additional assessment should take into account the frequency, intensity, and duration of the relevant behavior. Was the refusal a single act prompted by fear or frustration, or has the behavior been consistent across time, settings, and health care professionals? Can the ISDB be characterized as a periodic outburst, or is it a consistent pattern of behavior? Even when the clinician is satisfied that the ISDB is the result of a value-oriented decision on the part of a competent older adult who has access to all relevant information and options, it seems prudent to discuss the behavior across two or three visits where family members and various health professionals might be present.

Above all else, the clinician needs to be aware of the legal and professional issues surrounding these very difficult cases. Bongar (1991) has presented the legal aspects with regard to suicidal patients, and their implications with respect to malpractice. He notes that lawsuits resulting from patient suicides are among the most common brought against therapists. Many guidelines are provided to lessen the probability of malpractice suits in such cases, and a special focus is given to providing reasonable care that meets both clinical and legal standards. Among the suggestions Bongar makes are to consult frequently with colleagues in difficult cases of suicidal patients, to thoroughly and regularly document actions and the course of treatment, and to involve the family in the therapy plan. In summarizing these issues of risk management, Bongar recommends that psychologists "take affirmative steps to ensure that they have the requisite knowledge, training, experience, and clinical resources prior to accepting high-risk patients into their professional care. This requires that all of these mechanisms be in place *before* the onset of any suicidal crisis" (p. 704).

Other Psychotherapeutic Approaches

Although the emphasis in this chapter has been on cognitive–behavioral assessment and interventions, a number of other approaches have been and are being used with suicidal older persons. Such approaches include interpersonal, family, and psychodynamic therapy. Butler et al. (1991) asserted that, provided there is no severe brain damage, the elderly are good candidates for individual and group psychotherapy techniques.

Interpersonal Therapy

Interpersonal therapy (IPT) has been used successfully in the treatment of depression (Klerman, Weissman, Rounsaville, & Chevron, 1984) and combines several therapeutic approaches from a psychosocial viewpoint that emphasizes role transitions and disputes, pathological grief, and social skills training. For elderly clients, attention to role transitions such as retirement, widowhood, and dependence brought about by physical illness is certainly beneficial. IPT also emphasizes the importance of activity levels, problem solving, and cognitive misattributions in a manner similar to that of cognitive–behavioral approaches.

Family Therapy

Family therapy can be helpful for many suicidal patients, including older adults (Richman, 1986, 1993). Because the members of dysfunctional families are often at risk for suicide and other self-defeating behaviors, family therapy may be useful in helping to address such problems.

In the case of elderly patients, family composition varies. Some older adults still live with their spouse and, occasionally, even with their adult children, whereas others live alone in relative isolation. It is often essential to help depressed and suicidal patients maintain contact with their family and friends in order to reduce feelings of loneliness and desperation. Also, many elderly patients need to replace social bonds that have been broken through death or relocation.

Family conflict can be a precipitant to suicidal crises. The family may have become rigid, inflexible, or intolerant of the suicidal member (Richman, 1993). Therapy may be needed to improve flexibility and reduce critical attitudes directed toward the suicidal patient, and destructive patterns of family interaction (e.g., blaming one person for problems within the family) need to be confronted and reduced. Also, communication skills are important. Therapy can help to encourage the direct expression of emotions within the family.

When working with the elderly suicidal client, it can often be important to solicit family involvement in monitoring depression and suicidal behavior and to challenge irrational assumptions made by the older person. Such assumptions might include feeling that they are a burden to spouse and children, anticipating nursing home placement when no plans are actually being discussed, or blaming oneself for problems of adult children such as divorce or addiction.

Psychodynamic Therapy

Psychodynamic approaches to suicide examine negative emotions that may underlie the urge to die, such as self-hate, strong feelings of loneliness, and aggressive feelings toward others (Maltsberger, 1992). Apart from orientation-specific terminology, the psychodynamic approach is compatible with other forms of therapy. In this orientation, the therapist working with suicidal clients needs to evaluate the client's internal and external resources that are available for managing the emotional distress they are experiencing (Lovett & Maltsberger, 1992). It is often important for the therapist to use empathy to gain access to the client's frame of reference in order to understand any subjective feelings of loneliness or failure. By working from the "inside," therapist and client may better be able to make changes that enhance the client's feelings of self-worth (Lovett & Maltsberger, 1992). In general, psychodynamic therapists emphasize the need for more emotional support and less neutrality when dealing with the depressed older person.

Countertransference can become an important issue when working with suicidal clients. The emotional intensity of a suicidal crisis can disrupt therapists' ability to remain objective and detached. Therefore, it is essential for them to be aware of their own feelings during the course of therapy (Maltsberger & Buie, 1974). Some clinicians may respond with anger toward the suicidal client, especially if suicidal feelings become a recurrent issue throughout therapy. Other therapists may become anxious and overly cautious, refusing to take risks that may be beneficial to the client, whereas still others may respond with feelings of omnipotence, overstepping the boundaries of the therapeutic relationship in an attempt to rescue and protect the client (Maltsberger & Buie, 1974). If therapists can remain aware of their own feelings about the client and about suicide, they will be better able to remain objective and effective.

Biological Treatments

Medications (for overviews, see Goldblatt & Schatzberg, 1992; Slaby & Dumont, 1992) and psychotherapy can be used successfully in combination in many cases. The use of antidepressant and other psychotropic medications is both appropriate and potentially effective for older adults. At the same time, however, the side effects of medications and the generally lower dosages indicated for the elderly are important issues when prescribing (Butler et al., 1991; Morgan, 1989). There are also the related factors of probable polypharmacy in older adults and possible drug interactions, as well as drug noncompliance, that must be kept in mind (Butler et al., 1991).

Especially with severely depressed patients, the best treatment often involves the use of both psychotherapy and antidepressant medications. For some patients, antidepressant medications are effective in the early stages of treatment, when they would otherwise be too depressed to even discuss their problems. Positive indicators for antidepressant drug therapy include vegetative symptoms, loss of appetite, weight loss, middle or late insomnia, fatigue, low morning mood, and a family history of depression. A personal or family history of depression that previously responded positively to a particular medication suggests that the same medication is likely to work again (see Stern, Rush, & Mendels, 1980). Poor response to antidepressant medications is suggested by the presence of chronic symptoms, hypochondriacal symptoms, mood-incongruent psychotic features, and a family history of schizophrenia.

The two main classes of antidepressant medications are tricyclic antidepressants (TCAs) and monoamine oxidase inhibitors (MAOIs). TCAs work by preventing the reuptake of norepinephrine (NE) and serotonin, thereby prolonging their activity. Response time ranges from 3 days to 3 weeks before a therapeutic effect is noted. A drug may need to be used for up to 8–10 weeks before it can be decided whether it is effective for a particular patient. Any immediate response is likely to be a placebo effect. Antidepressants are not addicting, have no effect on nondepressed individuals, and do not elevate mood in nondepressed people, so they are not abused drugs. However, they can be lethal in overdose (see Kragh-Sørensen, 1993; Sterling-Smith, 1974). This poses a special concern when working with suicidal patients. Also, dosages must be adjusted to the slowed metabolism often seen in elderly patients; the level of medications can be measured through blood monitoring. If the blood level is adequate, some tricyclic antidepressants are effective in 70% to 90% of patients. Because of the slower metabolism in many elderly patients, blood levels reflect their metabolic rate more accurately than they reflect the ingested dosage.

Drug therapy is not curative in the true sense of the word. However, it is believed that medications help to hold the depressive symptoms at bay until natural remission occurs (Lader, 1980). After symptoms are under control, the dosage can be gradually reduced to the lowest level at which effectiveness can be maintained. Maintenance therapy is usually continued for six months after remission to prevent a resurgence of symptoms. Then, the physician can try to reduce the dosage gradually. If no symptoms reappear, the drug may be reduced further or discontinued altogether.

Tricyclic antidepressants have a number of side effects (see Table 2). Anticholinergic effects include sedation, dry mouth, blurred vision, light-headedness, rapid heart rate, constipation, and urinary retention. Cardiovascular side effects include tachycardia, heart rate increases of 15 to 20 beats per minute, and postural hypotension (when the person stands up, their blood pressure suddenly drops, causing dizziness). Amitriptyline, trazodone, and imipramine have the most dramatic cardiovascular effects, whereas nortriptyline, desipramine, and doxepin have the least cardiovascular effects. Some TCAs can be sedating (amitriptyline, doxepin) and, therefore, are best used when the patient displays anxiety, agitation, or insomnia. The patient can take a full day's dose at bedtime so that the sedating effects are useful instead of disruptive. Other TCAs are less sedating (e.g., imipramine), and some may have a stimulant effect (e.g., protriptyline, desipramine, nortriptyline). These drugs can cause insomnia if taken in the evening, but can also be helpful if taken in the morning. When using antidepressant medications, much of the assessment involves side effects. If side effects are too severe, the dose should be lowered or the medication changed. Fortunately, over time, many of the side effects are reduced (see Pollack & Rosenbaum, 1987).

MAOIs (e.g., Nardil, Parnate) pose more dangers than TCAs and are often used with patients who do not respond to TCAs. They are best reserved for patients with atypical depression (cases presenting with weight gain instead of weight loss and hypersomnia instead of insomnia). Monoamine oxidase (MAO) is a natural enzyme found in the brain that deactivates many transmitters (e.g., NE, serotonin [5-HT], dopamine, tyramine). MAOIs catalyze the deamination of biogenic amines into inactive derivatives and inhibit MAO. This leads to an increase of available transmitters because the enzymes that destroy NE and serotonin have been blocked.

Common side effects of MAOIs include restlessness, insomnia, constipation, loss of appetite, nausea, vomiting, dry mouth, blurred vision, postural hypotension, headaches, dizziness, and weakness. A hypertensive crisis can occur during which the patient experiences a severe headache, often starting in the occipital lobe of the brain and radiating forward, palpitations, nausea, vomiting, sweating, clammy skin, and visual disturbances such as photophobia (sensitivity to light). In severe cases, there can be fatal intracranial hemorrhaging. MAOIs can create severe hypertension when substances containing tyramine have

Table 2

Tricyclic Antidepressants: Drugs That Prevent the Reuptake of Norepinephrine and Serotonin, Thereby Prolonging Their Activity

Trade name	Generic name	Average daily dose	Potency	Sedation	Anticholinergic	Cardiovascular
Adapin	Doxepin	75–150	High	High	Low	Low
Asendin	Amoxapine	200–300	Moderate	Low	Moderate	Moderate
Desyrel	Trazodone	150–600	Low	Mild	Mild	Very high
Elavil	Amitriptyline	75–200	Highest	High	Highest	High
Endep	Amitriptyline	75–200	Highest	High	Highest	High
Ludiomil	Maprotiline	150–300	Moderate	High	Low	High
Norpramin	Desipramine	100–200	Moderate	Stimulant	Moderate	Low
Pamelor	Nortriptyline	75–150	Moderate	Low	Moderate	Low
Sinequan	Doxepin	75–150	High	High	Low	Low
Tofranil	Imipramine	100–200	High	Medium	High	Moderate
Triavil	Amitriptyline	75–200	Highest	High	Highest	High
Vivactil	Protriptyline	15–40	Very high	Stimulant	High	Low

Note. Sedating drugs are useful when agitation or insomnia are present. Nonsedating drugs are needed when psychomotor retardation occurs. Common anticholinergic side effects include dry mouth, blurred vision, tachycardia, dizziness, constipation, and urinary retention. Common cardiovascular side effects include postural hypotension (sudden drop in blood pressure when standing). Triavil is a combination of Trilafon and Elavil.

been ingested (e.g., red wine) or injected (e.g., Demerol). Thus, patients taking MAOIs must observe strict dietary restrictions, avoiding many common foods such as cheese, chocolate, beer, wine, and raisins (see McCabe & Tsuang, 1982), because eating foods with tyramine can dramatically increase blood pressure.

A few new medications are considered serotonin reuptake inhibitors. For example, Prozac (fluoxetine hydrochloride) differs from TCAs and MAOIs in that it works by inhibiting the reuptake of serotonin in the nervous system. Although Prozac is potentially effective in cases where other antidepressants have failed, it has numerous side effects, including headaches, nervousness, insomnia, drowsiness, nausea, and diarrhea.

Another medical approach to treatment involves ECT, or electroconvulsive therapy, in which electricity is used to produce a convulsive seizure (see Fink, 1988; Sackeim, 1988; Weiner & Coffey, 1988). The nervous system is based on a series of electrochemical impulses. If an unsuccessful attempt has been made to alter brain chemistry through drugs, it may be possible to alter the electrical functioning of the brain through ECT. ECT produces a considerable but short-lived increase in cerebral blood flow along with an altered cerebrovascular permeability that results in increased sodium levels in the brain. The early use of ECT without anesthesia sometimes resulted in bone fractures during the grand mal seizure. The use of general anesthesia reduced many of these dangers from the seizures. Atropine is used to produce a short-term anesthesia along with a muscle relaxant. Electricity at 110 to 260 volts is applied for 0.5 seconds and six to eight treatments are usually needed to be clinically effective. The physician may then use tricyclics for three to six months to prevent relapse.

ECT can be useful in cases where medications have been tried but found to be ineffective, or where the patient is acutely suicidal and the physician is concerned that the patient might overdose on antidepressant medications. Also, patients with delusional depression often show a poor response to TCAs but a good response to ECT. It has been estimated that 50% of antidepressant nonresponders will respond to ECT.

The side effects of ECT may include short-term (30 minutes) disorientation and confusion and long-term difficulties forming new memories. Often, by six to nine months after treatment, the ability to form new memories has recovered, but events occurring for two weeks around the time of the ECT may be lost forever. The severity of memory deficits increases with the number of ECT treatments, and there is a cumulative effect across treatment episodes. More than 50 ECT treatments can cause permanent memory deficits. Unilateral and bilateral ECT are equally effective. However, unilateral left ECT tends to cause verbal memory deficits, whereas unilateral right ECT tends to cause nonverbal memory deficits. Bilateral ECT causes deficits in both verbal and nonverbal memory.

The use of ECT in cases of severe depression with suicidal ideation may be quite effective for older adults, as it is for those of younger ages. That is, age per se does not seem to contraindicate the use of ECT (Butler et al., 1991; Morgan, 1989; Osgood, 1985).

Clinical Case Number 4.1: Hazel

This case briefly illustrates the way in which many of the issues discussed in this chapter may present themselves clinically. Hazel was a 79-year-old widow living alone in a home that she and her recently deceased husband had owned for over 40 years. She came to an outpatient mental health clinic complaining of anxiety and depression. The anxiety symptoms met the criteria for panic disorder. Hazel indicated that she had suffered these attacks for years but that they had increased in frequency and intensity following her husband's death seven months earlier. The symptoms of depression included dysphoria, loss of appetite ("I used to cook all the time for my husband, now I just start to cry when it is supper time"), difficulty in decision making, and extreme feelings of loneliness. Hazel also stated that she had suicidal thoughts two to three times a week ("I just want to be with my husband") and had a specific suicide plan (carbon monoxide poisoning by sitting in her car in a closed garage with the motor running).

Hazel had no children, but she did have two older sisters whom she saw regularly, and a dog to which she was extremely attached. She included the dog in her suicide plan because she was concerned that no one would look after it and that it would probably be "put to sleep" anyway. Her other complaints included chronic pain from arthritis, feeling overwhelmed by the demands of home maintenance that her husband had handled, and the necessity of learning to drive again (her husband had always done almost all of the driving).

Hazel had no previous psychiatric history, with the exception of the panic attacks. There appeared to be no prior history of depression and no earlier suicidal ideation or attempt. During her interview, she stated that she simply felt as though her life was over in terms of roles and tasks and that although she currently enjoyed relatively good health and independence, she was concerned about future debilitation (her husband had died in a nursing home after an 18-month struggle with cancer). Her reasons for living centered around her two sisters, her religious values (which prohibited suicide), and a moderate level of hope regarding the possibility that her psychological condition might improve. Hazel responded well to a combined psychopharmacological and cognitive–behavioral intervention. (These and other approaches will be considered at length in chapter 5.)

Hazel's case demonstrates many of the points that have been discussed in this chapter and elsewhere in this book. The interaction of psychological, social, and medical problems was clearly present, along with suicidal ideation and planning. She had never before been to a therapist, and she was torn between a desire to act on her suicidal thoughts and the recognition that she needed help. She did seek help, but in far too many other cases the suicidal impulse may be acted on without seeking professional assistance.

Counseling and Intervention With Individuals From Minority Groups and From Different Cultures

A final issue that should be noted involves therapy and intervention with racial/ethnic minorities and clients from different cultural backgrounds. Because the large majority of suicide attempts and completions, particularly in old age, are made by Whites in the United States, most suicide interventions involve White counselors/therapists and White clients. Although there are many impediments to the use of mental health and related services among minority groups, in therapy encounters where the cultural backgrounds of the client and therapist differ, a variety of special knowledge, sensitivities, experience, and perhaps even techniques is required for effective assessment and intervention (Korchin, 1980; Santos & VandenBos, 1982). Only a limited number of major points can be covered here, so more extensive reading on the topic is encouraged (e.g., Henderson, 1979; Jackson, 1981; Jones & Korchin, 1982; Korchin, 1980; Marsella & Pedersen, 1981; Pedersen, 1985, 1991; Pedersen, Draguns, Lonner, & Trimble, 1981; Ramirez, 1991; D. W. Sue, 1990; "White American Researchers," 1993). Unfortunately, few publications have focused on suicide assessment and intervention with minorities or minority elderly. Therefore, it is necessary to integrate facts, concepts, and conclusions that are available separately from the suicide or minority counseling literature and apply these to the special and specific problems of suicide counseling with minority group members.

A recurrent theme in the literature on this topic is that minorities generally underuse mental health and crisis intervention services (e.g., Korchin, 1980; S. Sue, 1977). Clearly, this should not be interpreted to mean that there is a lack of mental health problems among these groups. Unfortunately, minority persons tend to use such agencies only as a last resort, often after they have exhausted resources in their natural support systems and problems have become so chronic and severe that the outlook for treatment and alleviation of symptoms is poor. This, of course, has important implications for suicide intervention because it suggests that minority clients are more likely to be at higher risk when they are seen, for example, at community mental health centers or when they contact crisis intervention services. Minority persons may underuse mental health services for a number of reasons, including language problems and barriers, the stigma attached to needing such services, low awareness of community mental health programs, negative past experiences with agencies and society in general, and the lack of interest in and sensitivity to the needs of clients from different cultures (McIntosh & Santos, 1984).

It is generally agreed that to be more effective in such work, the therapist should have certain specialized knowledge, training, and experience. This would include adjusting counseling techniques and taking into account the cultural background, experiences, and expectations of the client. If this is not done, the counselor not only may be ineffective in helping the person in a suicidal crisis because of misinterpretation and misunderstanding of messages being given, but may even contribute to the severity of the client's situation. Cultural sensitivity is also helpful in facilitating the development of trust, rapport, and empathy, which are crucial to a good counseling relationship and self-disclosure (Vontress, 1971).

McIntosh and Santos (1984; see also Santos, Hubbard, & McIntosh, 1983) briefly provided separate consideration of the counseling and intervention issues specific to African Americans, Native Americans, Asian Americans, and Hispanics, but the therapist should keep in mind that there are other minorities, including White American ethnic groups, that may also have characteristics and backgrounds that require the use of modified counseling approaches. As Pedersen (1981) has pointed out, the need for "cultural awareness . . . permeates the whole field of counseling, and is not limited to exotic populations" (p. 22). Just as the diversity and uniqueness of racial minorities must be recognized, it is also essential to be aware of the heterogeneity among White ethnic subgroups. The uniqueness of the individual, of course, must always be kept in mind by the therapist. Draguns (1981) expressed it well when he said that "all of us are like all other persons, like some other persons, and like no other person" (p. 18). Effective therapy requires sympathetic understanding and knowledge of the unique characteristics, culture, and language of the client. This is true with respect to elderly clients in the same way as for minority clients.

Summary

In this chapter, we have attempted to provide an overview of some of the clinical issues that may be involved in dealing with suicidal older adults. We used a cognitive–behavioral approach as a model for understanding the multiple factors contributing to hopelessness, depression, and suicide in geriatric clients. Clearly, psychotropic medication, psychiatric inpatient programs, and other therapeutic approaches, including those with a psychodynamic, existential, gestalt, or client-centered perspective, might also be used. However, the cognitive aspects of hopelessness, the tendency for older adults to evaluate their past and future in terms of outcomes and expectations, and the increasing incidence of negative events in old age all provide a basis for the use of the cognitive–behavioral approach.

Key features that tend to differentiate elderly suicides from those seen in younger groups include precipitating factors such as chronic illness, death of a spouse, and social exit events like retirement, along with variables related to the suicidal behavior itself, such as lethality of method, probability of rescue, and indirect self-destructive behavior. The next chapter will consider these and other issues from an assessment and intervention perspective.

References

Alloy, L. B., Abramson, L. Y., Metalsky, G. I., & Hartledge, S. (1988). The hopelessness theory of depression: Attributional aspects. *British Journal of Clinical Psychology, 27,* 5–21.

Arbore, P. (1990). Effective intervention and negative emotional reactions to suicidal elders. In B. Genevay & R. S. Katz (Eds.), *Countertransference and older clients* (pp. 40–53). Newbury Park, CA: Sage.

Beck, A. T., Brown, G., Berchick, R. J., Stewart, B. L., & Steer, R. A. (1990). Relationship between hopelessness and ultimate suicide: A replication with psychiatric outpatients. *American Journal of Psychiatry, 142,* 190–197.

Beck, A. T., Steer, R., Kovacs, M., & Garrison, B. (1985). Hopelessness and eventual suicide: A ten year prospective study of patients hospitalized with suicidal ideation. *American Journal of Psychiatry, 142,* 559–563.

Beck, A. T., Weissman, A., Lester, D., & Trexler, L. (1974). The measurement of pessimism: The Hopelessness Scale. *Journal of Consulting and Clinical Psychology, 42,* 861–865.

Benson, R., & Brodie, D. (1975). Suicide by overdoses of medicines among the aged. *Journal of the American Geriatrics Society, 23,* 304–308.

Bongar, B. (1991). *The suicidal patient: Clinical and legal standards of care.* Washington, DC: American Psychological Association.

Butler, R. N., Lewis, M., & Sunderland, T. (1991). *Aging and mental health: Positive psychosocial and biomedical approaches* (3rd ed.). New York: Merrill.

Cohen, G. D. (1990). Psychopathology and mental health in the mature and elderly adult. In J. E. Birren & K. W. Schaie (Eds.), *Handbook of the psychology of aging* (3rd ed., pp. 359–371). New York: Academic Press.

Draguns, J. G. (1981). Counseling across cultures: Common themes and distinct approaches. In P. B. Pedersen, J. G. Draguns, W. J. Lonner, & J. E. Trimble (Eds.), *Counseling across cultures* (rev. & exp. ed., pp. 3–21). Honolulu: University Press of Hawaii.

Fink, M. (1988). Convulsive therapy: A manual for practice. *Review of Psychiatry, 7,* 482–497.

Goldblatt, M., & Schatzberg, A. (1992). Medication and the suicidal patient. In D. Jacobs (Ed.), *Suicide and clinical practice* (pp. 23–41). Washington, DC: American Psychiatric Press.

Gove, W. R., & Hughes, M. (1980). Reexamining the ecological fallacy: A study in which aggregate data are critical in investigating the pathological effects of living alone. *Social Forces, 58,* 1157–1177.

Greene, S. M. (1981). Levels of measured hopelessness in the general population. *British Journal of Clinical Psychology, 20,* 11–14.

Henderson, G. (Ed.). (1979). *Understanding and counseling ethnic minorities.* Springfield, IL: Charles C Thomas.

Hill, R. D., Gallagher, D., Thompson, L. W., & Ishida, T. (1988). Hopelessness as a measure of suicidal intent in the depressed elderly. *Psychology and Aging, 3,* 230–232.

Hubbard, R. W. (1992). Mental health and aging. In D. Ripich (Ed.), *Handbook of geriatric communication disorders* (pp. 97–112). Austin, TX: Pro-Ed.

Jackson, J. J. (1981). *Minorities and aging.* Belmont, CA: Wadsworth.

Jones, E. E., & Korchin, S. J. (Eds.). (1982). *Minority mental health.* New York: Praeger.

Kahn, A. (1990). Principles of psychotherapy with suicidal patients. In S. J. Blumenthal & D. J. Kupfer (Eds.), *Suicide over the life cycle: Risk factors, assessment, and treatment of suicidal patients* (pp. 441–467). Washington, DC: American Psychiatric Press.

Kethley, A., & Ehrlich, P. (1990). Benjamin Rose Institute: A model community long-term care system. In Z. Harel, P. Ehrlich, & R. Hubbard (Eds.), *The vulnerable aged: People, services, and policies* (pp. 276–294). New York: Springer.

Klerman, G. L., Weissman, M. N., Rounsaville, B. J., & Chevron, E. S. (1984). *Interpersonal therapy of depression.* New York: Academic Press.

Korchin, S. J. (1980). Clinical psychology and minority problems. *American Psychologist, 35,* 262–269.

Kragh-Sørensen, P. (1993). Pharmacotherapy of the suicidal patient. *Acta Psychiatrica Scandinavica, 87*(Suppl. 371), 57–59.

Lader, M. (1980). *Introduction to psychopharmacology.* Kalamazoo, MI: Upjohn.

Lovett, C. G., & Maltsberger, J. T. (1992). Psychodynamic approaches to the assessment and management of suicide. In B. Bongar (Ed.), *Suicide: Guidelines for assessment, management, and treatment* (pp. 160–175). New York: Oxford University Press.

Maltsberger, J. T. (1991). Psychotherapy with older suicidal patients. *Journal of Geriatric Psychiatry, 24,* 217–234.

Maltsberger, J. T. (1992). The psychodynamic formulation: An aid in assessing suicide risk. In R. W. Maris, A. L. Berman, J. T. Maltsberger, & R. I. Yufit (Eds.), *Assessment and prediction of suicide* (pp. 25–49). New York: Guilford Press.

Maltsberger, J. T., & Buie, D. (1974). Countertransference hate in the treatment of suicidal patients. *Archives of General Psychiatry, 30,* 625–633.

Marsella, A. J., & Pedersen, P. B. (Eds.). (1981). *Cross-cultural counseling and psychotherapy.* New York: Pergamon Press.

McCabe, B., & Tsuang, M. (1982). Dietary considerations in MAO Inhibitor regimens. *Journal of Clinical Psychiatry, 43,* 178–181.

McIntosh, J. L. (1987). Suicide: Training and education needs with an emphasis on the elderly. *Gerontology and Geriatrics Education, 7,* 125–139.

McIntosh, J. L., & Santos, J. F. (1984). Suicide counseling and intervention with racial/ethnic minorities. In C. L. Hatton & S. M. Valente (Eds.), *Suicide: Assessment and intervention* (2nd ed., pp. 175–194). Norwalk, CT: Appleton-Century-Crofts.

Morgan, A. C. (1989). Special issues of assessment and treatment of suicide risk in the elderly. In D. Jacobs & H. N. Brown (Eds.), *Suicide: Understanding and responding: Harvard medical school perspectives* (pp. 239–255). Madison, CT: International Universities Press.

Osgood, N. J. (1985). *Suicide in the elderly: A practitioner's guide to diagnosis and mental health intervention.* Rockville, MD: Aspen.

Pedersen, P. B. (1981). The cultural inclusiveness of counseling. In P. B. Pedersen, J. G. Draguns, W. J. Lonner, & J. E. Trimble (Eds.), *Counseling across cultures* (rev. & exp. ed., pp. 22–60). Honolulu: University Press of Hawaii.

Pedersen, P. B. (Ed.). (1985). *Handbook of cross-cultural counseling and therapy.* Westport, CT: Greenwood.

Pedersen, P. B. (Ed.). (1991). Special issue: Multiculturalism as a fourth force in counseling. *Journal of Counseling & Development, 70*(Whole No. 1).

Pedersen, P. B., Draguns, J. G., Lonner, W. J., & Trimble, J. E. (Eds.). (1981). *Counseling across cultures* (rev. & exp. ed.). Honolulu: University Press of Hawaii.

Pollack, M., & Rosenbaum, J. (1987). Management of antidepressant-induced side effects: A practical guide for the clinician. *Journal of Clinical Psychiatry, 48,* 3–8.

Ramirez, M., III. (1991). *Psychotherapy and counseling with minorities: A cognitive approach to individual and cultural differences.* New York: Pergamon Press.

Richman, J. (1986). *Family therapy for suicidal people.* New York: Springer.

Richman, J. (1993). *Preventing elderly suicide: Overcoming personal despair, professional neglect, and social bias.* New York: Springer.

Sackeim, H. A. (1988). Mechanisms of action of electroconvulsive therapy. *Review of Psychiatry, 7,* 436–457.

Santos, J. F., & Hubbard, R. W. (1990). Training needs for work with the vulnerable elderly. In Z. Harel, P. Ehrlich, & R. Hubbard (Eds.), *The vulnerable aged: People, services, and policies* (pp. 295–306). New York: Springer.

Santos, J. F., Hubbard, R. W., & McIntosh, J. L. (1983). Mental health and the minority elderly. In L. D. Breslau & M. R. Haug (Eds.), *Depression and aging: Causes, care, and consequences* (pp. 51–70). New York: Springer.

Santos, J. F., & VandenBos, G. R. (Eds.). (1982). *Psychology and the older adult: Challenges for training in the 1980's.* Washington, DC: American Psychological Association.

Slaby, A. E., & Dumont, L. E. (1992). Psychopharmacotherapy of suicidal ideation and behavior. In B. Bongar (Ed.), *Suicide: Guidelines for assessment, management, and treatment* (pp. 187–203). New York: Oxford University Press.

Sterling-Smith, R. (1974). A medical toxicology index: An evaluation of commonly used suicidal drugs. In A. T. Beck, H. Resnick, & D. Lettieri (Eds.), *The prediction of suicide* (pp. 214–220). Bowie, MD: Charles Press.

Stern, S., Rush, A. J., & Mendels, J. (1980). Toward a rational pharmacotherapy of depression. *American Journal of Psychiatry, 137,* 545–552.

Sue, D. W. (Ed.). (1990). *Counseling the culturally different: Theory and practice* (2nd ed.). New York: Wiley.

Sue, S. (1977). Community mental health services to minority groups: Some optimism, some pessimism. *American Psychologist, 32,* 616–624.

Vontress, C. (1971). Racial differences: Impediments to rapport. *Journal of Counseling Psychology, 18,* 7–15.

Weiner, R. D., & Coffey, C. E. (1988). Indications for use of electroconvulsive therapy. *Review of Psychiatry, 7,* 458–481.

White American researchers and multicultural counseling. (1993). *Counseling Psychologist, 21*(Whole No. 2).

5

Suicide Assessment and Intervention With the Elderly

This chapter will deal with the psychological assessment of suicide potential in the elderly and with possible interventions. Although in some cases, suicide may be attributed to other diagnoses (e.g., schizophrenia), the focus here will be on suicidal behavior as it occurs during periods of depression. In addition to factors related to physical vulnerability, choice of method, and the presence of physical illness, the subtle and unique changes in the way depression expresses itself in older individuals are clinically significant as well. For example, the cognitions that may prompt suicidal ideation in the elderly may differ significantly from those of younger adults. Although feelings of hopelessness and helplessness are common in suicidal clients across the life span (Weishaar & Beck, 1992), in the elderly they may reflect certain conditions related to the aging process that are not often encountered in younger clients. (Some of these conditions were summarized in chapter 4, Table 1).

Clinical Themes in the Assessment of Suicidal Elderly Clients

The normal aging process is characterized by a gradual erosion of certain skills and abilities rather than the sudden and dramatic drops associated with pathological aging. Elderly clients

---

Some portions of this chapter are substantially revised and expanded from McIntosh and Santos (1984).

may be aware of, and think in catastrophic terms about, the gradual process of attrition that may occur in their intellectual abilities, memory, physical stamina, or sexual capabilities. These changes are potentially destructive to their self-esteem.

Attitudes and fears about death represent one of the more important ways in which older adults, and particularly those considering suicide, may differ from their younger counterparts. Although older persons have relatively low death fears in comparison with younger individuals, they are concerned about *how* they are going to die and about practical matters related to wills and estates (Kastenbaum & Aisenberg, 1972). Thus, thoughts related to suicide as a death-controlling act can be expected to emerge from such concerns. In other words, if the elderly patient is strongly focused on death, this may well heighten concerns about cognitive decline or painful death, and suicide may come to be seen as a means of controlling such losses and problems. Attention to certain practical matters, as well as pressure for family meetings to discuss inheritance, funeral plans, and so forth, may well be regarded as indirect suicidal warnings. In some cases, the threatened loss of an estate or other resources to medical and long-term care bills may lead the older adult to consider suicide as an altruistic act that involves doing what is best for the family.

The elderly person's sense of personal control over his or her life has other clinical implications. The relationships among stress, locus of control, and learned helplessness in the elderly have been considered by a number of authors (Baltes & Baltes, 1986; Rodin, 1987). From a clinical perspective, it is important to note that one response to a sense of loss of control or external locus of control regarding life events (including health status and bodily functioning) may be pathological attempts to reassert control over one's life. Such attempts might include refusal to follow medical advice or other death-tempting/provoking acts. In other cases, more direct suicidal behavior may be in part motivated by an attempt to control future events that are viewed as being uncertain, uncontrollable, and generally negative in outcome.

Older adults are also more prone to reminiscence than younger persons, and although the life review process may generally be regarded as a healthy practice for many older persons (see, e.g., Butler, 1975), it may also lead, in some cases, to depressive rumination about failures and lost opportunities and to the belief that such outcomes can be neither accepted nor corrected. This type of despair typically surfaces in statements suggesting that the individual has outlived his or her usefulness. Marshall (1975) proposed that the elderly may alter their perspective of their life from a time-spent to a time-left orientation and that this may encourage a more healthy acceptance of their mortality. Of course, the pathological distortion of this process may lead to accepting death as a form of self-punishment or as a means of avoiding perceived failure in the future.

In terms of assessment, themes such as these may surface during an evaluation of the client's life satisfaction, family support systems, and cognitions about the present and future. Such themes, when seen in later life and particularly when accompanied by dysphoria and withdrawal, should not be considered as a part of normal developmental issues but as potential suicidal indicators.

The careful assessment of losses experienced by the elderly client may also shed some light on suicidal potential. Serious and limiting physical illnesses represent one form of loss, but even minor medical problems may be viewed in catastrophic terms by the older person. Cataracts may be viewed as signifying impending blindness, bronchitis as respiratory failure, and minor surgery as a major setback that threatens nursing home placement. Furthermore, there are two other important and unique dimensions relating to loss in the elderly that need to be considered. First, anniversary reactions related to the loss of a spouse or job or to other exit events may be highly significant for the older person. As a result, identifying important dates associated with losses should be included as part of assessment procedures with the elderly. Second, the death of an adult child can be particularly devastating for an older adult because it is "off time" (Neugarten, 1968) and usually unexpected and may represent the loss of a supportive individual on whom the client has depended or might expect to be dependent in the future. As life expectancy continues to increase for the elderly, the death of adult children through accidents or illness may be expected to become a more common experience. Although little research has been reported on this developing trend, it may well emerge as having considerable clinical significance.

Clinical Case Number 5.1: Laura

Laura was a 79-year-old widowed White woman who had been hospitalized after threatening to kill herself. It was her second psychiatric hospitalization, having been hospitalized for depression approximately 40 years earlier. At the time of her initial hospitalization, she was treated as an inpatient for one week and was not prescribed any psychotropic medications.

During her interview in connection with her most recent admission, Laura appeared to be depressed and tearful. In such cases, when a patient is in a crisis state, it is usually best to openly discuss any suicidal ideation in order to more effectively evaluate the presence and severity of reality distortions (A. Stone & Shein, 1968) and to estimate the lethality of suicidal intent. Laura's plan for attempting suicide involved ingesting alcohol and pills, both of which were available in her home. Upon her arrival at the hospital, her daughter brought a large grocery bag filled with various prescription and nonprescription medications that had been in the patient's medicine cabinet.

Laura lived alone in a small apartment located in a housing project for the elderly, but because she had many friends living nearby, she had not been socially isolated. She was retired and lived on a small pension after having worked as a librarian for 40 years. Her husband, who had died 13 years previously, was a dentist with a small practice. They had two daughters. As a result of her upbringing, Laura had been a conscientious and dependent girl. She was an only child with a close attachment to her parents. Even after getting married and having children, she and her husband continued to live with Laura's parents. The arrangements were reversed when, after her husband's graduation from dental school, they purchased a two-family home in a nearby community and Laura's parents moved into the downstairs apartment. A few years later, Laura's father died of a heart attack.

Shortly thereafter, Laura and her husband sold the duplex and purchased a larger, single-family home. Laura's mother then moved in with them, and as a result, Laura spent a large part of her time nursing her mother back to health during periods of illness. Laura's mother died one year before Laura's husband.

Both of Laura's daughters were married and lived nearby. The older daughter visited or called her mother several times a week, but the younger one had distanced herself emotionally from her mother, and this had been a source of much distress for Laura.

At the time of her hospitalization, Laura displayed severe problems in two of the areas assessed by the Brief Psychiatric Rating Scale (Overall & Gorham, 1962), namely, depressed mood and somatic concern. She also reported mild to moderate levels of anxiety about the future, guilt about past events, and feelings of emotional withdrawal. Her complaints of significant emotional distress focused on two central precipitants involving her inadequate relationship with her youngest daughter and the progressive loss of her vision. She seemed to focus on these problems to the exclusion of others, stating for instance, "There's nothing that I want except my family and my health."

The deterioration of physical health is among the most devastating losses suffered by the elderly (Jarvik, 1983), because it has an influence on almost every aspect of their lives. Medical problems are often related to both depression and suicide in all age groups (MacKenzie & Popkin, 1987), but especially among the elderly (see chapter 3; M. Miller, 1979; Sainsbury, 1963). In Laura's case, she had been diagnosed as suffering from a macular degeneration that was causing a progressive bilateral loss of vision. This was especially disconcerting because of her previous career as a librarian and the fact that her two most enjoyable leisure activities had been reading and playing the piano. Thus, in this case as in many others, a loss of vision can lead to a loss of independence and social isolation because of reduced mobility (Salzman & Shader, 1979). This became a major factor in Laura's dysphoria and pessimism, and in this context she stated, "I think I could take everything that was dished out to me except the eyesight." She also stated that she would no longer be interested in dying "if I got my eyesight back." Although the fore-warning of an impending stressful event often allows a person to prepare for it (Wilkie, Eisdorfer, & Staub, 1982), Laura was allowing the information about her impending loss of vision to build negative expectations about her future. It was felt that she would benefit from cognitive therapy to help her recognize and modify her maladaptive cognitions about her physical ailments (Emery, 1981). The therapist decided to proceed at a cautious pace because providing assurance too quickly (e.g., "Don't worry, everything will turn out all right") can be perceived as shallow and make clients feel they have not been listened to or understood (Morgan, 1981).

Other than her visual problems, Laura appeared to be in good physical health. Two months earlier she had an an-giogram that failed to identify any major coronary obstruc-tions, but since that time she had felt anxious and had lost her appetite. She showed a strong tendency to focus on somatic symptoms. Her complaints of physical and emotional distress had been escalating over the past two months, and she had become increasingly depressed after she was hospitalized for cardiac tests four months earlier. Laura complained of an-hedonia to the extent that even her favorite leisure activi-ties were no longer enjoyable. However, despite her visual limitations and reported difficulties in concentrating, she con-tinued to request additional books from the hospital library so that she could continue reading. Also, she became quite animated when discussing the elderly gentleman who had recently proposed marriage to her.

The patient complained of a severely depressed mood. The morning after being hospitalized, her Beck Depression Inven-tory (BDI) score (Beck, Ward, Mendelson, Mock, & Erbaugh, 1961) was 24. The same afternoon, her BDI score was 28, and that evening it was 30. Such a reverse diurnal variation is often characteristic of nonmelancholic depression. Her score on the Hamilton Rating Scale for Depression (Hamilton, 1960) was 20, indicating a moderate level of depression. No sleep disturbance was noted, and no psychomotor agitation or re-tardation was observed.

Her assessed level of suicidality varied according to the instrument used. On the Scale for Suicide Ideation (Beck, Ko-vacs, & Weissman, 1979) as modified by I. Miller, Norman,

Bishop, and Dow (1986), the patient obtained a moderate total score of 23. The Hopelessness Scale (Beck, Weissman, Lester, & Trexler, 1974) has also been found to be an appropriate measure in evaluating depressed elderly (Hill, Gallagher, Thompson, & Ishida, 1988), and on this instrument, Laura obtained a total score of 15, reflecting a high degree of pessimism and hopelessness. Finally, on the Risk Estimator for Suicide (Motto, Heilbron, & Juster, 1985), her score of 609 indicated a very high risk of suicide. It is interesting to note that during a clinical interview, Laura stated that she was "too much of a coward to do it." Her suicidal ideation focused on passive and indirect means, as reflected in statements such as "If somebody else would kill me, that would be great."

Laura was quite sociable and had many friends. In terms of a formal assessment of social supports (see Lin, Dean, & Ensel, 1986), she identified eight good friends with whom she regularly spent time. She reported having pleasant conversations with her four closest friends on a daily basis, including both small talk and discussions of emotional problems. She also belonged to a local recreational group and a singing group and frequently played cards with her friends. Unfortunately, her depressive cognitions were distorting and negating the value of her social supports: As she said, "What good can friends do if I'm blind?" She was also preoccupied with her inadequate relationship with her daughters. Even though she had received numerous telephone calls from her friends inquiring sincerely as to how she was doing, she minimized their significance, stating, "But they're not family." She displayed a tendency that is fairly common among high-suicide-risk patients, denying the existence of social bonds (Achté, 1988). Despite this, Laura's previous socialization tendencies were deemed as being important in her treatment because prior coping behavior provides a good indication of current coping capability (Hendin, 1981).

In relation to Laura's concerns about her family, it should be pointed out that older patients often have inappropriate beliefs and expectations regarding the role their adult children should serve in their lives (Emery, 1981). It is common for them to become dependent on their grown children for emotional support and companionship. Therefore, an important aspect of their treatment might be based on the promotion of self-reliance (Gallagher & Thompson, 1981).

Laura reported many recreational outlets. Using the Pleasant Events Schedule for Older Persons (Teri & Lewinsohn, 1982), she identified a variety of events that she both enjoyed doing and had done in the past month. Using the classification of leisure activities developed by Tinsley, Teaff, Colbs, and Kaufman (1985), she reported enjoying reading, playing the piano, playing cards, raising house plants, knitting, watching television, joining a singing group, and attending social groups and religious meetings. Her major problem in connection with leisure activities involved her difficulties in reading because of her impaired vision.

The decision was made to encourage Laura to develop the abilities that she still retained, rather than having her dwell on those that had been lost (Gallagher & Thompson, 1981). She could still read using a magnifying glass but was fearful that her vision would progressively deteriorate. She disliked the idea of audio books for the blind, primarily because of the handicapped implications. Tinsley et al. (1985) suggested that if a person is unable to participate in a certain preferred recreational activity, they may obtain similar psychological benefits by substituting equivalent leisure activities. In Laura's case, reading could be classified as a comfortable solitude activity, similar to raising house plants or collecting antiques or photographs. Although photography would not be a viable alternative because of her visual problems, Laura had expressed an interest in minor gardening, and this was suggested as an activity that might help her to satisfy her need for quiet solitary recreation.

When asked about her emotion-regulating coping strategies, Laura reported that she discussed her problems with a close friend because she found this useful in broadening her views of the situation. She would occasionally remind herself to take one day at a time, but this remained difficult for her. However, she had not resorted to clearly maladaptive strategies such as abusing alcohol or other drugs. On occasion she had vented her emotions; she stated, "I cry a lot." Strengthening religious beliefs is a common coping strategy for many elderly persons (Koenig, George, & Siegler, 1988), but this approach had not been adopted by Laura.

An important area to assess because of its direct relevance to suicide prevention involves the reasons for living that may be identified by the patient. Suicidal patients have been found to report significantly fewer reasons for living than nonsuicidal patients (Linehan, Goodstein, Nielsen, & Chiles, 1983). In Laura's case, when asked why she might prefer to live, she spontaneously said because "my friends would miss me [if I died]." When asked if she could think of any other reasons, she said no and laughed. Such a generalized negative evaluation of reasons for living seems to be a core factor in the hopelessness expressed by many suicidal patients and certainly warrants careful evaluation in the course of therapy.

The DSM-III-R Multiaxial Diagnosis for Laura was as follows:

Axis I: Major Depressive Disorder, Recurrent Episode Nonpsychotic, Nonmelancholic, Moderate Severity

Axis II: Dependent Personality Traits

Axis III: Macular Degeneration

Axis IV: Psychosocial Stressors: Friction with daughter, physical illness
Severity: 3 = moderate (predominantly enduring circumstances)

Axis V: Current GAF: 50
Highest GAF past year: 70

Laura's case clearly reflects the interrelationships between suicidality and medical illness. Not only did her visual problems restrict her primary leisure activity, they also forced her to become more dependent on her daughters. This seemed to aggravate an already problematic relationship between Laura and her daughters and tended to promote suicidal threats.

Clinical Case Number 5.2: Hal, Part 1

The second case example involves Hal, a 70-year-old widowed White man who was hospitalized following a suicide attempt by drug overdose. He had taken 14 Enduron pills (a common diuretic) and then, in a moment of indecision, telephoned his sister before collapsing on the floor of his apartment. Although he was unable to speak on the phone, his sister realized that it was Hal who had called, and tried calling him several times. When she could not get through, she went to his apartment and found him lying on the floor. She drove him to the emergency room of a nearby hospital. Several days later, he was transferred to a large psychiatric hospital for evaluation and treatment.

Although Hal's telephone call after ingesting the pills may suggest a manipulative quality about his attempt, it is also possible that this might have been a direct cry for help. In either case, one cannot rule out the possibility of true suicidal intent (Hendin, 1981). In fact, most attempters appear to exhibit some ambivalence over their death, and often hope to be rescued. Nevertheless, there is a relationship between suicide attempts and eventual completions (Avery & Winokur, 1978) in that many unsuccessful attempters eventually die by suicide (Motto, 1965). Approximately 10% of attempters will commit suicide within 10 years following the initial attempt (Weiss & Scott, 1974). Thus, when working with someone who has a history of suicidal behavior, the therapist should not assume that the client did not intend to die or that they will not attempt suicide again. Also, a clinician can obtain much useful information about current suicidal potential by knowing the circumstances surrounding a previous attempt or attempts.

In Hal's case, he had been widowed for five years and lived alone in a small apartment. He had been a production supervisor until his retirement eight years before. During the majority of his adult years, Hal's main social outlet had been his wife, who unfortunately died of cardiac problems just two months after Hal retired. Since that time, he had become quite socially isolated, his only real social contact being the frequent visits with his younger sister, who lived in a nearby community. In this and many similar instances, retirement and the death of one's spouse are the two most common traumatic events and precipitants of a depressive episode in the elderly (Wilkie et al., 1982). In Hal's case, both of these events occurred within a relatively brief period of time, thus enhancing the overall impact of the stressors (Miller, 1979). It should also be noted that elderly widows who have relied on their spouses for the majority of their social support have been found to be more vulnerable to suicide than those with a more extensive social support network (Miller, 1979). In addition, under similar circumstances, widowers are at much greater suicide risk than widows (see chapter 1).

Although it might be expected that Hal would have attempted suicide shortly after his wife's death, it should be pointed out that it can take time before the full impact of such a loss becomes apparent. In Hal's case, the close occurrence of his retirement and his wife's death may have pushed him to the point where the desire to live and a wish to die had become equally strong. This conflict of life and death wishes appears to be a common struggle in the early stages of those considering suicide (Kovacs & Beck, 1977). Under such circumstances, even relatively minor problems may be enough to tip the scales in favor of suicide (Miller, 1979).

At the time of his initial interview, Hal was neatly and casually dressed. He was cooperative throughout the interview and showed no signs of psychomotor retardation or agitation. However, he did complain of a dysphoric mood, which he attributed to his persistent guilt feelings regarding his sexual urges. Although never acting on these urges, he reported occasional sexual fantasies and dreams with sexual content, both of which upset him greatly. His mood remained serious as he discussed his feelings of depression and hopelessness, calmly indicating that "I've never been happy since I left work." Although he still reported occasional suicidal ideation, it seemed limited to a passive wish that he was dead. He denied any active suicidal intent at the time of the interview, stating, "Every time I try (suicide), I end up worse than before."

Hal was alert and oriented throughout the initial interviews. His short- and long-term memory appeared to be intact. Although he complained about problems with concentration, he showed no difficulty in dealing with the material being discussed in the interviews. Hal described himself as a compulsive worrier, saying, "I've always been nervous and tense" and "I feel like I have so many problems I'll never get out from under them; I worry about everything."

Clinical Case Number 5.3: Karl, Part 1

Karl was a 58-year-old divorced White man who was initially seen as an inpatient in a private psychiatric hospital. He was voluntarily hospitalized because of severe depression and suicidal ideation. He was a recovering alcoholic who had been in Alcoholics Anonymous for the past 20 years and had been abstinent since he joined the AA program. He had a master's degree in education and worked as an instructor in the local public school system.

Karl had been divorced for the past six years and had a son attending college out of state and a daughter who worked full-time and lived with her mother. Karl reported much enjoyment from his infrequent chats with his daughter, but he indicated that, in the course of these conversations, he often gave her unsolicited advice and attempted to direct her life. This was usually met with resistance and rebuff on her part and often terminated their interaction.

During a clinical interview shortly after his admission to the hospital, Karl refused to leave his bed, initially participating in the interview with a sheet over his head. He openly discussed his depression in terms of low self-esteem and persistent social withdrawal, stating, "I see myself as a waste," and complained of a variety of depressive symptoms, including a dysphoric mood, feelings of dejection and discouragement, anhedonia, and a loss of the mirth response. Despite the variety and severity of depressive symptoms that Karl displayed, he reported none of the usual somatic manifestations of depression such as a loss of appetite, weight, or energy or diurnal variation of his symptoms. He presented himself as severely depressed and seemed to lack the social supports and coping skills necessary for managing the problems in his life.

A client such as Karl, who lacks psychological, personal, or social resources, is typically more vulnerable to the effects of stress (Osgood, 1985). On the basis of demographic factors, he also was likely to be at risk for potentially lethal suicidal behavior. He reported persistent suicidal ideation, often involving thoughts of jumping from a local bridge, but he claimed, "I don't have the guts to do it." He continued to view this action as an option, yet denied he would ever carry out the plan.

On the BDI (Beck et al., 1961), Karl had a total score of 37, thus reflecting a severe level of depression. This score was obtained despite the fact that he had failed to answer two questions. Similarly, on the Dysfunctional Attitudes Scale (Weissman, 1978), he achieved a total score of 242, suggesting the presence of extensive depressogenic cognitions. His Minnesota Multiphasic Personality Inventory (MMPI) Depression scale t score was 120, again reflecting a severe level of depression. On the Beck Hopelessness Scale (Beck et al., 1974), Karl's total score of 19 indicated extreme difficulty visualizing the future because of severe pessimism and a loss of hope. He seemed always to be anticipating failure and misfortune, thus eroding his motivation to perform most tasks. He was quite discouraged about most activities, his self-confidence was low, and his self-evaluation was characterized by feelings of helplessness and worthlessness.

Karl's depressive symptoms predominantly appeared in the cognitive sphere, with specific irrational negative thoughts leading to self-deprecation, self-criticism, and low self-esteem. He demonstrated the presence of distortions in each sphere of the cognitive triad, including a negative view of himself, his world, and his future. He tended to recall much negative information and underestimated the amount of positive reinforcement that he had received. Karl appeared to internalize the cause of negative events while externalizing the locus of positive events. He also displayed an extreme response to criticism, as reflected in statements such as "It doesn't matter what I do; I'm always the jerk." For example, while attending a group meeting for the inpatients on his unit, the group leader politely asked him to move to a different chair. Although responding appropriately during the situation, in a therapy session later that day he reported thinking to himself, "You can't do anything right" because he couldn't even find a proper place to sit. He showed signs of a strong self-critical attitude, a poor self-image, and persistent self-attributions for failure. He reported feelings of inadequacy and worthlessness, as well as self-blame and guilt, and described a futile and nihilistic view of his life, stating that he had "a meaningless existence; there's no point to my life."

Karl's social functioning was severely impaired, and he was almost totally lacking in social supports. This is an important consideration because an aging person lacking a confidante may be at increased risk for suicidal behavior (M. Miller, 1979). Because he was a quiet and introspective man, Karl had difficulties meeting people and making friends. He admitted to persistent and deliberate self-imposed social withdrawal, saying, "I stay as far away from people as I possibly can" because "very few people want me around." Thus, his social resources were clearly limited and even while in the hospital, he often retreated to the solitude of his bedroom, at times even hiding under the sheets.

Karl's personality functioning was also impaired. On the MMPI, he obtained significant elevations on six of the clinical scales. His profile (Welsh code: 2874*60"13'5-9/F"L-K/; Welsh, 1948) suggested severe depression, suicidal ruminations, and schizoid tendencies. He seemed unable to express his emotions in an adaptive manner and was likely to react to very minor irritants as though they were major threats. He displayed what appeared to be a long-standing pattern of social isolation and social rejection. On the Millon Clinical Multiaxial Inventory (Millon, 1982), he attained elevations on the Avoidant, Schizoid, Dependent, and Schizotypal scales. His scores also suggested a dependent coping style characterized by passive resignation and chronic worrying. His fear of rejection had resulted in extended periods of loneliness and solitude. His tendency to avoid emotional arousal prevented him from experiencing rewarding social interactions. Furthermore, Karl's self-image of weakness and frailty often made the ordinary responsibilities of daily living seem unwieldy.

The official DSM-III-R diagnosis of this patient was as follows:

Axis I: 296.23 Major Depression, Single Episode, Severe, Nonpsychotic, Nonmelancholic 300.40 Dysthymia

Axis II: 301.90 Mixed Personality Disorder with Dependent, Avoidant, and Passive–Aggressive features

Axis III: None

Axis IV: Psychosocial Stressors: Financial limitations
Severity: 4 = Moderate

Axis V: Current GAF: 40
Highest GAF past year: 60

Assessment Measures

The test-battery approach illustrated in these case scenarios reflects the wide variety of measures that are available for evaluating and monitoring affect, suicidal thoughts, and intent. This approach seems well advised because of the importance of ongoing measurement, because many of these states and processes may fluctuate on a daily to weekly basis. The test battery allows for a tracking of fluctuations in mood while identifying underlying irrational thoughts that tend to promote depressive and suicidal ideation. In addition, personality variables can also be examined. The appendix contains an annotated review of some of the most useful measures in assessing the elderly suicidal patient (similarly, see Eyman & Eyman, 1992; Rothberg & Geer-Williams, 1992).

Interventions

Most of the interventions that are used with younger adults may also be used with elderly persons. However, there are some important differences that should be identified on the basis of social and psychological factors that are associated with aging. For example, there should be an awareness of the cohort experiences of the elderly, along with their personal exposure to loss and trauma and their available coping resources, in order to implement more effective age-appropriate interventions. Obviously, each new cohort of older persons brings with it a different background based on a unique set of historical experiences. One interesting and important example of such emerging changes and challenges may well be reflected in the upcoming generation of career women who will be facing retirement.

An illustration of a cohort-sensitive approach would involve the use of a variety of formal and informal support systems in managing suicidal behavior in the elderly. For example, researchers have documented that although religiosity does not appear to increase significantly with age, the current cohort of older persons are often highly religious (regular church attendance, private religious behavior, and high self-ratings of religiosity) and have been so throughout their lives (see Mindel & Vaughn, 1978). For this reason, the use of clergy and pastoral counselors as adjuncts in the therapeutic process should be given consideration, particularly when the patient's background reveals a high degree of religiosity.

Family support systems may also provide important resources in the development of a treatment plan. The roles that spouses and adult children of the aged may play will vary substantially from the parent and sibling roles encountered in younger suicidal clients. This is particularly true in terms of accessibility, degree, and type of existing interdependence (e.g., economic, emotional, or social) and the resources that they can bring to the situation, such as commitment of time to monitor the older adult's behavior or the ability to provide and arrange for pleasant activities and experiences. When feasible, family members can and should play an important role in the treatment process. The reasons-for-living approach, behavioral contracting regarding communication with significant others prior to a suicide attempt, and the availability of social reinforcement are all influenced by and, to some extent, dependent on family involvement. Future cohorts—with smaller families increasingly headed by single parents, fewer individuals available for support, and possible changing roles for elder family members—will undoubtedly require therapists to make changes in treatment approaches with older adults and their adult family members.

A great deal of emphasis has been given to the importance of cautiousness in old age (Botwinick, 1984). Although the vast majority of the research on this topic has involved laboratory experiments with specific learning tasks, the findings offer some interesting hints for clinical treatment as well. Essentially, cautiousness has been viewed as a multivariate construct. Older adults have been found to value accuracy over speed of response in that they prefer to omit answers rather than guess (e.g., Botwinick, 1984, chapter 10), and they may need more certainty of correctness prior to responding or choosing a problem-solving option. Because any therapeutic approach involves change, the manner in which the notion of change is structured or presented to the older client may be important for the acceptance and effectiveness of therapy. In cognitive–behavioral approaches, goals are typically concrete and specific, with periodic measures of improvement built into the course of treatment. This may be a particularly appropriate treatment style for the elderly because they often require more reassurances and information about the process and more reward for attempts that involve risk taking.

Loneliness in the later years of life has also received a great deal of attention (Peplau & Perlman, 1982; Young, 1982) and clearly has relevance for working with suicidal elderly. Osgood (1985) has conceptualized loneliness along dimensions that are similar to some models of depression: The subjective experience of loneliness is based on the individual's cognitions regarding his or her social world and relationships, the decline in the availability and type of social reinforcement to which the person is historically accustomed, and an affective orientation emphasizing basic human needs for intimacy and relationships.

The treatment of individuals following unsuccessful suicide attempts has been a sorely neglected problem area, and few empirical investigations have been conducted to critically evaluate the types of treatments that have been used with these cases. Group approaches have been successfully used in the treatment of depressed elderly (Gallagher & Thompson, 1981) and suicidal adults (Patsiokas & Clum, 1985), and they appear to offer effective means for decreasing social isolation, promoting social skills, increasing opportunities for social reinforcement, and developing peer support. Of course, as with many psychological disorders, individual psychotherapy should be considered prior to group placement in order to handle the crisis phase of a suicide attempt as well as potential relapses. Although the present review focuses on cognitive–behavioral techniques, it should be acknowledged that other interventions (e.g., pharmacological, psychodynamic) may be useful as well (see chapter 4).

A continuation of two case examples presented earlier may help clarify some of the treatment issues likely to arise in depressed and suicidal elderly patients.

Clinical Case Number 5.2: Hal, Part 2

While still a psychiatric inpatient, Hal was treated with antidepressant medications. Initially, 25 mg of Imipramine at bedtime was used and gradually increased to 100 mg. It should be noted that because of lowered metabolism rates in the elderly, such low doses are gradually increased while the presence and severity of side effects are continuously monitored (Salzman, 1982). Unfortunately, in this case the medication seemed to have little effect on Hal's mood so that psychological treatments were initiated as the major intervention.

Individual psychotherapy in this case included both cognitive and behavioral strategies designed to help Hal deal with his depression, guilt, and social isolation. Cognitive restructuring was used to reduce his unrealistic high standards for himself because they consistently resulted in feelings of failure.

Sexuality was discussed with the patient to help identify and reduce his feelings of guilt. Since his wife died, Hal had not had any heterosexual contact. However, he did have sexual urges and found this greatly upsetting, feeling that he was being unfaithful to his deceased wife. Many discussions were needed to explore this sexuality issue, because Hal found it difficult to openly discuss the topic. Cognitive restructuring helped to reduce his guilt over sexual matters, and as the guilt lessened, his self-acceptance increased, leading to improved affect.

Although he still tended to be quite serious, Hal began to show episodes of happiness that included spontaneous smiling and laughter. While still in the hospital, occupational therapy activities were emphasized for him as a means of increasing his socialization level, and he was also encouraged to spend more time interacting with the staff and other patients on the unit. Together, these measures were effective in increasing Hal's social activities and initiation of social contact with other patients. As a result, he would strike up conversations or suggest playing cards or other activities.

Hal's perfectionistic standards were challenged through the use of behavioral tasks designed to alter his excessively high goals. For example, he was initially encouraged to participate in card games with other patients on the unit. Although agreeable to this, when later asked how it went, he would typically describe the experience as "terrible." The reason for this was that Hal was not a card player and usually had to learn the rules to new games, so that he frequently lost and found that to be upsetting. Therefore, an attempt was made to shift his focus in these activities to emphasize the opportunities that they provided to socialize, no matter who won the game. Gradually, he showed an increased enjoyment in the activity itself rather than just the end result.

Social activities played a major part in Hal's treatment plan, where the goal was to forcibly expose him to behavior that might be socially rewarding (Brink, 1979). Because of his extreme social withdrawal prior to hospitalization, steps were taken to ensure that he remained more active after his discharge. It would have been a mistake to simply return him to the same social situation that had precipitated his suicide attempt (Krieger, 1978), so prior to his discharge from the hospital, Hal was enrolled in an activity group for the elderly through the local community mental health center, and he was assisted in structuring a weekly planner of social activities similar to that suggested by Gallagher and Thompson (1981). In preparation for this, he had identified 14 activities from the Pleasant Events Scale (Lewinsohn, Munoz, Youngren, & Zeiaa, 1978) that he enjoyed and that fit his life-style and finances. He agreed to engage in two different activities each day so that he performed each at least once a week (see Figure 1).

Upon discharge, Hal was referred to a local psychiatrist for the management of his medications and to provide continued psychotherapy sessions. He was also encouraged to continue working on reducing his feelings of guilt, increasing his socialization, and setting appropriate standards for himself and his behavior.

Clinical Case Number 5.3: Karl, Part 2

A comprehensive treatment program was initiated for Karl in order to provide specific interventions to deal with each of his problem areas (Zarit, 1980) (described in Part 1 of Karl's case presentation earlier in this chapter). Another consideration in this instance that has been emphasized by several authors involves the importance of the temporal aspects of treatment (Frederick & Resnik, 1970; Overholser & Spirito, 1990). Building on the work of Moss and Hamilton (1956), Overholser and Spirito (1990) incorporated new treatment approaches into a temporal model that coordinated the timing of interventions with targeted problem areas (see Table 1). Different

Name: _____

Please check off each activity at least once during the week.

Please check off one activity (or more) each day.

	Monday	Tues.	Wed.	Thur.	Friday	Sat.	Sunday
Go for a walk							
Play cards							
Visit YMCA							
Visit Library							
Call a friend							
Write a letter to a friend							
Listen to music							
Lunch w/ sister							
Buy yourself something							
Watch a movie with a friend							
Give someone a compliment							
Visit a museum							

Figure 1.   Sample Pleasant Events Weekly Checklist.

interventions were used at each of the following three stages of adjustment after the suicidal crisis: the acute crisis phase, the convalescence phase, and the recovery phase.

Although antidepressant medications were initially attempted in Karl's treatment, they were found to be ineffec-

Table 1

Stages in the Treatment of Suicidality

A. Acute crisis
  1. Assess and monitor suicidal ideation
  2. Remove immediate risk factors
  3. Assess the need for medications
  4. Hospitalize when necessary

B. Convalescent phase
  1. Cognitive therapy for depression
  2. Reinforce reasons for living
  3. Promote realistic expectations
  4. Adjunctive therapy as needed

C. Recovery phase
  1. Encourage problem-solving skills
  2. Promote active coping strategies
  3. Develop adequate social supports
  4. Follow relapse prevention guidelines

Note. From "Cognitive–Behavioral Treatment of Suicidal Depression," by J. C. Overholser, and A. Spirito, 1990, in E. L. Feindler and G. R. Kalfus, *Adolescent Behavior Therapy Handbook* (p. 217), Springer Publishing Company, Inc., New York 10012. Copyright 1990 by Springer Publishing Company. Used by permission.

tive in reducing his depressive symptoms. This outcome is in agreement with the research that has shown a better response to medications with symptoms of endogenous as compared with exogenous depression. More important, avoiding the use of medications also serves to restrict access to drugs, a commonly used suicide method (McFarland & Beavers, 1984). Karl's psychotherapy began while he was still an inpatient, and continued for several months after his discharge. During this time, daily therapy sessions were provided in an attempt to challenge and change Karl's negative thoughts and to promote the development of more adaptive coping strategies. These sessions often lasted 50 to 90 minutes per day, five days a week.

Working with Karl was extremely difficult because his negative attitudes affected every aspect of his life, including therapy. However, his resistance to treatment was used to full advantage in bringing his cognitive distortions into the reality of the therapy hour. Because of the importance of the alliance between therapist and client (Emery, 1981), the early sessions were used to establish a solid therapeutic relationship. It should be emphasized that therapists working with suicidal persons need to be aware of the countertransference issues that may be involved in working with patients who display a great deal of hopelessness, apathy, and general nonresponsiveness during the early stages of treatment (see chapter 4).

After a few sessions, Karl quickly learned that the therapeutic atmosphere was nonthreatening and could even be enjoyable. He began arriving early for his sessions, often avoiding his other meetings in order to spend more time with the therapist. This avoidance was tactfully introduced in the therapy sessions, and Karl began attending his other meetings on a more consistent basis. This approach was considered to be an essential part of socializing the client into therapy and also developing proper expectations for what should occur during and between sessions (Gallagher & Thompson, 1983). In essence, Karl needed to learn that the sessions were not simply to be used for emotional venting, but to address specific skill deficits. A learning model was used that incorporated homework assignments to be completed between sessions. In this way, therapy was not limited only to the time spent in the therapist's office, but continued throughout the week.

Karl frequently displayed depressogenic cognitions, viewing himself as totally devoid of positive qualities. The result was that, when confronted with problems, he was unable to step outside of his restricted idiosyncratic view of the situation and objectively evaluate it. His primary appraisal was to quickly read possible harm or threat into many innocuous situations, and his secondary appraisal typically failed to identify coping strategies that he could use other than escape or avoidance. In other words, from a cognitive perspective

Karl overestimated the probability of threat and used emotional rather than problem-solving behaviors in responding to threats that did arise.

Attributional biases have frequently been found to be involved in geriatric depression (Maiden, 1987), and in Karl's case, he attributed any positive events that occurred for him as being due to unstable factors such as luck. However, when a problem arose or failure occurred, he tended to attribute it to global internal factors (e.g., he was "such a jerk"). For example, at one group meeting, he entered a few minutes late, and the room was filled to capacity. The group leader politely said to him, "Sit here, you can have my seat." A few minutes later, two other members came in, and because there was no place left to sit, they sat on the windowsill. Because nothing was said to these late-arriving members, Karl felt that he had been picked on. Although he was treated kindly but differently, he felt that he had been treated much worse. In the next therapy session, the therapist asked him to shift roles and evaluate the situation as if he had been one of those who sat on the windowsill. It then became apparent to him that under those circumstances, he would have felt neglected. This helped to demonstrate to him how he interpreted ambiguous cues in a negative manner.

Karl also reported persistent difficulties in expressing both positive (e.g., love) and negative (e.g., anger) emotions to others. During one session, he did have the courage to ask the therapist to turn off a radio. Although the music had bothered him since his initial session, it was only after nine visits that Karl finally felt comfortable enough to express to the therapist what he felt would be a devastating criticism. When he stated that he found the radio distracting, the therapist praised him for directly expressing his feelings and promptly turned off the radio. This was used for further discussion of the risks and benefits of direct social communication.

In therapy, an attempt was made to address the deficits in Karl's social skills in order to reduce his social isolation. He was assisted in learning to express his emotions in an adaptive and constructive manner. He was also encouraged to participate in more social activities, in spite of his reluctance and resistance to do so. Group therapy was also used to supplement his individual therapy sessions because group meetings have been found to be useful in helping withdrawn clients socialize on a regular basis and develop friendships (Wolff, 1971).

Karl also appeared to possess several passive–aggressive personality traits. It was common for him to feel intense resentment and irritability over minor misunderstandings, but rather than take a more active approach, Karl would typically use passive and indirect means to cope with the problem. For example, when talking to a friend over a cup of coffee, another person interrupted the conversation to greet Karl's friend. Karl was quite enraged over the intrusion but was unable to deal with it in a constructive manner. Instead, he stood up, made up some reason why he had to leave, and politely excused himself. The resentment and anger lingered for several days.

Psychological assessment was repeated one month after Karl's initial evaluation. This follow-up revealed that Karl continued to experience severe levels of depression as measured by the BDI (total = 33) and the MMPI Depression scale (t score = 120). His score on the Beck Hopelessness Scale had not been greatly reduced (total = 17). Furthermore, although showing a slight reduction in anger and rebelliousness (MMPI-Pd = 78), his anxiety (MMPI-Pt = 105) and alienation (MMPI-Sc = 118) had increased.

Karl seemed to deal with problems by quickly arriving at one possible solution (often not the best one), and if that failed, he would feel dejected and hopeless. Both self-blame and self-pity were evident. He needed to better recognize when problems existed and to identify the skills that were needed to effectively cope with the situation (Gallagher & Thompson, 1981). During outpatient therapy sessions, Karl showed a willingness to try the different coping strategies that had been discussed and to temporarily set aside his usual style of criticizing all alternatives and denying his ability to change. He was confronted with his tendency to run into the brick wall instead of going around it when his goal was blocked. In such circumstances, Karl reported feeling overwhelmed with the many tasks required of him and, paradoxically, would do nothing. He needed much assistance in identifying and planning the intermediate steps necessary in reaching a goal. The type of rigidity that Karl demonstrated has been found to be an important risk factor for suicide (Neuringer, 1964) in that it can reduce the ability to identify reasonable solutions to a problem (T. Ellis, 1986). Only when a client can see that many alternatives and solutions actually exist does the hopelessness eventually subside (M. Stone, 1980).

Cognitive therapy (Beck, Rush, Shaw, & Emery, 1979) was used to help Karl identify and replace his depressogenic outlook with more objective and realistic appraisals. During the course of therapy he displayed great difficulty in overcoming his negative cognitions, his fear of negative evaluation, and his suppressed hostility. Many of his overly critical attitudes seemed to be related to his internalization of parental attitudes, and after several probing questions Karl was able to see how he had internalized many of these attitudes typically displayed by his father. He described a number of incidents during his childhood when his father would criticize him for inadequate performance. Even at times when Karl felt proud of his achievements, his father would indicate that these efforts were not good enough. During the course of treatment, Karl was gradually able to understand how these developmental antecedents led to his current negative attitudes.

Karl displayed frequent use of non sequiturs in his reasoning. For example, his depressive reasoning would lead him to adopt the interpretation that "my life has problems, therefore my life is a complete waste." It was pointed out to him that this was comparable to an advertisement stating, "Our new cars come with a complete set of brand new tires; therefore our car is the best car available." He was able to see that the tires are only a small part of a car and that all new cars come with brand new tires. This logic was then applied to his own reasoning. With assistance, he was able to understand and accept that his problems were only a small part of his life and that everyone has some problems with which they must deal. Finally, a realistic automobile ad was used to parallel his life evaluation, stating, "Our car starts easily, gets good gas mileage, and rarely breaks down, but the brakes need replacing and the clutch sticks when shifting into reverse. Therefore, it is still a good car, not the best, but a good solid car." This rational approach in arriving at a realistic conclusion was useful in helping Karl see the extent and severity of his problems in relation to his strengths. Like many suicidal patients, he needed help in realizing that his harsh interpretation of his life situation was not the only view and usually not the most accurate one (Bedrosian & Beck, 1979).

Religion has been discussed as a coping strategy commonly used by the elderly (Koenig et al., 1988), and Karl's religious beliefs were certainly a potential therapeutic strength along with his desire to increase his acceptance of himself to other people. His spiritual strengths were emphasized to him in therapy as they related to his suppressed anger and his self-deprecation. His religiosity was used to facilitate the notion of "Christian acceptance of self and others," and on the basis of his interest in the spiritual life, a therapy analogy was implemented. A car was described, requiring the smooth running of four cylinders: affective, behavioral, cognitive, and spiritual. It was pointed out that inadequate functioning in any of the cylinders would disturb the smooth functioning of the entire system so that all four must be evaluated and modified as needed.

Rational emotive techniques (A. Ellis, 1962) were also used to help Karl see the relationship between his belief system and his subsequent emotional distress. For example, one day between sessions, he drove across town to attend an Alcoholics Anonymous meeting but forgot that the site of the meetings had been moved some time before. When he arrived at the wrong address and found himself alone, he considered it to be a serious problem and referred to himself as "a jerk". The therapist attempted to point out that other interpretations of the situation were possible and would likely result in different emotional reactions. Thus, the message directed toward Karl was that it was not the situation per se, but his cognitive interpretation of what had happened, that resulted in his negative emotional state.

Therapy was also useful in helping Karl identify a number of positive factors in his life (reasons for living), and with some assistance, he showed improvement in focusing more attention on these positive aspects. In this way, he was able to develop a more accurate and balanced view of his current life situation, and he acknowledged that although he was "not yet out of the tunnel," he was "starting to see the light at the end."

One strategy that was found to be useful in overcoming Karl's global negativistic approach was self-monitoring. Daily homework journals served as useful adjuncts (Brink,

1979) both to demonstrate the relationship between activity and mood and to apply what had been learned in sessions (Gallagher & Thompson, 1981). In Karl's case, this strategy involved asking him to list the positive aspects of his life. Although he initially found the task to be quite difficult, he was able to identify several important areas that he still valued. This process was shaped to the point where he completed a daily form asking for a list of "the five positive things that happened today." Typically, this involved receiving various personal or business phone calls or participating in minor social encounters. Eventually, the procedure progressed to asking him to identify some of the positive aspects of events that he found to be aversive. This technique was useful not only in demonstrating to Karl that most events contain some positive and some negative aspects, but, more important in forcing him to begin actively searching for the positive side of things.

The last stages of therapy involved a relapse prevention model that emphasized the fact that the client must learn that although stress is an inevitable part of life, increasing one's sensitivity to the early symptoms of depression can lead to early interventions designed to prevent a deeply depressive state (Gallagher & Thompson, 1981). In this case, Karl was able to identify specific problematic situations that were likely to elicit negative affective reactions, and to prepare to cope with them. This exercise was useful in helping him to prevent a major setback from occurring in response to minor aggravations. Finally, follow-up telephone contacts, which have been found to be useful in reducing the risk of subsequent suicidal behavior, were used (Liberman & Eckman, 1981): The therapist used occasional telephone contacts to remind Karl of the progress he had made and the coping skills that he had developed. In this way, his progress was maintained despite a variety of stressful life events that subsequently occurred.

Warning Signs of Suicide

Before concluding a consideration of assessment and treatment, a brief discussion of the recognition of those elderly who are at risk of suicide seems warranted. There is considerable evidence to indicate that the vast majority (at least three fourths) of suicides provide a number of possible warning signs to those around them (Bernstein, 1978–1979; Murphy & Robins, 1968; Rudestam, 1972). In addition, many of these clues occur in the presence of others over a period of time. The opportunity for the identification of suicidal tendencies is nearly always present, and awareness of relevant clues allows an informed and attentive observer to recognize the persons who are potentially at risk. Knowledge of the mental health services that are available in the community also helps in providing family and friends with resources for referral and a source of help for the troubled suicidal individual.

There have been many listings of warning signs of suicide published in the literature, and one of the most useful was provided by Shneidman (1965). Osgood (1982, 1992, chapter 6) provided essentially the same clues as Shneidman but emphasized older adults in discussing them. Shneidman (1965) proposed that there were four categories of warning signs of suicide: syndromatic, verbal, behavioral, and situational clues. He suggested that patterns of clues should be sought because, in most cases, single clues are not adequate in assessing the potential for suicidal behavior. He discussed several syndromes or patterns that tend to be associated with high suicide risk. The most obvious of these is depression along with its various and well-known symptoms (i.e., sleep or eating habit changes, dysphoria, etc.). Among the other syndromes, however, is a category labeled *dependent–dissatisfied* that should have special relevance for older adults who are unhappy in a dependency situation. This might be particularly relevant among older adults who find themselves dependent on family members or others following physical illness and debility, or perhaps under circumstances of financial problems or necessity.

Other warning signs relate to the clues that suicidal persons may provide in the things that they say and do as well as in the circumstances under which they are living. The individual contemplating suicide may provide verbal hints to others that range from the obvious to the indirect. It is generally suggested that explicit verbal expressions of suicidal thoughts or preoccupation with death be regarded as serious and that immediate action be taken to obtain professional assistance for the individual and to determine the level of seriousness. Such direct statements are considered to be the most obvious of warning signs. This is particularly true in the case of the elderly, who often may be more intent on dying by their own actions than younger groups. All clues should be dealt with seriously so that intervention may be provided if the situation is deemed appropriate.

Other clues from the suicidal person may not be as obvious as using the word "suicide" or its synonyms or discussing death. Less direct statements may nonetheless provide signs that, together with others, make up a pattern indicating that suicidal ideation does exist. Examples include statements such as "I'm tired of life," "I won't be around much longer," and "How do you leave your body to science?". These comments should not be ignored, because they offer an opportunity to discuss possible thoughts of suicide or depression.

In addition to the verbalizations of suicidal persons, their actions may also reveal their ruminations about self-destruction. Shneidman (1965) suggested that past suicide attempts are an important diagnostic clue because those who have attempted previously are likely to be at higher risk in the future. Clearly, on some past occasion(s) these individuals, when faced with stress or problems, have responded with a suicide attempt. Thus, other warning signs, when combined with past suicidal behavior, warrant serious attention and immediate action.

Of course, awareness of an individual's past attempt(s) may not exist, or the person may have never made any previous attempt. Other behavioral signs may include writing or changing a will, giving away prized possessions, or making funeral arrangements. Often the behavioral clues may simply involve a subtle difference or change in the normal "manner" of the individual, so that he or she seems to be "not themselves." More obvious behaviors would include buying a gun or obtaining quantities of medications that might be used in a suicide attempt. Suicidal as well as depressed persons often lose interest in activities that they normally value or find pleasure in performing. When any of these behaviors or changes occurs in combination with other verbal or situational clues,

Use for conclusion

suicide should be regarded as a possibility, and seeking pro-fessional assistance or encouraging the older person to obtain help is recommended.

With respect to situational clues, it is obvious that many of the circumstances in which older adults find themselves de-mand attention because they are associated with a high risk of suicide. These situational indicators have been discussed throughout this book and are particularly relevant for those individuals for whom there is an impending loss or those for whom a loss has already taken place. The loss may involve a loved one through death, physical separation, marital discord or divorce, or other interpersonal problems. The loss may not involve a person, but rather a job through dismissal, retirement, or layoffs; the death of a pet; or a required relocation of resi-dence. Other traumatic circumstances might involve the loss of function associated with a stroke, heart attack, or some other physical debility (e.g., hearing, vision, loss of bladder and/or bowel control). Diagnosis or fear of terminal illness may — *Con.* also present an intolerable situation. Economic problems, whether real or feared, as well as social isolation and/or loss of social activities or mobility, may create intolerable stress for the older adult.

It is important to emphasize that many of the situations and problems noted above are common in old age, and most older adults adapt to them relatively well. However, for those who must endure severe multiple stressors, or who lack adequate personal coping skills and social support resources, these situ-ations can greatly increase the possibility of suicide. Recogniz-ing the high-risk nature of these situations, especially when they exist along with other clues, may permit timely intervention be-fore any overt suicidal action is taken.

Summary

Suicidal elderly persons represent a particularly high-risk group for psychologists and other mental health professionals. They appear to be more serious and violent in their thoughts and acts, and also more vulnerable to the physical effects of an attempt. It would be inaccurate to conclude that aging itself is depressing and, therefore, results in higher suicide rates. What is more likely is that when those who are predisposed to depression encounter the emerging and sometimes irreversible losses of aging, the likelihood of a suicidal attempt may increase. The existence of more physical health problems in old age is a significant factor that distinguishes elderly suicides from those of younger age groups. Other important differences involve family changes, increases in dementia, and psychosocial exit events such as retirement and widowhood.

A comparison of old age with adolescence, another life stage with a high incidence of suicide, reveals some intriguing similarities between these groups for future research and theory (see Rappoport, 1972). Both adolescence and old age are periods of significant physical changes (puberty and senescence) in which body awareness and physical concerns are prominent. Both involve periods of social ambiguity in which important transitions (from child to adult, adult to older adult) occur that may lead to increased social alienation. Cognitively, anxiety about the future is common to both age groups, as is the potential for catastrophic, all-or-none thinking related to what lies ahead (adulthood for the adolescent, debility or death for the elderly). Clinicians who work with older adults should understand and keep these similarities and differences in mind.

As the number of elderly in this country continues to grow, mental health professionals can expect to encounter increasing numbers of older clients with a variety of psychological problems. It is indeed disturbing to realize that the growing rates of drug abuse and addictions, as well as suicidal attempts, in younger age groups suggest that future generations of elderly may be at an even higher risk of suicide than the current cohort of older persons.

References

Achté, K. (1988). Suicidal tendencies in the elderly. *Suicide and Life-Threatening Behavior, 18,* 55–65.

Avery, D., & Winokur, G. (1978). Suicide, attempted suicide, and relapse rates in depression. *Archives of General Psychiatry, 35,* 749–753.

Baltes, M. M., & Baltes, P. B. (1986). *The psychology of control and aging.* Hillsdale, NJ: Erlbaum.

Beck, A. T., Kovacs, M., & Weissman, A. (1979). Assessment of suicidal intention: The Scale for Suicidal Ideation. *Journal of Consulting and Clinical Psychology, 47,* 343–352.

Beck, A. T., Rush, A. J., Shaw, B., & Emery, G. (1979). *Cognitive therapy of depression.* New York: Guilford Press.

Beck, A. T., Ward, C., Mendelson, M., Mock, J., & Erbaugh, J. (1961). An inventory for measuring depression. *Archives of General Psychiatry, 4,* 561–571.

Beck, A. T., Weissman, A., Lester, D., & Trexler, L. (1974). The measurement of pessimism: The Hopelessness Scale. *Journal of Consulting and Clinical Psychology, 42,* 861–865.

Bedrosian, R., & Beck, A. T. (1979). Cognitive aspects of suicidal behavior. *Suicide and Life-Threatening Behavior, 9,* 87–96.

Bernstein, M. (1978–1979). The communication of suicidal intent by completed suicides. *Omega, 9,* 175–182.

Botwinick, J. (1984). *Aging and behavior* (3rd ed.). New York: Springer.

Brink, T. (1979). *Geriatric psychotherapy.* New York: Human Sciences Press.

Butler, R. N. (1975). *Why survive? Being old in America.* New York: Harper & Row.

Ellis, A. (1962). *Reason and emotion in psychotherapy.* Secacus, NJ: Citadel.

Ellis, T. (1986). Toward a cognitive therapy for suicidal individuals. *Professional Psychology: Research and Practice, 17,* 125–130.

Emery, G. (1981). Cognitive therapy with the elderly. In G. Emery, S. Hollon, & R. Bedrosian (Eds.), *New directions in cognitive therapy* (pp. 84–98). New York: Guilford Press.

Eyman, J. R., & Eyman, S. K. (1992). Psychological testing for potentially suicidal individuals. In B. Bongar (Ed.), *Suicide: Guidelines for assessment, management, and treatment* (pp. 127–143). New York: Oxford University Press.

Frederick, C., & Resnik, H. (1970). Interventions with suicidal patients. *Journal of Contemporary Psychotherapy, 2,* 103–109.

Gallagher, D., & Thompson, L. (1981). *Depression in the elderly: A behavioral treatment manual.* Los Angeles: University of Southern California Press.

Gallagher, D., & Thompson, L. (1983). Cognitive therapy for depression in the elderly. In L. Breslau & M. Haug (Eds.), *Depression in the elderly* (pp. 168–192). New York: Springer.

Hamilton, M. (1960). A rating scale for depression. *Journal of Neurology, Neurosurgery and Psychiatry, 23,* 56–62.

Hendin, H. (1981). Psychotherapy and suicide. *American Journal of Psychotherapy, 35,* 469–480.

Hill, R. D., Gallagher, D., Thompson, L. W., & Ishida, T. (1988). Hopelessness as a measure of suicidal intent in the depressed elderly. *Psychology and Aging, 3,* 230–232.

Jarvik, L. (1983). The impact of immediate life situations on depression: Illnesses and losses. In L. Breslau & M. Haug (Eds.), *Depression and aging: Causes, care, and consequences* (pp. 114–120). New York: Springer.

Kastenbaum, R., & Aisenberg, R. (1972). *The psychology of death*. New York: Springer.

Koenig, H., George, L., & Siegler, I. (1988). The use of religion and other emotion-regulating coping strategies among older adults. *Gerontologist, 28*, 303–310.

Kovacs, M., & Beck, A. T. (1977). The wish to live and the wish to die in attempted suicides. *Journal of Clinical Psychology, 33*, 361–365.

Krieger, G. (1978). Common errors in the treatment of suicidal persons. *Journal of Clinical Psychiatry, 39*, 649–651.

Lewinsohn, P. M., Munoz, R. F., Youngren, M. A., & Zeiaa, A. M. (1978). *Control your own depression*. Englewood Cliffs, NJ: Prentice-Hall.

Liberman, R. P., & Eckman, T. (1981). Behavior therapy vs. insight-oriented therapy for repeated suicide attempters. *Archives of General Psychiatry, 38*, 1126–1130.

Lin, N., Dean, A., & Ensel, W. (1986). *Social supports, life events, and depression*. New York: Academic Press.

Linehan, M., Goodstein, J., Nielsen, S., & Chiles, J. (1983). Reasons for staying alive when you are thinking of killing yourself: The Reasons for Living Inventory. *Journal of Consulting and Clinical Psychology, 51*, 276–286.

MacKenzie, T., & Popkin, M. (1987). Suicide in the medical patient. *International Journal of Psychiatry in Medicine, 17*, 3–23.

Maiden, R. (1987). Learned helplessness and depression: A test of the reformulated model. *Journal of Gerontology, 42*, 60–64.

Marshall, V. (1975). Age and awareness of finitude in developmental gerontology. *Omega, 6*, 113–127.

McFarland, B., & Beavers, D. (1984). Preventive strategies and program evaluation methods for chronically mentally ill suicide attempters. *Comprehensive Psychiatry, 25*, 426–437.

McIntosh, J. L., & Santos, J. F. (1984). Suicide counseling and intervention with racial/ethnic minorities. In C. L. Hatton & S. M. Valente (Eds.), *Suicide: Assessment and intervention* (2nd ed.). Norwalk, CT: Appleton-Century-Crofts.

Miller, I., Norman, W., Bishop, S., & Dow, M. (1986). The Modified Scale for Suicidal Ideation: Reliability and validity. *Journal of Consulting and Clinical Psychology, 54*, 724–725.

Miller, M. (1979). *Suicide after sixty: The final alternative*. New York: Springer.

Millon, T. (1982). *Millon Clinical Multiaxial Inventory manual* (3rd ed.). Minneapolis, MN: National Computer Systems.

Mindel, C. H., & Vaughn, C. E. (1978). A multidimensional approach to religiosity and disengagement. *Journal of Gerontology, 33*, 103–108.

Morgan, H. G. (1981). Management of suicidal behaviour. *British Journal of Psychiatry, 138*, 259–260.

Moss, L., & Hamilton, D. (1956). The psychotherapy of the suicidal patient. *American Journal of Psychiatry, 112*, 814–820.

Motto, J. (1965). Suicide attempts: A longitudinal view. *Archives of General Psychiatry, 13,* 516–520.

Motto, J., Heilbron, D., & Juster, R. (1985). Development of a clinical instrument to estimate suicide risk. *American Journal of Psychiatry, 142,* 680–686.

Murphy, G. E., & Robins, E. (1968). Communication of suicidal ideas. In H. L. P. Resnik (Ed.), *Suicidal behaviors: Diagnosis and management* (pp. 163–170). Boston: Little, Brown.

Neugarten, B. N. (1968). *Middle age and aging.* Chicago: University of Chicago Press.

Neuringer, C. (1964). Rigid thinking in suicidal individuals. *Journal of Consulting Psychology, 28,* 54–58.

Osgood, N. J. (1982). Suicide in the elderly: Are we heeding the warnings? *Postgraduate Medicine, 72,* 123–126, 128, 130.

Osgood, N. J. (1985). *Suicide in the elderly: A practitioner's guide to diagnosis and mental health intervention.* Rockville, MD: Aspen.

Osgood, N. J. (1992). *Suicide in later life: Recognizing the warning signs.* New York: Lexington Books.

Overall, J., & Gorham, D. (1962). The Brief Psychiatric Rating Scale. *Psychological Reports, 10,* 799–812.

Overholser, J. C., & Spirito, A. (1990). Cognitive–behavioral treatment of suicidal depression. In E. L. Feindler & G. R. Kalfus (Eds.), *Adolescent behavior therapy handbook* (pp. 211–231). New York: Springer.

Patsiokas, A., & Clum, G. (1985). Effects of psychotherapeutic strategies in the treatment of suicide attempters. *Psychotherapy, 22,* 281–290.

Peplau, L., & Perlman, D. (Eds.). (1982). *Loneliness: A sourcebook of current theory, research, and therapy.* New York: Wiley.

Rappoport, L. (1972). *Personality development: The chronology of experience.* Glenview, IL: Scott, Foresman.

Rodin, J. (1987). Personal control through the life course. In R. P. Abeles (Ed.), *Life span perspectives and social psychology* (pp. 103–119). Hillsdale, NJ: Erlbaum.

Rothberg, J. M., & Geer-Williams, C. (1992). A comparison and review of suicide prediction scales. In R. W. Maris, A. L. Berman, J. T. Maltsberger, & R. I. Yufit (Eds.), *Assessment and prediction of suicide* (pp. 202–217). New York: Guilford Press.

Rudestam, K. E. (1972). The "noncommunicating suicide": Does he exist? *Omega, 3,* 97–102.

Sainsbury, P. (1963). Social and epidemiological aspects of suicide with special reference to the aged. In R. H. Williams, C. Tibbitts, & W. Donahue (Eds.), *Processes of aging: Social and psychological perspectives* (Vol. 2, pp. 153–175). New York: Atherton.

Salzman, C. (1982). A primer on geriatric psychopharmacology. *American Journal of Psychiatry, 139,* 67–74.

Salzman, C., & Shader, R. (1979). Clinical evaluation of depression in the elderly. In A. Raskin & L. Jarvik (Eds.), *Psychiatric symptoms and cog-*

nitive loss in the elderly: Evaluation and assessment techniques (pp. 39–63). New York: Hemisphere.

Shneidman, E. S. (1965). Preventing suicide. *American Journal of Nursing, 65,*(5), 111–116.

Stone, A., & Shein, H. (1968). Psychotherapy of the hospitalized suicidal patient. *American Journal of Psychotherapy, 22,* 15–25.

Stone, M. (1980). The suicidal patient: Points concerning diagnosis and intensive treatment. *Psychiatric Quarterly, 52,* 52–70.

Teri, L., & Lewinsohn, P. (1982). Modification of the Pleasant and Unpleasant Events Schedules for use with the elderly. *Journal of Consulting and Clinical Psychology, 50,* 444–445.

Tinsley, H., Teaff, J., Colbs, S., & Kaufman, N. (1985). A system of classifying leisure activities in terms of the psychological benefits of participation reported by older persons. *Journal of Gerontology, 40,* 172–178.

Weishaar, M. E., & Beck, A. T. (1992). Clinical and cognitive predictors of suicide. In R. W. Maris, A. L. Berman, J. T. Maltsberger, & R. I. Yufit (Eds.), *Assessment and prediction of suicide* (pp. 467–483). New York: Guilford Press.

Weiss, J., & Scott, K. (1974). Suicide attempters ten years later. *Comparative Psychiatry, 15,* 165–171.

Weissman, M. M. (1978). The myth of involutional melancholia. *Journal of the American Medical Association, 242,* 742–744.

Welsh, G. S. (1948). An extension of Hathaway's MMPI Profile Coding System. *Journal of Consulting Psychology, 12,* 343–344.

Wilkie, F., Eisdorfer, C., & Staub, J. (1982). Stress and psychopathology in the aged. *Psychiatric Clinics of North America, 5,* 131–143.

Wolff, K. (1971). The treatment of the depressed and suicidal geriatric patient. *Geriatrics, 26,* 64–69.

Young, J. E. (1982). Loneliness, depression and cognitive therapy: Theory and application. In L. Peplau & D. Perlman (Eds.), *Loneliness: A sourcebook of current theory, research and therapy* (pp. 379–406). New York: Wiley.

Zarit, S. (1980). *Aging and mental disorders: Psychological approaches to assessment and treatment.* New York: Free Press.

6

Prevention, Ethics, and Unresolved Issues

Thus far, this book has presented the major epidemiological and risk factors associated with elder suicide, along with the theoretical explanations that have been advanced to account for these risk factors, and the problems associated with the assessment and treatment of suicide in older adults. This final chapter will offer some measures that might be used in the prevention of elderly suicide and a discussion of the ethics of suicide in late life, including the right to suicide and physician-assisted suicide. The chapter will conclude with a brief coverage of important questions for which answers are still needed regarding suicide in old age.

Prevention of Elder Suicide

Prevention must be addressed at the primary, secondary, and tertiary levels to be effective. *Primary prevention* refers to the elimination of factors and circumstances that may be associated with or tend to produce suicidal behavior prior to the actual occurrence of the behavior. This involves true prevention in that the core reasons that can ultimately lead to suicide are eliminated before they can produce self-destructive behavior. Some possible primary measures will be noted later in this chapter. The term *secondary prevention* is appropriate when suicidal

---

Some portions of this chapter are substantially revised and expanded from Osgood and McIntosh (1986).

behavior or other problems already exist for the individual and treatment is initiated to eliminate the behavior or lessen the problem. The vast majority of current suicide prevention efforts are directed at this level, including crisis intervention and therapy. Several issues of secondary prevention will be discussed below. Finally, suicidal behavior often produces problems even following treatment or the elimination of causative factors, and this level of prevention is referred to as *tertiary prevention*. In chapter 1, the problems of suicide survivors were discussed, and it is this group, those who survive the suicide death of a loved one, that is the major target of postvention or tertiary prevention. Other frequently ignored issues of postvention involve the care of those who have attempted suicide in the past but who are not currently suicidal, and the family and friends of those who have survived a nonfatal attempt. Virtually no systematic study has dealt with these groups, and therefore, little is known about the problems and aftereffects that attempted but unsuccessful suicidal attempts may produce in their lives.

It has often been pointed out that older adults generally do not seek and, therefore, are underrepresented in the clientele of suicide prevention programs, crisis intervention centers, and general mental health agencies (Felton, 1982; Gatz & Smyer, 1992; Lasoski, 1986; McIntosh, Hubbard, & Santos, 1981; Redick & Taube, 1980). These programs, of course, are the primary services that are available in our communities to prevent suicide. The reasons for their underutilization by older persons are many, including lack of awareness of their existence, the conviction that such services are not intended for older adults, the cost of services and the lack of insurance coverage to pay for them, and mistrust of any kind of agencies and institutions among the current cohorts of older adults. Although elderly persons may tend to harbor negative attitudes towards mental health services in general, it is also true that the mental health delivery system has not emphasized elder care and is definitely lacking in the number of professionals trained in geriatric areas or specialties (Santos & VandenBos, 1982).

A national survey of suicide prevention resources for the elderly that was funded and initiated by the American Association for Retired Persons (AARP; Mercer, 1989) revealed virtually no programs specifically established to work with the highest risk group for suicide—the older population. Only two suicide prevention or crisis agencies were found to have such an objective (one in San Francisco and another in Dayton, Ohio). These two programs included components that were organized to confront the special problems of older adulthood and suicide, and even included an outreach component. Although additional services and educational programs have since been established to deal with elderly suicide (e.g., Pratt, Schmall, Wilson, & Benthin, 1991), along with programs for at-risk elders that will undoubtedly benefit all potentially suicidal persons (e.g., Raschko, 1990), the number is still small, so that the need has remained inadequately met. It should be pointed out that innovative programs will be required to reach those who are at high risk but who do not typically use mental health services, if they are to be provided effective services.

Intervention Program Descriptions

Center for Elderly Suicide Prevention and Grief Related Services. Originally part of the San Francisco Suicide Prevention Center, the Center for Elderly Suicide Prevention and Grief Related Services includes two components within its Geriatric Program related to suicide intervention (additional components include an Elder Abuse Program that provides for assessment and follow-up of possible cases of abuse, and a grief program for those of any age). This multifaceted and innovative center serves clients 60 years of age and above and represents a model for the development of similar services elsewhere. One of its programs, a Friendship Line, is primarily intended to provide 24-hour crisis intervention as well as referrals and information for elders who call or for those who call on their behalf. The telephone line functions much as any crisis intervention line does, with the essential difference that it has a stated and advertised mission to serve the older adult population. Presumably, this would increase the likelihood that older adults will contact the service. Unlike other suicide prevention and crisis intervention services, which might have as few as 1% to 2% of their callers above age 60 (e.g., McIntosh et al., 1981), this program's fall 1992 newsletter noted that it had received 8,300 calls, of which 1,254 were first-time users, during the fiscal year 1991–1992. Callers are able to talk to professionally trained and supervised volunteers who provide emotional support and human contact 24 hours each day. It is likely that most of these callers would not contact traditional crisis intervention services.

A second component of the center's services involves the Geriatric Outreach Program, which provides ongoing home visits and telephone contact to those elderly who are isolated or homebound. In fiscal year 1991–1992, the center made 14,385 calls to or on behalf of clients, along with 779 home visits. This component is intended to deal with the social circumstances that are often present in suicidal elders, such as living alone or in social isolation, and the infrequent use of traditional inpatient or outpatient mental health services. Volunteers who take part in this service receive additional training in gerontological areas, and, consistent with the Friendship Line approach, the emphasis of contacts is on emotional support and counseling.

The Geriatric Outreach Program also makes telephone calls to remind older adults to take their medications on schedule, and elders can arrange to call the center daily so that if they fail to call, a physician or the police are alerted. In addition, for elders who are changing residence, a volunteer can be requested to assist them with their move and help to provide emotional support in this time of stress and change. Finally, older clients can request a volunteer to act as their advocate in negotiations with social service agencies or health care providers, or to express concerns that they might have with their family or physician. This latter service may be especially useful because the current cohort of older adults appears to be reluctant to question their physician or ask for second opinions for fear of offending or being perceived as rude. For example, Rollin (1985) described her mother's reluctance to be impolite to her physician, even to the point of not indicating what her ailments or discomfort were, because she felt that it was impolite for one to say that one is sick (see Public Case Number 3.1). Seeking a second medical opinion regarding treatment for her ovarian cancer was extremely difficult, and after reluctantly agreeing to a second opinion, she objected vehemently to what she perceived as a cruel and insensitive bedside manner by the second physician (voiced of course to her daughter and not to the physician). Thus, this type of advocacy service for older adults is likely to be especially needed and helpful in many cases.

Gatekeepers Program and Elderly Services. The Spokane Community Mental Health Center provides a different model of outreach, service delivery, and crisis intervention than does the program in San Francisco. Older adults with mental health problems who are referred by any source receive an in-home evaluation in which information crucial to assessment, case management, and treatment is gathered by trained staff of the community mental health center. Crisis intervention is available around the clock as well. The most unique aspect of this approach to elderly suicide prevention is its Gatekeepers Program. Responding to the well-established lack of self-referrals by older adults noted above, businesses and other organizations whose employees are in frequent contact with older adults, and especially isolated elders, have cooperated to provide these employees with special training to recognize the signs and symptoms associated with a need for help and refer such cases to Elderly Services. The diversity of the gatekeepers is impressive and would seem to greatly increase the likelihood of recognition and subsequent referral. The gatekeepers include meter readers and credit and repair personnel for power, electric, and gas utilities; fuel oil dealers; bank personnel; managers and owners of apartments and mobile homes; cable TV personnel; fire, police, and ambulance personnel; appraisers with the tax assessor's office; pharmacists; and telephone and taxi employees. In rural areas of the county, there are also mail and newspaper carriers, grain and farm utility dealers, and ministers.

As an indication of the effectiveness of the Gatekeepers Program, data (R. Raschko, Director of Elderly Services, personal communication, June 25, 1992) for the first six months of 1991 show that 49% of the referrals of suicidal elders to Elderly Services were from gatekeepers. During that time, there were 86 total referrals of suicidal older adults, 42 of which were by gatekeepers (24% were referred by hospitals and physicians,

14% by relatives, 13% by social agencies). Without the gate-keepers program, these 42 suicidal elderly might not have been recognized, referred, or helped.

The Dayton, Ohio Suicide Prevention Center also offers an independently developed Gatekeepers Program. Part of its program offerings include a training videotape and manual designed to educate the staff of nursing homes to recognize depressed and suicidal older adults. The videotape and manual may be purchased but are also loaned to area nursing homes on request (Mercer, 1992, p. 436). This resource targets another group of high-risk elders (see chapter 3).

Link-Plus. Life Crisis Services, a St. Louis crisis intervention center, has approached the problem of older adult suicide from within a more conventional suicide prevention scheme but at the same time provides a service specifically designed for and targeted at depressed elderly persons. The Link-Plus program uses traditional phone crisis intervention. This model is one that is already familiar to crisis centers. Therefore, it simply builds on the skills and services such centers already provide, and as a result, it is cost-efficient and can be adopted readily within existing frameworks.

As is common with other crisis intervention services, older adults (age 60 and above) represent only approximately 3% of Life Crisis's callers despite widespread publicity about the availability of the hotline. Thus, the need for a program specifically focused on this high-risk group was apparent. Link-Plus is an intervention service for immediate suicidal and other crises, but more descriptively and accurately, it is a general telephone case management program for depressed elders. Callers to Link-Plus are assessed by trained case managers/crisis center personnel both as individuals and with respect to their social network. The physical, psychosocial, and mental health needs of the individual are determined and matched with community services. Following the initial contact and the coordinating and arranging of links to agencies, supportive counseling and problem solving continue to be available to the older adult client. Regular, ongoing telephone contact and monitoring are maintained with the client until the case manager determines that it is no longer needed.

Clients are identified for Link-Plus through Life Crisis hotline calls, community professionals, and especially hospitals and home health care agencies. Those who are referred to Link-Plus are most often depressed, lonely elderly persons who live alone. Clients are typically in contact with the service for five to six months (L. Judy, Executive Director of Life Crisis Services, personal communication, October 14, 1993).

Each of these programs serves as a possible model for intervening with actively depressed or suicidal older adults. As such, they represent possible secondary prevention efforts.

Primary Prevention Measures

Primary prevention measures, as well as those intended to provide interventive services, tend to follow almost directly from the motivations and factors that are likely to produce elderly suicidal ideation and behavior. For instance, concern about physical health may be lessened or prevented by regular medical examinations and early detection and treatment of even minor health problems. Of course, the accessibility, availability, and affordability of good medical services are essential to this approach. Regular exercise and activities such as sports and recreation may also improve overall physical health and functioning, particularly if the pattern is instituted earlier in life and maintained through the later years. However, there is clear evidence that even exercise programs begun in late life, in consultation with a physician, can have a beneficial effect for older adults.

The impact of economic losses and related problems might be lessened in a number of ways. Although welfare programs do not eliminate all problems, the availability of needed financial support through programs, along with other benefits that are available to all, may reduce the impact of economic factors that have been associated with elderly suicide. Careful financial planning and savings programs for older adulthood and the retirement years would also lessen some of the financial burdens of later life. The availability of affordable catastrophic or long-term care insurance for elders would certainly help to relieve some of the economic as well as psychological burdens on those who experience poor health in their old age.

The motivations for suicide that may result from social and role losses are also amenable to change. Work role losses, for instance, among elderly men, might be minimized if they were encouraged to remain active in their occupational roles as long as they desired and could handle the job. Similarly, more effective programs might be developed to assist older persons in developing second or third careers or in finding new roles that encourage feelings of worth and importance. Long-range planning for retirement, emotionally as well as economically, certainly offers the potential to combat role losses and changes that might contribute to suicidal motivations in old age.

Loss of family and other interpersonal relationships may be lessened by encouraging and maintaining close family ties among living relatives. Arranging for elderly persons to become or continue to be involved in community groups and organizations helps to combat isolation and loneliness and also widens their social networks. For these same reasons, the "recruiting" of significant others has been proposed, which includes actively involving family members of various relationships in the therapy plan for elderly individuals and maintaining contact with the family (Brent, Kupfer, Bromet, & Dew, 1988; Liptzin, 1991). An intriguing and related approach is the strategy of providing support and other training services for the family caregivers of depressed older adults, as in the case of family caregivers of those with Alzheimer's disease (Hinrichsen, Hernandez, & Pollack, 1992; Parmelee & Katz, 1992). Because depressed individuals tend to be difficult to deal with on a full-time and continuing basis, caregivers may themselves become depressed, so that support not only may contribute to improved care of the depressed person but at the same time may lessen the possibility of mental health problems for the caregivers (thus simultaneously accomplishing both secondary and primary prevention and potentially eliminating the need for eventual tertiary prevention).

Recognizing that the elderly do not often self-refer to intervention services, several possible changes for improvement in the delivery and nature of such resources have been advanced. Prominent among these has been the emergence of new methods to identify and assist suicidal and troubled older persons. Examples of these would be the promotion of "buddy system" phone calls and visits and the use of senior citizens' centers as means of achieving early identification and referral of those who may be suicidal. It has often been suggested that the elderly do not call or use crisis and suicide prevention centers because they do not identify with the service or those who provide it. If, in fact, this is the case, the recruitment and employment of elders in these centers may well result in an increased identification and number of contacts. The establishment of separate crisis intervention or suicide prevention centers for older adults (such as the programs described above) may also prove to be an effective alternative. As with any service delivery system, however, a well-organized and active outreach component with properly trained personnel that are able to identify and assist older suicidal persons is essential. Such a component may need to recommend a variety of services, provide transportation to such services, or perhaps even deliver mental health services to the elderly in the community. An approach similar to that of Alcoholics Anonymous (AA) has also been suggested as a model for the provision of intervention services that would provide support by going to those in need in times of crisis rather than requiring that they go to a service site on a formal appointment basis. This approach, as in AA, might also make use of the help of those who have previously been in the same circumstances and to whom the older person in trouble may turn in time of crisis and suicidal ideation.

Osgood, Brant, and Lipman (1991, chapter 8) outlined several suggestions for changes in institutions in relation to elderly suicide prevention. With respect to this institutional change, they noted the research of Mishara and Kastenbaum (1973), in which a token-economy ward was effective in lessening indirect self-destructive behaviors (see chapter 3 of the present volume) compared with those of residents in traditional custodial care wards of the same facility. Osgood et al. (1991, p. 138) suggested that self-destructive behaviors can be prevented if institutions more adequately meet the personal needs of the residents for freedom, choice, privacy, autonomy, and space. Goffman (1961) had outlined these dimensions and what their loss entails, along with the mortification of the self that "total institutions" produce. The absence of these basic human needs as contributors to suicide are apparent in the commonalities of suicide described by Shneidman (1985; see chapter 2 of the present volume). In addition to these basic needs, however, Osgood et al. suggested that the environmental design of long-term care facilities should also take into account the physical, sensory, and perceptual changes of old age (a long-standing issue for institutionalized and community-dwelling elderly; see, e.g., Blank, 1988; Regnier & Pynoos, 1987), and, on the basis of the results of a survey, they further recommend that staff development and improvement are needed if direct and indirect suicidal behavior among institutional residents is to be reduced.

As indicated elsewhere (McIntosh, 1987), education is a crucial aspect of any successful suicide prevention effort for older adults. This education should be provided to the lay public, of course, and particularly to those who are frequently in contact with the aged in a variety of settings. The target groups include mental health professionals, health care providers (doctors, nurses, orderlies), emergency medical technicians, firefighters, law enforcement personnel, and members of the clergy. Of special importance would be educational and training programs for nursing home administrators and staff, senior citizens' center personnel and volunteers, nutrition staff and meals-on-wheels volunteers, social services personnel, and those in a variety of disciplines that work with the elderly (for example, the AARP and the American Association of Suicidology have developed a brochure addressing elderly suicide that is targeted for distribution to volunteers such as those who work with meals-on-wheels; McIntosh, 1993). Funeral directors should also be included as a target group because they routinely encounter the bereaved, including the survivors of suicide.

It is essential that the education and training of new professionals and volunteers in these various fields include information about suicide and aging, and the provision of continuing education to those professionals who have already completed their training and who are working with older persons should not be overlooked. Although the depth of coverage and the inclusion of intervention and therapy training (the latter predominantly for mental health professionals) will vary somewhat among the various disciplines involved in geriatric work, all training should include basic aspects of suicide education (Farberow, 1969; Heilig, 1970; Maris et al., 1973). With regard to geriatric suicide, some basic training in gerontology would certainly be useful and appropriate.

Core education and training content should include several components if it is to effectively prepare professionals and others to deal with the complex, multifactor phenomenon of elderly suicide. McIntosh (1987) outlined this core education in some detail, but for the present purposes a brief description of its components would include (a) eliminating dangerous and erroneous myths surrounding suicide and suicidal behavior; (b) discussing the identification of suicidal persons, in terms of both the demographic and situational factors that are associated with high risk and the cognitive and other components that are important for an understanding of suicide (e.g., Shneidman, 1985); (c) training to know and recognize the warning signs and clues of suicide noted in chapter 5; (d) teaching the assessment of potential lethality as a part of assessing suicidal risk; (e) informing about the availability and existence of community resources to which referrals may be made; (f) increasing awareness and knowledge of the variety of suicidal behaviors that may be exhibited by the elderly, including both direct and indirect self-destructive behaviors; and (g) sensitizing professionals about the problems associated with suicide survivorship at all ages, including possible effects that the suicide death of a loved one might produce in terms of bereavement and grief, the possibility of suicide by bereaved individuals, and the existence of community resources for the bereaved (often through bereavement support groups). A final component of such education would provide accurate knowledge about aging and old age as a point of reference for the experiences and problems of suicidal elders. The development and implementation of suicide education programs would certainly offer a significant possibility for reducing the number of elders who take their own lives. Bennett (1967, p. 175), for instance, estimated that educating the public as well as professionals to recognize suicidal persons and to be knowledgeable about community resources could prevent as many as 50% of all self-destructive acts.

As noted in chapter 2, Shneidman (1985), Maris (1981), and Clark (1993) have contended that there are lifelong patterns that characterize the suicidal person. If they are correct, those who may be vulnerable to the problems of old age might be identified earlier in life, and more effective coping methods may be taught along with other possible interventions that will enable them to better adapt to problems later in life. In any event, training in and encouragement of coping and adaptive responses to difficult life circumstances should certainly be possible at younger ages and should provide alternative approaches to dealing with the problems of late life (and even earlier, as with the aging of parents and others).

Other societal and community measures that might also lower the number of elderly suicides include more careful and responsible prescribing and dispensing of medications, particularly those that are lethal. Similarly, better controlled and lessened availability of other lethal methods of suicide, such as firearms, would probably have an important effect. Vigorous and effective treatment and prevention of alcohol abuse and alcoholism as well as depression should be incorporated into any large-scale prevention program to reduce geriatric suicide. Rabins (1992), for instance, suggested that the mental health of older adults could be improved if there was more effective use of present resources, as well as communication between practitioners in the medical and mental health professions.

The societal and other measures proposed here will certainly require some time to institute and will be expensive to implement in terms of both monetary and personnel resources. However, Rachlis (1970) stated that these efforts would be worthwhile on several levels. "Helping the aging now is in a sense buying insurance for the younger generations. Supportive health and social welfare services developed today will provide security in the later years for the presently young and middle-aged. They will enter late life with assurance that help will be available to deal with the inevitable losses of aging" (p. 25). The implications of the aging of our society and of the growing size of the cohorts that will reach older adulthood in the future have been noted already in chapter 1 and are especially relevant to Rachlis's comments.

As discussed in chapter 1, some authors (e.g., Pollinger-Haas & Hendin, 1983) have suggested that suicide rates in the future will be much higher than those of today as a result of the size of the baby boomer cohort. McIntosh (1992) pointed out that this increase is only one of several possible predictions with respect to the elderly. Other prognosticators have not included in their scenarios the possibility that the large population of baby boomers may themselves have a major impact on future suicide trends by changing the nature of older adulthood. As the baby boomers pass through adulthood on their way to 2010, they may be better prepared for their retirement and may be better off economically in their old age than previous generations. It has already been predicted that they will be better educated and perhaps healthier than the current elderly, both factors being associated with better adjustment to aging. It is also possible that as a large, potentially potent political force, baby boomers may demand and receive more attention to the problems of aging and the aged along with a greater allocation of social and economic resources (e.g., Russell, 1993, chapters 24–30; Torres-Gil, 1992, chapter 5).

As noted earlier, present and past cohorts of elderly (i.e., the pre-boomers) have underused crisis intervention and suicide prevention programs as well as general mental health services. However, the baby boomers are more likely to have positive attitudes toward such services because of their education and their experiences with them. Therefore, it is unlikely that they would be reluctant to receive help from these sources, and in that case, the potential for suicide prevention would be improved. Finally, it is certainly possible that many of the baby boomers who are most vulnerable and predisposed to depression and suicide will have died by suicide before reaching older adulthood. Therefore, the surviving cohort members as a group may generally be at lower suicide risk than previous cohorts in their old age.

A final aspect of elderly suicide prevention leads directly to the final topic of this book and involves the motivation of older adult suicide. Much has been written about the negative attitudes toward aging and the elderly and the ageism that exists in subtle and more obvious ways in our society. The continued existence of mandatory retirement ages sends a message that the old are no longer needed or wanted by society and its institutions. They tend to be viewed as expendable, as having lived long enough, and perhaps as having outlived their usefulness. The high value of youth and the devaluing of old age are apparent daily in advertisements, television, and other media. A recent reflection of this ambivalent or even negative feeling toward aging and the aged has emerged in the debates over the rationality of suicide and assisted suicide.

Ethical Issues in Elder Suicide

This book has so far reflected the assumption that the prevention of elderly suicide is desirable and should be at least part of the justification of research efforts on this topic. Although this point of view reflects the position of the authors, there is certainly not total agreement regarding suicide prevention either among the old or in general. The arguments and concerns regarding the right of old, sick, and frail persons to end their lives have been advanced by both advocates and opponents. Although our society permits the existence of groups that attempt to facilitate or assist those who wish to commit suicide (e.g., the Hemlock Society), at the same time in communities across the country there are agencies whose purpose it is to prevent suicide. Public surveys (e.g., Gallup poll, "Fear of Dying," 1991) have indicated the general opinion that healthy individuals do not have a moral right to commit suicide (80% no, 16% yes), nor do those who are a heavy burden on their family (61% no, 33% yes). However, these same respondents suggested that persons in great pain (66% yes, 29% no) and those with incurable diseases (58% yes, 36% no) do have a moral right to commit suicide. In addition, attitudinal research (e.g., Deluty, 1988–1989) has suggested that people regard suicide as more acceptable when the person's precipitating illness is cancer and when the person committing suicide is elderly.

Both sets of arguments surrounding the ethical issues of elderly suicide will be briefly presented here. Some special issues that have arisen in recent years and their impact on the pro and con arguments will also be noted, including the topic of physician-assisted suicide. Detailed writings on the moral, rational, legal, ethical, and philosophical aspects of suicide are available for the reader wishing more information (e.g., Basson, 1981; Battin, 1982; Battin & Maris, 1983; Battin & Mayo, 1980; Englehardt & Malloy, 1982; Litman, 1980; Maris, 1982; Szasz, 1971, 1986; Wennberg, 1989). It should be made clear at this point that suicide and assisted suicide are being addressed here and not those issues involving the prolongation of life by extraordinary means (i.e., life support machines such as respirators) and those individuals who are in comas or other circumstances where they cannot speak for themselves but may have a "living will." These issues, of course, are not entirely different from those of suicide and assisted suicide, but they are distinct enough to be handled separately under the more general context of euthanasia.

A basic premise of many advocates of elderly suicide involves a "right to die," a "right to self-determination," and "death with dignity" as key components (e.g., Bromberg & Cassel, 1983; Chesser, 1967, chapter 12). In her book *Common Sense Suicide: The Final Right,* Portwood (1978) advocates a right to suicide among elderly persons who believe it is time for them to die. She discusses the changes that occur with advancing age, particularly the losses and the often negative physical, social, and economic changes. She uses a "balance sheet suicide" concept in which a sane and competent older adult, "thinking logically [can] set off the unacceptable or intolerable aspects of his or her life against the chances for betterment and find the result weighted on the side of death" (p. 33). However, under such circumstances, the person may decide that the positive aspects outweigh the intolerable negative aspects and, therefore, choose to live. Portwood's goal is to make this choice available and provide a mechanism to effect a respectable and voluntary death when "the absence of life has become more attractive than its presence" (p. 52). She argues that the quality as well as the quantity of life must be considered.

Public Case Number 6.1: Jo Roman

Jo Roman was a 61-year-old social worker who had decided three years previously that she would control the time of her death. She was an outspoken advocate for rational suicide and had gone so far as to designate a target age for her death based on her age at the time and her knowledge of the lives of her relatives. That date, nearly 17 years in the future, was modified when she developed breast cancer with a diagnosis that it was irreversible and terminal. In her mind's perfect world, she had envisioned an "exit house" wherein death was aided, but in the real world, none existed. She wrote a book with that title (Roman, 1980) in which she explained her ideas about such a facility, and at the same time she set out to create a dying atmosphere in her home in anticipation of her own death. She and her husband arranged for PBS to film a weekend with her family and friends in which her decision and suicide were openly discussed. "Choosing Suicide" was broadcast on the PBS network in June 1980, one year after her death, and following the airing of the documentary film, a panel of national experts discussed her case and the concept of rational suicide. The forum was certainly one of which Jo would have approved, even if she disagreed with the opinions of some of the panelists.

Jo had chosen the day for her death, and she spent the week with her family and working on a "life sculpture." When the chosen time came, she went to her room and took an overdose of Seconal that killed her in her sleep. She justified her actions as a rational decision to commit suicide and went to great lengths to provide evidence for that decision. In a review of her book, Maris (1982) argued that her suicide was not rational and, in fact, was the final act in a life that constituted a "suicidal career" as he had outlined the concept in his 1981 book *Pathways to Suicide.*

Humphry's (1991) publication of *Final Exit* added an additional dimension to the right-to-suicide debate by providing a frank and explicit "how-to" manual intended for the terminally ill. It is probable in Ida Rollin's case (Public Case Number 3.1) that the information in Humphry's book would have been used to bring about her death. Betty Rollin (1985) related her search for specific information about how to effectively and painlessly help her mother die. However, she was unable to find enough information until she contacted a physician overseas, even though she had found one of Humphry's earlier books, which did not provide enough explicit information to be of practical help to her. In addition to raising a number of ethical issues, Humphry's (1991) *Final Exit* may also have an uncertain impact on elderly suicide. This best-selling book is now widely available nationwide, and its detailed "prescription" could increase the number of those who commit suicide in what they decide to be appropriate circumstances. However, it might also be argued that the book will help some of those who may not commit suicide, by providing comfort, psychological relief, and a choice in dealing with their terminal condition. It is even possible that Humphry's strong negative opinions regarding certain methods of suicide, such as firearms, will dissuade those who have ready access to these methods. However, the overall impact of this book is difficult to ascertain.

An additional argument often made for the right of the elderly to commit suicide suggests that it is their choice because it does not affect or infringe on the rights of others or harm society (e.g., Alvarez, 1969; Beckwith, 1979; Narveson, 1983; Portwood, 1978). Lebacqz and Englehardt (1980) have justified suicide in terminal illness because in such a situation the person cannot fulfill his or her obligations to others and, therefore, is not bound by obligations to them. Invoking the concept of self-determination and the right to autonomy, Szasz (1971, 1986) and others (Battin, 1991; Bromberg & Cassel, 1983; Sartorius, 1983) have noted that societal intervention with suicide is often paternalistic, violates individual rights, and is unjustified because suicidal ideation does not indicate that a mental illness (which may call into question the ability to make rational, considered decisions) is invariably present.

Beyond the issue of the right to commit suicide when an old person has made the rational decision to die, Beckwith (1979) listed six reasons "why [aged] dying persons should be permitted to shorten their painful lives by suicide and why such suicide is beneficial and praiseworthy" (p. 231). These reasons are as follows:

First and foremost, by timely suicide those dying painfully can end their own suffering immediately. . . . Second, suicide may prevent a degrading or even disgusting death. . . . Third, timely suicide will usually save family and friends the very unpleasant and depressing experience of watching the slow, painful, and degrading death of someone they care for. . . . Fourth, timely suicide by the dying will drastically reduce the often very high cost of dying slowly. . . . Fifth, dying persons who commit suicide for the above reasons demonstrate the kind of self-control, logical thinking, and considerations for others that most intelligent people respect and admire. . . . Finally, if we legalize and facilitate timely and painless suicide by the dying, we will not only enable them to gain the benefits described above, but will also enable all people to look forward to death with less fear. (pp. 231–232)

In her "Apologia for Suicide," Barrington (1969) argued that a disabled elderly individual in poor health and in need of constant care and attention may feel that they are a burden to the younger person or persons who must provide that care. In effect, the young person may be caught in a "bondage" type of situation, whether willingly or unwillingly, and the older adult may want to "release" them but has no real choice in being forced to live. On the basis of this interpretation, Barrington argued for the option of voluntary termination of life. Brandt (1975) identified as morally defensible acts of suicide that are a response to terminal illness, because these acts may involve release from terrible pain or avoidance of medical expenses that are a burden to the surviving family members.

Leering, Hilhorst, and Verhoef (1979) suggested that the wish to die in old age may simply be "conscious acceptance of the end of life at life's end" (p. 184). Death, therefore, is to be viewed as a natural part of the life cycle.

With a different argument and circumstances in mind, Prado (1990) presented a case for *preemptive suicide* in advanced old age. Under such circumstances, suicide may not be only a rational and honorable act but, indeed, may even be "the wisest course of action" (p. 1). Prado defined preemptive suicide as the "rational way of avoiding not actual, intolerable conditions, but foreseen demeaning decline" (p. 1). His objective was "to enable consideration of suicide as an *elective* choice, rather than as always the most drastic of responses" (p. 2). Preemptive suicide thus may occur "well in advance of conditions which entail diminishment of self and loss of personal autonomy" (p. 17). Prado chose the term *surcease suicide* to refer to those acts that constitute an "escape from pressing and desperate circumstances such as terminal illness" (p. 6), but he did not argue for or justify this type of action, nor assisted suicide.

In advanced age, the individual might reach a point at which life can only continue in a diminished capacity that is unacceptable to the cognitively "reflective" aging person. For Prado, once we have become the person that we wish to become, any significant changes in that status are undesirable (i.e., in terms of loss of self, autonomy, intellect, or dignity). Although Prado provided no examples, an Associated Press story of a couple seems to appropriately illustrate a preemptive suicide ("Couple," 1990). In this account, a relative of a husband and wife in their forties received a videotape, a will, a cremation receipt, and some other personal effects in the mail. The videotape showed the couple explaining that they had reached an age and a point in life where "they have gone as far as they are going to go" (p. A6) and that they had decided to end their life now rather than live into old age. After viewing the tape, the relative rushed to the home but found the couple already dead there. The husband had shot his wife and then himself. They had no children. On the basis of the available facts, but with more information and details about their reasoning, this event could fulfill Prado's criteria for a preemptive suicide.

In addition to emphasizing the sanctity of life, along with religious and other moral arguments, some who feel that suicide should be prevented raise a number of counterarguments to those presented above. One of the most frequently mentioned positions suggests that suicide is not, or is rarely, "rational" (e.g., Maris, 1982). It has been proposed that suicidal persons may be mentally ill and most often depressed. Thus, depression may cloud judgment and influence reasoning abilities so that depressed and suicidal individuals have difficulty recognizing or generating alternative solutions to their problems (see chapter 2 and Shneidman, 1985). As Brandt (1975) suggested, they may fail to realize their *best* solution. In this sense, therefore, suicide may represent not a rational choice weighed against all possible alternatives, but only a choice from among a few severely restricted alternatives. Although the terminally ill are most often presented as examples of those who choose suicide, Siegel and Tuckel (1984–1985) noted that cancer patients seem to have no elevated suicide risk when compared with the general population. Thus, it may well be that those terminally ill who wish to end their lives may not be as representative of elderly suicides in general as is often suggested (see chapter 3).

A less common argument involves the contention that there is no *right* to commit suicide, and in fact, Kass (1993) argued that "there is no firm philosophical or legal argument for a 'right to die'" (p. 34). Maris (1982) also pointed out that there are no guarantees that life will be easy or painless, and indeed, there are no such guarantees about dying either. Maris further argued that these elements are part of the unpredictable "human condition," which requires struggle and adaptation, so that harsh conditions do not excuse or legitimize suicide.

It has also been argued that suicidal persons are almost always ambivalent (see Shneidman, 1985, and chapter 2 of the present volume). That is, they wish to die and at the same time want very much to live but just may not see any way possible to go on living. Such ambivalence would seem to argue against an absolute, rational, and clear choice being made. Of course, the irreversibility of the self-destructive act must also be emphasized, along with the question as to whether the person might still choose suicide at a later time. Might the situation improve, given some time? Travis (1991) argued that no one is capable of knowing when their life is bad enough or sufficiently meaningless to end it.

Although the advocates of a right to suicide suggest that the act affects only the one who dies, it has also been pointed out that society loses any benefits the deceased might provide to others or that others might gain by caring for them (Travis, 1991). Society also loses any skills and special knowledge that the individual might possess. In addition, people have obligations to others because people are involved in social relationships. Perhaps most important, suicide *does* affect others.

The survivors (see chapter 1) often feel socially stigmatized and, perhaps, guilty in connection with the death, as well as the manner in which death occurred, so that suicide may influence the grief process in a negative fashion (Dunne, McIntosh, & Dunne-Maxim, 1987).

Siegel and Tuckel (1984–1985) argued that the legal sanctioning of suicide could undermine related societal norms and eliminate clear guidelines in decision making, thus leading to disorientation and anxiety among those faced with making the decision. Others (e.g., Battin, 1980) have proposed that accepting and condoning rational suicide may lead to some individuals, and especially the old, being "manipulated" into suicide, perhaps against their will, because they feel obligated (i.e., a duty) to do so under certain circumstances. The end result would then be to actually lessen free choice. Similarly, Moody (e.g., Battin, McKinney, Kastenbaum, & Moody, 1984) has been concerned that the acceptance of suicide as rational will lead us "down the slippery slope" where it is difficult to draw the line where someone is a candidate for sanctioned suicide. "Suicide *on grounds of* old age, not simply during the period of old age" (Moody, 1984, p. 65) likewise becomes a matter of concern. All disabled elderly could thus be labeled as living a "meaningless" life, and the same might be said for those who are dependent on others (Post, 1990). Additionally, widespread acceptance of suicide may even encourage suicides that are not rational (Mayo, 1980).

Suicide among elders often appears to be more generally acceptable at least partially because they belong to that segment of the population that is closer to death anyway and partially because of ageism and the devaluing of older adults. An important related, but often ignored, issue concerns increasingly limited resources, especially in the domain of health care. Callahan (1987) is one of the primary advocates of the need to control medical costs, even if that requires the rationing of care based on age. Unfortunately, there are limits to the availability and allocation of health care and other resources that will ultimately have to be set in a society that is aging, where the elderly as a group requires a disproportionate amount of financial resources. Callahan's position and proposals have led to much and often heated debate on the basis of practical considerations as well as humanitarian issues (e.g., Barry & Bradley, 1991; Binstock & Post, 1991; Callahan, 1990, 1993; Homer. & Holstein, 1990; Hunt, 1993). This quandary is of course related in a broad sense to that of suicide and older adults, and Battin (1987), for one, has addressed the issue of older adults, suicide, and rationing in the context of these cost-conscious times. She has identified two options, one to limit or deny treatment to control costs, and another to encourage suicide among the elderly. Clearly, this is a difficult decision if these are, in fact, the only options. It is somewhat reminiscent of the world portrayed by Matheson (1954/1969) in his short story "The Test," where an elderly gentleman is preparing for a test required of all older adults every five years. The test examines a wide range of cognitive, psychomotor, and common tasks of daily living, and failure results in the elder being put to death by the government. As this man prepares for the test, it becomes obvious that he will not pass. Rather than face the inevitable, he obtains medications from a sympathetic druggist, goes to his room the night before his scheduled exam, and takes the pills, which kill him in his sleep. Although the events are fictionalized, the message that this story conveys regarding the extremes of such practices are unsettling to contemplate.

In dealing with the availability of suicide from a different perspective, Roman (1980), discussed her fantasy (Public Case Number 6.1), as described earlier, of an "exit house" where assistance would be available to those who wish to die. Others (e.g., Meserve, 1975; Pressey, 1977) have advocated similar legitimized and institutionalized procedures to facilitate swift and painless deaths for those older persons who have rationally decided to die. Science fiction has likewise depicted societally sanctioned suicide clinics where those who wish to expire may find assistance and easily available lethal methods (e.g., Vonnegut's 1970 "Welcome to the Monkey House"). The most recent serious and highly publicized of these concepts and methods was advanced by Dr. Jack Kevorkian (1991), who proposed a medical specialty for which he coined the term *obitiatry*. Such physicians would practice assisted suicide, or

what he refers to as "medicide." Given his growing and controversial record to date, Kevorkian undoubtedly considers himself
to be the first "obitiatrist."

Public Case Number 6.2: Dr. Jack Kevorkian (aka "Dr. Death")

Jack Kevorkian is a retired Michigan pathologist who described his position regarding physician-assisted suicide and
issues of death in general in *Prescription: Medicide* (1991). He
argued strongly for individual self-determination of death
and recounted the history and events surrounding his decision to assist in the deaths of some of those who requested his help. Among the information contained in the
book is a discussion of his "Mercitron," the name he gave
to the suicide machine that was used by a "patient," Janet
Adkins. Following the Adkins suicide, Dr. Kevorkian was
given the nickname by the public media of "Dr. Death," and
later both his Michigan and California medical licenses were
suspended.

Kevorkian has been charged in connection with some of
the early deaths, but thus far, in all but one case the charges
were dropped without a trial. Charges of violating Michigan's law against assisted suicide have been brought in one
of the latest deaths and legal proceedings have begun. Speaking primarily through his attorney, Kevorkian has vowed to
continue to help others die and says that he will test and de-
feat any laws that are passed to stop his assistance to those
who ask his aid in dying, even if it means that he is im-
prisoned. His actions and the subsequent publicity resulted
in the passage of a Michigan law banning physician assisted
suicide, because no such law previously existed in the state.
The neighboring state of Indiana currently has a similar law
awaiting final passage.

As might be expected, Kevorkian's activities, along with
the issue of physician-assisted suicide, have created a tremendous amount of discussion and debate on a national scale
(e.g., "Assisted Suicide," 1992; Conwell & Caine, 1991; Crigger, 1992; Hendin & Klerman, 1993; "Medicide," 1992; Miller,
1991; Portenoy, 1991; Quill, 1991; Rosenbaum & Forsythe,

1990). Few, including its advocates, would argue that physician-assisted suicide should be available without strict guidelines. An exception, of course, is Kevorkian, who has been quoted as opposing as immoral nearly every law that has been proposed to regulate this action. He generally rejects criteria such as those that would limit access to assisted suicide to the terminally ill who are judged to be within six months of death. Even more troubling, however, was his statement that "any disease that curtails life even for a day is terminal" (Stone, 1992, p. 6A). It has been pointed out that Kevorkian's actions and words are actually harming rather than facilitating serious efforts to make more strictly regulated and justifiable physician-assisted suicide available (e.g., Gibbs, 1992).

Among the most commonly cited conditions that might indicate or justify physician-assisted suicide are those that have been spelled out in regulating euthanasia in the Netherlands (e.g., Capron, 1992; de Wachter, 1992; van der Wal, van Eijk, Leenen, & Spreeuwenberg, 1992a, 1992b). To be an appropriate candidate for euthanasia in the Netherlands, one must satisfy the conditions that

> there is intolerable suffering with no prospect of improvement; the patient is mentally competent to choose euthanasia; the patient requests euthanasia voluntarily, repeatedly, and consistently over a reasonable period of time; and two physicians, one of whom has not participated in the patient's care, agree that euthanasia is appropriate. (Orentlicher, 1991/1992, p. 58)

Quill, Cassel, and Meier (1992) also proposed a number of clinical criteria specifically for physician-assisted suicide. These include incurable disease with severe, intractable suffering; a request that is not due to inadequate control of pain ("comfort care"); a request that must be freely, clearly, and repeatedly made; judgment that must not be distorted; a doctor–patient relationship; consultation with another physician; and full, descriptive documentation of the process to be used. To this list, Quill et al. added that the wishes of the family must not take precedent over those "of a competent patient" (p. 1382). Whatever the criteria that may eventually be adopted, it seems clear that adequate pain management measures and perhaps a reconsideration of pain alleviation principles will be needed. It should also be pointed out that the hospice movement is challenged by this issue and must act to provide adequate options other than suicide for the dying who desire and are in need of terminal care and support.

Obviously, only a few aspects of this volatile issue have been covered here. This topic has only begun to emerge as a crucial legal, social, and moral issue for the immediate future. As in any such issue involving extremely divergent viewpoints and case examples, it is easy to lose sight of a middle ground and less than clear-cut examples. In the face of a rapidly progressive medical technology, diminished resources, and exploding health care costs, the multifaceted aspects of suicide are a largely neglected but important topic that must be addressed. Camus (1955), in *The Myth of Sysiphus*, went so far as to say that "there is but one truly serious philosophical problem, and that is suicide. Judging whether life is or is not worth living amounts to answering the fundamental question of philosophy" (p. 3). The elderly as a group are certainly caught in the middle of the moral dilemmas relating to the unresolved issues of assisted suicide, and it is obvious that the problems are not going to go away.

Unresolved Issues in Elder Suicide

Despite more recent information on and attention to the topic of elderly suicide, there remain many puzzling and unanswered questions. With respect to demographic and epidemiological aspects of the problem, there are many uncertainties. For instance, what is the actual level of suicide among the old? How many suicides are underreported each year? What are the most important factors that have been responsible for the long-term declines in elderly suicide? What has contributed to the short-term increases of the 1980s? What factors have produced the tremendous differences that have been observed across sex and race/ethnicity in elderly suicide?

Research findings have produced information that allows for a better understanding of the motivations for elderly suicide, but obviously, many more and better investigations are needed to help clarify the many important questions that still remain to be answered. For instance, what can be learned by studying low-risk populations that may help in developing preventive measures for high-risk groups such as the elderly? Most older adults experience the majority of factors that are associated with a high risk for suicide. Therefore, why is it that more older adults do not commit suicide? How accurate are the studies of the elderly in institutions with regard to the levels of direct and indirect suicidal behaviors that occur? What is the level or incidence of indirect self-destruction in community-dwelling elderly? What is the nature of the causative relationship between terminal illness and suicide? Does retirement and the adjustments required to cope with it increase suicide risk? How are the elderly who survive the suicide of their loved ones different from those survivors who are younger? How do elderly versus younger suicides differentially impact survivors?

Therapy and assessment of suicide potential among older persons also involve many unresolved questions. What therapy techniques or combination of techniques can be identified that are likely to be most effective in preventing elderly suicides? What warning signs are most predictive of elderly suicide potential? What measures can be best used to increase the number of elderly self-referrals to traditional crisis intervention and mental health services? What new approaches may be available to assist in the early identification of suicidal older persons? How might physical pain be more effectively managed to eliminate its influence on suicidal behavior?

The chapter on theories of suicide (chapter 2) as they relate to older adults emphasized the tremendous need for a unifying, integrated theory that would take into account the biological, psychological, social, and other factors that contribute to a suicidal outcome. There is also the need for more research that is theory driven in the overall field of suicidology, and geriatric suicide in particular. Other theoretical questions also exist. Are the commonalities that Shneidman (1985) has suggested among all those who die by suicide somehow different for the old? How important are various specific and identifiable factors in leading to suicide? What are the most effective deterrents to suicide for those who, theoretically, should be at highest risk? What characteristic coping styles lead to higher and lower suicide risk in old age?

Finally, the emerging issues relating to the ethics of suicide, particularly among old, frail, and terminally ill elderly, along with physician-assisted suicide, raise numerous questions. For instance, what type of person or case would likely be a justifiable candidate for rational suicide? Should there be age criteria, diagnostic limitations, time frames, and so forth that apply? Should assisted suicide be regarded as the exclusive realm and responsibility of physicians, and are physicians really trained and prepared to make such judgments? Do physicians receive enough training about depression (and mental health) to be able to recognize its presence or absence? What are the roles, if any, of nurses, psychologists, psychiatrists, and other mental health professionals in any processes and procedures that may be involved? Should euthanasia or physician-assisted suicide be legalized? If so, should it proceed on a state-by-state basis or should the laws be national in scope? If legalized and accepted, how do we safeguard against abuses in determining appropriate versus inappropriate candidates? There are many such questions, but the answers that we can currently provide are not easy or clear.

The United Nations has offered a set of Principles for Older Persons that relate to the well-being of elders. Although in proposal form, these principles were summarized in the statement "Add life to the years that have been added to life by assuring all older persons: independence, participation, care, self-fulfillment and dignity" ("Proposed UN Principles," 1991, p. 1). It would be difficult not to agree with this general principle, although the steps to implement it are not completely clear and will certainly require much time and effort in our own and other societies. Suicide is only one extreme response to the absence of many of these ingredients in the lives of older persons. Assuring that the elderly are able to realize these ingredients would go a long way in eliminating the frustrated psychological needs that Shneidman (1985) suggested are the common stressors leading to suicide.

Of course, the answers to these and many other questions about elderly suicide must await findings from future researchers, theoreticians, and practitioners. Clearly, much more emphasis must be given to the needs and problems of the elderly in this society, and their sheer numbers in the future will demand more attention. In providing services such as those that may help to deal with problems such as suicide, it will certainly be necessary to face up to the deficiencies in our current systems and develop new and more effective procedures for the identification, referral, and treatment of older, suicide-prone people.

These and the other issues mentioned in this chapter involving the prevention of elderly suicide are a matter of urgency not only for the current generations of elderly but also for the immediate future, before the baby boomers reach older adulthood. Future rates of geriatric suicide will certainly be influenced by the nature of the experiences of each cohort in its journey through older adulthood. Suicide represents a premature death at any age, and the premature deaths of older adults constitute a loss of talent and resources that we as a society cannot accept. We must improve and increase our efforts to reduce such avoidable tragedies. The late Frank Church, former chairman of the Senate Special Committee on Aging (quoted in a document prepared for the 1971 White House Conference on Aging), expressed some thoughts that are relevant to this issue when he said,

> I think there is no country, that has the means as we do, that has done as badly in providing for the elderly as we have here in the United States. This is one of the greatest travesties, I think, of the contemporary American way. It's one of the most conspicuous of our failures. We have our successes, we have much to be proud of in this country, but this treatment of the elderly is something that we ought, by right, to be ashamed of, and I think that's why it cries out so for attention. (p. 67)

References

Alvarez, W. C. (1969, October). Is suicide by an old, dying person a sin and a crime? [Editorial]. *Geriatrics, 24*(10), 77–78.

Assisted suicide. (1992, February 21). *CQ Researcher, 2*(Whole No. 7), 145–168.

Barrington, M. R. (1969). Apologia for suicide. In A. B. Downing (Ed.), *Euthanasia and the right to die* (pp. 152–172). London: Peter Owen.

Barry, R. L., & Bradley, G. V. (Eds.). (1991). *Set no limits: A rebuttal to Daniel Callahan's proposal to limit health care for the elderly.* Urbana: University of Illinois Press.

Basson, M. D. (Ed.). (1981). Rational suicide. *Progress in Clinical and Biological Research, 50,* 179–212.

Battin, M. P. (1980). Manipulated suicide. *Bioethics Quarterly, 2,* 123–134.

Battin, M. P. (1982). *Ethical issues in suicide.* Englewood Cliffs, NJ: Prentice-Hall.

Battin, M. P. (1987). Choosing the time to die: The ethics and economics of suicide in old age. In S. F. Spicker, S. R. Ingman, & I. R. Lawson (Eds.), *Ethical dimensions of geriatric care: Value conflicts for the 21st century* (pp. 161–189). Dordrecht, The Netherlands: D. Reidel.

Battin, M. P. (1991). Rational suicide: How can we respond to a request for help? *Crisis, 12,* 73–80.

Battin, M. P., & Maris, R. W. (Eds.). (1983). Suicide and ethics [Special issue]. *Suicide and Life-Threatening Behavior, 13*(4).

Battin, M. P., & Mayo, D. J. (Eds.). (1980). *Suicide: The philosophical issues.* New York: St. Martin's Press.

Battin, M. P., McKinney, D., Kastenbaum, R., & Moody, H. R. (1984). Suicide: A solution to the problem of old age [Abstract]. In C. R. Pfeffer & J. Richman (Eds.), *Proceedings of the 15th annual meeting of the American Association of Suicidology* (pp. 78–81). Denver, CO: American Association of Suicidology.

Beckwith, B. P. (1979). On the right to suicide by the dying. *Dissent, 26,* 231–233.

Bennett, A. E. (1967, May). Recognizing the potential suicide. *Geriatrics, 22,* 175–181.

Binstock, R. H., & Post, S. G. (Eds.). (1991). *Too old for health care? Controversies in medicine, law, economics, and ethics.* Baltimore: Johns Hopkins University Press.

Blank, T. O. (1988). *Older persons and their housing: Today and tomorrow.* Springfield, IL: Charles C Thomas.

Brandt, R. B. (1975). The morality and rationality of suicide. In S. Perlin (Ed.), *A handbook for the study of suicide* (pp. 61–76). New York: Oxford University Press.

Brent, D. A., Kupfer, D. J., Bromet, E. J., & Dew, M. A. (1988). The assessment and treatment of patients at risk for suicide. *Review of Psychiatry, 7,* 353–385.

Bromberg, S., & Cassel, C. K. (1983). Suicide in the elderly: The limits of paternalism. *Journal of the American Geriatrics Society, 31,* 698–703.

Callahan, D. (1987). *Setting limits: Medical goals in an aging society.* New York: Simon & Schuster.

Callahan, D. (1990). *What kind of life: The limits of medical progress.* New York: Simon & Schuster.

Callahan, D. (1993). Response to Roger W. Hunt. *Journal of Medical Ethics, 19,* 24–27.

Camus, A. (1955). *The myth of Sysiphus, and other essays* (J. O'Brien, Trans.). New York: Knopf.

Capron, A. M. (1992). Euthanasia in the Netherlands: American observations. *Hastings Center Report, 22*(2), 30–33.

Chesser, E. (1967). *Living with suicide.* London: Hutchinson.

Church, F. (1971). From a special vantage point: A call for action. In M. Abrams & B. Robinson (Eds.), *46 national leaders speak out on options for older Americans* (p. 67). Washington, DC: National Retired Teachers Association and the American Association of Retired Persons.

Clark, D. C. (1993). Narcissistic crises of aging and suicidal despair. *Suicide and Life-Threatening Behavior, 23,* 21–26.

Conwell, Y., & Caine, E. D. (1991). Rational suicide and the right to die: Reality and myth. *New England Journal of Medicine, 325,* 1100–1103.

Couple, fearing age, mails tape before murder–suicide. (1990, August 2). *South Bend Tribune* (IN), p. A6.

Crigger, B.-J. (Ed.). (1992). Dying well? A colloquy on euthanasia and assisted suicide. *Hastings Center Report, 22*(Whole No. 2), 1–55.

Deluty, R. H. (1988–1989). Factors affecting the acceptability of suicide. *Omega, 19,* 315–326.

de Wachter, M. A. M. (1992). Euthanasia in the Netherlands. *Hastings Center Report, 22*(2), 23–30.

Dunne, E. J., McIntosh, J. L., & Dunne-Maxim, K. (Eds.). (1987). *Suicide and its aftermath: Understanding and counseling the survivors.* New York: Norton.

Englehardt, H. T., Jr., & Malloy, M. (1982). Suicide and assisting suicide: A critique of legal sanctions. *Southwestern Law Journal, 36,* 1003–1037.

Farberow, N. L. (1969). Training in suicide prevention for professional and community agents. *American Journal of Psychiatry, 125,* 1702–1705.

Fear of dying. (1991, January). *Gallup Poll Monthly,* No. 304, pp. 51–61.

Felton, B. J. (1982). The aged: Settings, services, and needs. In L. R. Snowden (Ed.), *Reaching the underserved: Mental health needs of neglected populations* (pp. 23–42). Beverly Hills, CA: Sage.

Gatz, M., & Smyer, M. A. (1992). The mental health system and older adults in the 1990s. *American Psychologist, 47,* 741–751.

Gibbs, N. (1992, December 28). Mercy's friend or foe? *Time,* pp. 36–37.

Goffman, E. (1961). *Asylums: Essays on the social situation of mental patients and other inmates.* Chicago: Aldine.

Heilig, S. M. (1970, Spring). Training in suicide prevention. *Bulletin of Suicidology,* No. 6, pp. 41–44.

Hendin, H., & Klerman, G. (1993). Physician-assisted suicide: The dangers of legalization. *American Journal of Psychiatry, 150,* 143–145.

Hinrichsen, G. A., Hernandez, N. A., & Pollack, S. (1992). Difficulties and rewards in family care of the depressed older adult. *Gerontologist, 32,* 486–492.

Homer, P., & Holstein, M. (Eds.). (1990). *A good old age? The paradox of Setting Limits.* New York: Touchstone.

Humphry, D. (1991). *Final exit: The practicalities of self-deliverance and assisted suicide for the dying.* Secaucus, NJ: Carol.

Hunt, R. W. (1993). A critique of using age to ration health care. *Journal of Medical Ethics, 19,* 19–23.

Kass, L. R. (1993). Is there a right to die? *Hastings Center Report, 23*(1), 34–43.

Kevorkian, J. (1991). *Prescription: Medicide—The Goodness of planned death.* Buffalo, NY: Prometheus.

Lasoski, M. C. (1986). Reasons for low utilization of mental health services by the elderly. In T. L. Brink (Ed.), *Clinical gerontology: A guide to assessment and intervention* (pp. 1–18). New York: Haworth.

Lebacqz, K., & Englehardt, H. T. (1980). Suicide and covenant. In M. P. Battin & D. J. Mayo (Eds.), *Suicide: The philosophical issues* (pp. 84–89). New York: St. Martin's Press.

Leering, C., Hilhorst, H. W. A., & Verhoef, M. J. (1979). Reflections on the wish to die at life's end. In H. Orimo, K. Shimada, M. Iriki, & D. Maeda (Eds.), *Recent advances in gerontology* (pp. 183–184). Amsterdam: Excerpta Medica.

Liptzin, B. (1991). The treatment of depression in older suicidal persons. *Journal of Geriatric Psychiatry, 24,* 203–215.

Litman, R. E. (1980). Psycholegal aspects of suicide. In W. J. Curran, A. L. McGarry, & C. S. Petty (Eds.), *Modern legal medicine: Psychiatry and forensic science* (pp. 841–853). Philadelphia: Davis.

Maris, R. W. (1981). *Pathways to suicide: A survey of self-destructive behaviors.* Baltimore: Johns Hopkins University Press.

Maris, R. W. (1982). [Review of *Exit house: Choosing suicide as an alternative*]. *Suicide and Life-Threatening Behavior, 12,* 123–126.

Maris, R. W., Dorpat, T. L., Hathorne, B. C., Heilig, S. M., Powell, W. J., Stone, H., & Ward, H. P. (1973). Education and training in suicidology for the seventies. In H. L. P. Resnik & B. C. Hathorne (Eds.), *Suicide prevention in the 70s* (DHEW Publication No. [HSM] 72-9054, pp. 23–34). Washington, DC: United States Government Printing Office.

Matheson, R. (1969). The test. In R. Matheson, *The shores of space* (pp. 60–78). New York: Bantum Books. (Original work published 1954)

Mayo, D. J. (1980). Irrational suicide. In M. P. Battin & D. J. Mayo (Eds.), *Suicide: The philosophical issues* (pp. 133–137). New York: St. Martin's Press.

McIntosh, J. L. (1987). Suicide: Training and education needs with an emphasis on the elderly. *Gerontology and Geriatrics Education, 7,* 125–139.

McIntosh, J. L. (1992). Older adults: The next suicide epidemic? *Suicide and Life-Threatening Behavior, 22,* 322–332.

McIntosh, J. L. (1993). *The suicide of older men and women: How YOU can help prevent a tragedy* [Brochure]. Washington, DC: American Association of Retired Persons and the American Association of Suicidology.

McIntosh, J. L., Hubbard, R. W., & Santos, J. F. (1981). Suicide among the elderly: A review of issues with case studies. *Journal of Gerontological Social Work, 4,* 63–74.

Medicide: New humanism or old euthanasia? (1992). *Society, 29*(5), 1–38.

Mercer, S. O. (1989). *Elder suicide: A national survey of prevention and intervention programs.* Washington, DC: American Association of Retired Persons.

Mercer, S. O. (1992). Suicide and the elderly. In F. J. Turner (Ed.), *Mental health and the elderly: A social work perspective* (pp. 425–453). New York: Free Press.

Meserve, H. C. (1975). Getting out of it. *Journal of Religion and Health, 14,* 3–6.

Miller, F. G. (1991). Is active killing of patients always wrong? *Journal of Clinical Ethics, 2,* 130–132.

Mishara, B. L., & Kastenbaum, R. (1973). Self-injurious behavior and environmental change in the institutionalized elderly. *International Journal of Aging and Human Development, 4,* 133–145.

Moody, H. R. (1984). Can suicide on the grounds of old age be ethically justified? In M. Tallmer, E. R. Prichard, A. H. Kutscher, R. DeBellis, M. S. Hale, & I. K. Goldberg (Eds.), *The life-threatened elderly* (pp. 64–92). New York: Columbia University Press.

Narveson, J. (1983). Self-ownership and the ethics of suicide. In M. P. Battin & R. W. Maris (Eds.), *Suicide and ethics* (pp. 240–253). New York: Human Sciences Press.

Orentlicher, D. (1992). Physicians cannot ethically assist in suicide. In M. Biskup & C. Wekesser (Eds.), *Suicide: Opposing viewpoints* (pp. 57–61). San Diego: Greenhaven. (Original work published 1991)

Osgood, N. J., Brant, B. A., & Lipman, A. (1991). *Suicide among the elderly in long-term care facilities.* New York: Greenwood.

Osgood, N. J., & McIntosh, J. L. (1986). *Suicide and the elderly: An annotated bibliography and review.* Westport, CT: Greenwood Press.

Parmelee, P. A., & Katz, I. R. (1992). "Caregiving" to depressed older persons: A relevant concept? [Editorial]. *Gerontologist, 32,* 436–437.

Pollinger-Haas, A., & Hendin, H. (1983). Suicide among older people: Projections for the future. *Suicide and Life-Threatening Behavior, 13,* 147–154.

Portenoy, R. K. (1991, July). Special issue on medical ethics: Physician-assisted suicide and euthanasia [Special issue]. *Journal of Pain and Symptom Management, 6*(5).

Portwood, D. (1978). *Common-sense suicide: The final right.* New York: Dodd, Mead.

Post, S. G. (1990). Severely demented elderly people: A case against senicide. *Journal of the American Geriatrics Society, 38,* 715–718.

Prado, C. G. (1990). *The last choice: Preemptive suicide in advanced age.* New York: Greenwood.

Pratt, C. C., Schmall, V. L., Wilson, W., & Benthin, A. (1991). A model community education program on depression and suicide in later life. *Gerontologist, 31,* 692–695.

Pressey, S. L. (1977). Any rights as to my dying? *Gerontologist, 17,* 296, 302.

Proposed UN principles for older persons. (1991). *Ageing International, 18*(1), 1–6.

Quill, T. E. (1991). Death and dignity: A case of individualized decision making. *New England Journal of Medicine, 324,* 691–694.

Quill, T. E., Cassel, C. K., & Meier, D. E. (1992). Care of the hopelessly ill: Proposed clinical criteria for physician-assisted suicide. *New England Journal of Medicine, 327,* 1380–1384.

Rabins, P. V. (1992). Prevention of mental disorder in the elderly: Current perspectives and future prospects. *Journal of the American Geriatrics Society, 40,* 727–733.

Rachlis, D. (1970, Fall). Suicide and loss adjustment in the aging. *Bulletin of Suicidology,* No. 7, pp. 23–26.

Raschko, R. (1990). The gatekeeper model for the isolated, at-risk elderly. In N. L. Cohen (Ed.), *Psychiatry takes to the streets* (pp. 195–209). New York: Guilford Press.

Redick, R. W., & Taube, C. A. (1980). Demography of mental health care of the aged. In J. E. Birren & R. B. Sloane (Eds.), *Handbook of mental health and aging* (pp. 57–71). Englewood Cliffs, NJ: Prentice-Hall.

Regnier, V., & Pynoos, J. (Eds.). (1987). *Housing the aged: Design directives and policy considerations.* New York: Elsevier.

Rollin, B. (1985). *Last wish.* New York: Linden Press.

Roman, J. (1980). *Exit house: Choosing suicide as an alternative.* New York: Seaview Books.

Rosenbaum, V. G., & Forsythe, C. D. (1990). The right to assisted suicide: Protection of autonomy or an open door to social killing? *Issues in Law and Medicine, 6,* 3–31.

Russell, C. (1993). *The master trend: How the baby boom generation is remaking America.* New York: Plenum Press.

Santos, J. F., & VandenBos, G. R. (Eds.). (1982). *Psychology and the older adult: Challenges for training in the 1980s.* Washington, DC: American Psychological Association.

Sartorius, R. (1983). Coercive suicide prevention: A libertarian perspective. In M. P. Battin & R. W. Maris (Eds.), *Suicide and ethics* (pp. 293–303). New York: Human Sciences Press.

Shneidman, E. S. (1985). *Definition of suicide.* New York: Wiley.

Siegel, K., & Tuckel, P., (1984–1985). Rational suicide and the terminally ill cancer patient. *Omega, 15,* 263–269.

Stone, A. (1992, October 28). "Dr. Death": No law is needed on euthanasia. *USA Today*, p. 6A.

Szasz, T. S. (1971). The ethics of suicide. *Antioch Review, 31,* 7–17.

Szasz, T. (1986). The case against suicide prevention. *American Psychologist, 41,* 806–812.

Torres-Gil, F. M. (1992). *The new aging: Politics and change in America.* New York: Auburn House.

Travis, R. (1991). Two arguments against euthanasia [Letter]. *Gerontologist, 31,* 561–562.

van der Wal, G., van Eijk, J. T. M., Leenen, H. J. J., & Spreeuwenberg, C. (1992a). Euthanasia and assisted suicide: I. How often is it practised by family doctors in the Netherlands? *Family Practice, 9,* 130–134.

van der Wal, G., van Eijk, J. T. M., Leenen, H. J. J., & Spreeuwenberg, C. (1992b). Euthanasia and assisted suicide: II. Do Dutch family doctors act prudently? *Family Practice, 9,* 135–140.

Vonnegut, K., Jr. (1970). Welcome to the monkey house. In K. Vonnegut, Jr., *Welcome to the monkey house* (pp. 28–47). New York: Dell.

Wennberg, R. N. (1989). *Terminal choices: Euthanasia, suicide, and the right to die.* Grand Rapids, MI: Eerdmans.

Appendix

Assessment Instruments

The *Beck Depression Inventory* (BDI; Beck, Ward, Mendelson, Mock, & Erbaugh, 1961) includes 21 items designed to assess different symptoms of depression. Each item is rated using a multiple-choice format, with different answers representing different levels of severity. Items assess the presence and severity of common depressive symptoms, including dysphoric mood, feelings of guilt, low self-esteem, crying, loss of interest in activities, sleep disturbance, loss of appetite, and suicidal thoughts. Scores greater than 9 reflect the presence of dysphoria, and scores greater than 17 are often associated with depressive states (Kendall, Hollon, Beck, Hammen, & Ingram, 1987). The BDI is useful in measuring the severity of depressive reactions and is sensitive to changes in depression over the course of treatment (Johnson & Heather, 1974). The BDI is short and easy to administer and gathers information that is clearly relevant to the concerns of a suicidal patient. Thus, the BDI can be incorporated into treatment as an ongoing assessment measure, monitoring changes in depressive symptoms over time.

The *Hamilton Rating Scale for Depression* (Ham-D; Hamilton, 1960) includes 17 items designed to quantify the severity of a depressive syndrome. Items are rated as part of a semistructured interview with the patient. Items include depressed mood, feelings of guilt, sleep disturbance, psychomotor agitation or retardation, and concerns about one's physical health. The main advantage of using the Ham-D is the clinical interview format (Hamilton, 1980). Professional ratings can incorporate information from several different sources (e.g., patient, family members, nursing staff) and are less susceptible to response biases in the depressed patient. However, the ratings are based on the judgment of the professional, and therefore, raters require adequate training in psychopathology and diagnosis (Hamilton, 1980).

The *Suicidal Intent Scale* (SIS; Beck, Schuyler, & Herman, 1974) includes 20 items to be scored by a professional after interviewing the patient. Items are designed to quantify the seriousness of the individual's intent to die, and rate the degree of premeditation and medical danger involved in a recent suicide attempt. Also, items evaluate the individual's expectations regarding their suicide attempt, their beliefs about death, and their attitudes about living versus dying. The SIS provides detailed information about suicidal tendencies so as to avoid global discussions of suicidal intent (Beck, Weissman, Lester, & Trexler, 1976). The SIS provides the framework for a clinical interview with the patient, gathering much useful information about previous suicidal behavior. This information can be valuable in therapy because a client who has attempted suicide once is likely to become suicidal again, usually for similar reasons and often using similar methods. Thus, previous suicidal behavior can guide the clinician into areas to be examined, challenged, and changed.

The *Scale for Suicidal Ideation* (SSI; Beck, Kovacs, & Weissman, 1979) includes 19 items to be rated by a clinician following an interview with the patient. The SSI provides useful scoring criteria for rating the frequency, intensity, and duration of suicidal thoughts. The SSI was modified (MSSI; Miller, Norman, Bishop, & Dow, 1986) to provide structured interview questions for assessing each of the items. Adequate interrater agreement and internal consistency estimates have been obtained for the MSSI. The MSSI is correlated with measures of depression (BDI) and hopelessness (Hopelessness Scale). Also, the MSSI discriminates between suicidal and nonsuicidal psychiatric inpatients (Miller et al., 1986). Perhaps most important, the MSSI provides the clinician with detailed information about the patient's suicidal thoughts, factors pushing the person toward death by suicide, and potential deterrents to attempting suicide. All of these issues can play an important role in the prevention and treatment of suicidal patients.

The *Hopelessness Scale* (HS; Beck, Weissman, Lester, & Trexler, 1974) includes 20 items to be rated by the client as true or false. Items assess the degree of pessimism and negative expectations reported by the individual. Total scores range from 0 to 20, with scores greater than 9 reflecting high levels of hopelessness and potential for suicidal behavior. Hopelessness is a good predictor of suicide risk, often being more strongly related to suicidal ideation (Beck, Kovacs, & Weissman, 1975; Kovacs, Beck, & Weissman, 1975) and suicidal intent (Wetzel, 1976) than is depression. In a 5- to 10-year follow-up study, scores from the HS predicted eventual death by suicide (Beck, Steer, Kovacs, & Garrison, 1985). Psychiatric inpatients who had obtained HS scores greater than 9 during their initial hospitalization were most likely to have died by suicide by the time of follow-up. Similar findings were obtained in a follow-up study of psychiatric outpatients (Beck, Brown, Berchick, Stewart, & Steer, 1990). In an investigation of hopelessness in the general population (Greene, 1981), 400 adults obtained a mean score of 4.45 with a standard deviation of 3.09. Thus, scores greater than 9 are more than one standard deviation above the mean for adults. Although scores rose gradually with the age of the subject, those over age 65 still scored substantially less than the cut-off ($M = 5.87$). Nonetheless, the HS is useful for identifying elderly patients at risk for suicidal thoughts (Hill, Gallagher, Thompson, & Ishida, 1988). Higher levels of hopelessness are associated with more negative views toward oneself, the environment, and the future (Nekanda-Trepka, Bishop, & Blackburn, 1983).

The *Reasons for Living Inventory* (Linehan, Goodstein, Nielsen, & Chiles, 1983) includes 48 self-rated items indicating the presence of different reasons for a person to stay alive despite tremendous problems in their life. Factor analyses identified six subscales, labeled Survival and Coping Beliefs, Responsibility to Family, Child-Related Concerns, Fear of Suicide, Fear of Social Disapproval, and Moral Objections to Suicide. The Reasons for Living Inventory was developed to help clinicians and patients retain an adaptive focus, rather than emphasizing maladaptive characteristics of suicidal patients. In most clinical settings, the inventory can be used to identify strengths and positive aspects of the patient's life and to try to enhance these life-saving features.

The *Paragraphs About Leisure Questionnaire* (Tinsley, Teaff, Colbs, & Kaufman, 1985) lists 18 common activities appropriate for most elderly people. Included are both social (e.g., playing cards, volunteer activities) and solitary (e.g., reading, gardening) activities. Patients are asked how well the various activities satisfy different psychological needs. Activities can be clustered into groups representing different psychological issues (e.g., need for companionship, expressive service). In clinical work, this scale can be useful in helping patients find useful ways to spend their time involved in enjoyable activities. Also, if the individual is unable to perform a preferred activity because of health or financial limitations, other similar activities may be identified and substituted.

The *Minnesota Multiphasic Personality Inventory* (MMPI; Hathaway & McKinley, 1940) includes 3 validity scales and 10 standard clinical scales designed to rate the severity of different forms of psychopathology. The MMPI includes a Depression scale, comprising 60 true–false statements rating the presence or absence of different depressive symptoms. Raw scores are converted into t scores, providing normative data about the frequency of different elevations. T scores above 70 are considered noteworthy. The MMPI Depression scale has demonstrated concurrent validity for assessing depression (Nelson & Cicchetti, 1991).

The *Millon Clinical Multiaxial Inventory* (MCMI; Millon, 1982) uses 175 true–false statements to gather information relevant to each of the 11 personality disorders. Several clinical scales are also included to address major depression, substance abuse, and psychotic thought processes. The MCMI has been revised (MCMI-II; Millon, 1987) but largely follows its original structure.

The *Mini-Mental State Exam* (MMSE; Folstein, Folstein, & McHugh, 1975) includes a short series of questions to be used as a screening measure of cognitive impairment. The questions are used to evaluate the patient's memory, orientation, attention, language, and other basic abilities. For example, attention is assessed by asking patients to begin at 100 and count backward by 7. The patient is given one point for each correct answer made performing five subtractions (i.e., 93, 86, 79, 72, 65). Scores on the MMSE range from 0 to 30, with lower scores reflecting an increased likelihood of cognitive impairment. Patients with dementia usually score much lower (7–14) than patients with depression (18–19) or other nonorganic psychiatric problems. It should be noted that some patients will present with dual diagnoses of dementia and depression, leading to lower scores in this population.

The *Dysfunctional Attitudes Scale* (DAS; Weissman & Beck, 1978) includes 40 statements that are rated on a 7-point scale from *totally agree* to *totally disagree*. Items attempt to capture common attitudes reported by patients who are prone to depressive episodes. Preliminary research has suggested that these negative attitudes are more stable than depressed moods (Weissman & Beck, 1978) and may serve to provoke depressed moods in vulnerable individuals. However, other studies have found the dysfunctional attitudes to be correlates of depression rather than causal variables (Silverman, Silverman, & Eardsley, 1984). Nonetheless, the DAS gathers information about cognitive distortions as a symptom of depression and provides information about problems that can be addressed through cognitive therapy. Scores above 120 reflect depressive cognitions.

References

Beck, A. T., Brown, G., Berchick, R., Stewart, B., & Steer, R. (1990). Relationship between hopelessness and ultimate suicide: A replication with psychiatric outpatients. *American Journal of Psychiatry, 147,* 190–195.

Beck, A. T., Kovacs, M., & Weissman, A. (1975). Hopelessness and suicidal behavior: An overview. *Journal of the American Medical Association, 234,* 1146–1149.

Beck, A. T., Kovacs, M., & Weissman, A. (1979). Assessment of suicidal intention: The Scale for Suicidal Ideation. *Journal of Consulting and Clinical Psychology, 47,* 343–352.

Beck, A. T., Schuyler, D., & Herman, I. (1974). Development of suicide intent scales. In A. T. Beck, H. L. P. Resnik, & D. Lettieri (Eds.), *The prediction of suicide* (pp. 45–56). Bowie, MD: Charles Press.

Beck, A. T., Steer, R., Kovacs, M., & Garrison, B. (1985). Hopelessness and eventual suicide: A 10-year prospective study of patients hospitalized with suicidal ideation. *American Journal of Psychiatry, 142,* 559–563.

Beck, A. T., Ward, C., Mendelson, M., Mock, J., & Erbaugh, J. (1961). An inventory for measuring depression. *Archives of General Psychiatry, 4,* 561–571.

Beck, A. T., Weissman, A., Lester, D., & Trexler, L. (1974). The measurement of pessimism: The Hopelessness Scale. *Journal of Consulting and Clinical Psychology, 42,* 861–865.

Beck, A. T., Weissman, A., Lester, D., & Trexler, L. (1976). Classification of suicidal behaviors: II. Dimensions of suicidal intent. *Archives of General Psychiatry, 33,* 835–837.

Folstein, M., Folstein, S., & McHugh, P. (1975). Mini-mental state: A practical method for grading the cognitive states of patients for the clinician. *Journal of Psychiatric Research, 12,* 196–197.

Greene, S. (1981). Levels of measured hopelessness in the general population. *British Journal of Clinical Psychology, 20,* 11–14.

Hamilton, M. (1960). A rating scale for depression. *Journal of Neurology, Neurosurgery and Psychiatry, 23,* 56–62.

Hamilton, M. (1980). Rating depressive patients. *Journal of Clinical Psychiatry, 41,* 21–24.

Hathaway, S., & McKinley, J. C. (1940). A multiphasic personality inventory (Minnesota): I. Construction of the schedule. *Journal of Psychology, 10,* 249–254.

Hill, R. D., Gallagher, D., Thompson, L. W., & Ishida, T. (1988). Hopelessness as a measure of suicidal intent in the depressed elderly. *Psychology and Aging, 3,* 230–232.

Johnson, D., & Heather, B. (1974). The sensitivity of the Beck Depression Inventory to changes of symptomatology. *British Journal of Psychiatry, 125,* 184–185.

Kendall, P., Hollon, S., Beck, A. T., Hammen, C., & Ingram, R. (1987). Issues and recommendations regarding use of the Beck Depression Inventory. *Cognitive Therapy and Research, 11,* 289–299.

Kovacs, M., Beck, A. T., & Weissman, A. (1975). Hopelessness: An indicator of suicide risk. *Suicide, 5,* 98–103.

Linehan, M., Goodstein, J., Nielsen, S., & Chiles, J. (1983). Reasons for staying alive when you are thinking of killing yourself: The Reasons for Living Inventory. *Journal of Consulting and Clinical Psychology, 51,* 276–286.

Miller, I., Norman, W., Bishop, S., & Dow, M. (1986). The Modified Scale for Suicidal Ideation: Reliability and validity. *Journal of Consulting and Clinical Psychology, 54,* 724–725.

Millon, T. (1982). *Millon Clinical Multiaxial Inventory Manual* (3rd ed.). Minneapolis, MN: National Computer Systems.

Millon, T. (1987). *Millon Clinical Multiaxial Inventory: II. Manual for the MCMI-II.* Minneapolis, MN: National Computer Systems.

Nekanda-Trepka, C., Bishop, S., & Blackburn, I. (1983). Hopelessness and depression. *British Journal of Clinical Psychology, 22,* 49–60.

Nelson, L., & Cicchetti, D. (1991). Validity of the MMPI depression scale for outpatients. *Psychological Assessment, 3,* 55–59.

Silverman, J., Silverman, J., & Eardsley, D. (1984). Do maladaptive attitudes cause depression? *Archives of General Psychiatry, 41,* 28–30.

Tinsley, H., Teaff, J., Colbs, S., & Kaufman, N. (1985). A system of classifying leisure activities in terms of the psychological benefits of participation reported by older persons. *Journal of Gerontology, 40,* 172–178.

Weissman, A., & Beck, A. T. (1978, November). *Development and validation of the Dysfunctional Attitude Scale.* Paper presented at the convention of the Association for Advancement of Behavior Therapy, Chicago.

Wetzel, R. (1976). Hopelessness, depression, and suicide intent. *Archives of General Psychiatry, 33,* 1069–1073.

Author Index

Page numbers in italics refer to listings in reference sections.

Abel, E. L., 114, *125*
Abrahams, R., 41, *59*
Abrams, R. C., 121, *125*
Abramson, L. Y., 79, *94*, 140, *158*
Achté, K., 38, *56*, 76, *94*, 169, *193*
Adelson, L., 21, *55*
Adkins, J., 2, 117–118, 221
Adler, A., 74, *94*
Aisenberg, R., 75–77, *97*, 164, *195*
Alexander, V., 53, *54*
Alexopoulos, G. S., 121–122, *125*
Allebeck, P., 108, *125*
Allen, N., 8, *54*
Alloy, L. B., 140, *158*
Alvarez, A., 68, 74, 89, *94*
Alvarez, W. C., 215, *227*
Anderson, W. F., 106, *128*
Angle, C. R., 37, *57*
Ansbacher, H. L., 75, *94*
Arbore, P., 138, *158*
Atchley, R. C., 67, *94*, 103–104, *126*
Augenbraun, B., 51, *54*
Austin, R. L., 105, *127*
Avery, D., 172, *194*

Bahn, A. K., 67, *96*, 105, *128*
Baker, F., 41, *59*
Baltes, M. M., 164, *194*
Baltes, P. B., 164, *194*
Barakat, S., 109, *127*
Barraclough, B., 108, *126*
Barraclough, B. M., 49, 51–52, *60*, 103, *130*
Barrett, T. W., 49–50, *54*
Barrington, M. R., 216, *227*
Barry, R. L., 220, *227*

Bartimus, T., 35, *54*
Barwick, C., 47, *59*
Basson, M. D., 227
Batchelor, I. R. C., 115, *126*
Battin, M. P., 116, 118, *126*, 213, 215, 219–220, *227*
Batzel, L. W., 108, *126*
Baum, A., 41, *56*
Beachy, L., 117, *126*
Beavers, D., 183, *195*
Beck, A. T., 38, *56*, 79, *95*, 105–106, *129*, 140, *158*, 163, 168–169, 173–175, 187–188, *194–195*, 197, 233–235, 237, *237*, *238–239*
Beck, M., 117, *126*
Beckwith, B. P., 215, *227*
Bedrosian, R., 188, *194*
Bennett, A. E., 209, *227*
Benson, R., 145, *158*
Benthin, A., 201, *231*
Berardo, F. M., 67, *95*
Berchick, R., 235, *237*
Berchick, R. J., 140, *158*
Bergman, D. B., 1, *3*
Berman, A. L., 1, *4*, *57*, 122, *126*
Bernstein, M., 190, *194*
Bettelheim, B., 7, 32–34, *54–55*, 122
Bille-Brahe, U., 36, *54*, *59*, *130*
Binstock, R. H., 220, *227*
Bishop, S., 169, *195*, 234–235, *238–239*
Bjerke, T., *59*
Blackburn, I., 235, *239*
Blank, T. O., 208, *227*
Blau, Z. S., 67, *95*, 102, *126*

241

Subject Index

About the Authors

JOHN L. MCINTOSH, PhD, is currently a professor of psychology on the faculty at Indiana University at South Bend, where he has taught since 1979. He completed his undergraduate work at Western Kentucky University and received his doctorate from the University of Notre Dame. Dr. McIntosh is review editor of *Suicide and Life-Threatening Behavior*. He is a member of the Board of Directors of the American Association of Suicidology (AAS). Dr. McIntosh holds the office of president of the association for 1993–94 and has previously served as secretary of the AAS Board of Directors. He was the 1990 recipient of the American Association of Suicidology's prestigious Shneidman Award, given to a person below the age of 40 who has made scholarly contributions in research to the field of suicidology. Dr. McIntosh was the program chair of the 1990 23rd annual AAS meeting in New Orleans.

JOHN F. SANTOS, PhD, is emeritus professor of psychology and former director of the GERAS Center at the University of Notre Dame. He is editor emeritus of *Gerontology & Geriatrics Education*, a multidisciplinary journal in the field of aging. He received his doctoral degree in psychology from Tulane University and completed postdoctoral work at the University of Texas. He served as project and program director at the Menninger Foundation in Topeka, Kansas, and was director of field studies for the Peace Corps and the Agency for International Development in Brazil. In addition, he was the Ford Foundation's Population Advisor for Mexico, Central America, and the Caribbean. He is a trustee of the Retirement Research Foundation and a member of the Board of Directors of the Alliance for Aging Research and has served on the National Advisory Council on Aging of the National Institute of Health in Washington.

RICHARD W. HUBBARD, PhD, is assistant professor of psychology at Indiana University at South Bend. He was formerly assistant director of the GERAS Program at the University of Notre Dame as well as the Director of Geriatric Education at the Medical School of Case Western Reserve University's Geriatric Education Center in Cleveland, Ohio. His doctoral degree in psychology was earned from the University of Notre Dame. He later completed the postdoctoral respecialization program in clinical psychology in the Department of Psychology at Case Western Reserve University and completed his APA Internship in clinical psychology at the Cleveland Veterans Administration Medical Center. Dr. Hubbard is a licensed psychologist in practice at the Stress Recovery Center in South Bend, Indiana.

JAMES C. OVERHOLSER, PhD, received his doctorate in clinical psychology from the Ohio State University. He completed his predoctoral internship and postdoctoral fellowship at the Brown University Program in Medicine, Providence, Rhode Island. He also served as research faculty at Brown University. Dr. Overholser is currently an associate professor in the Department of Psychology at Case Western Reserve University in Cleveland, Ohio. He provides clinical training and supervision through Case Western's graduate program and postdoctoral respecialization training program in clinical psychology. Dr. Overholser is actively involved in research on risk factors for suicide in adolescents and adults. He is the current President of the American Suicide Foundation of Northeast Ohio.